UNSUNG HEROES WEAR NO CAPES

EXHORTATIONS TO EXCELLENCE

UNSUNG HEROES
WEAR NO CAPES

12 Essential Virtues for
an Extraordinary Life

JIM B. NORTH

Published by Faith Notes Live! LLC
For more information, visit jimbnorth.com

ISBN (paperback): 978-1-961798-00-7
ISBN (ebook): 978-1-961798-01-4

Book design and production by www.AuthorSuccess.com

Printed in the United States of America

All quotes and interview material of Jim's guests granted by permission:

To the inspired life and vision of each reader.
I began with the end in mind, and that was you.

Contents

INTRODUCTION 1

Virtue #1 Love: The Master Key 11
What's behind the doorway of unlimited inner wealth

Virtue #2 Courage: Light in the Dark 31
Highlighting benefits of a commodity that conquers in every battle

Virtue #3 Honesty: Heavyweight Champ of the World 49
How keeping integrity makes you a winning person

Virtue #4 Friendship: Armor for Life's Good Fight 68
Examining standard equipment that multiplies superpower

Virtue #5 Optimism: Focus of Desire 88
Reasons to choose the magnificent view no matter the circumstance

Virtue #6 Hope: Wind for Your Sails 106
Methods for adjusting position to accomplish the mission

Virtue #7 Diligence: The Winner's Edge 125
Why the one drip at a time tool still works wonders

Virtue #8 Creativity: Setting Genius Free 144
This is the way to smash the box of limitations

Virtue #9   Gratitude: The Equalizer 165

Extreme benefit of a healthy attitude for a balanced life

Virtue #10   Faithfulness: The Great Connector   185

Advantages to being a strong finisher of tasks, dreams, missions, and objectives

Virtue #11   Mercy: Cutting Edge Humanity   204

Open invite to the secret rapid rewards system for maximized living

Virtue #12   Growth: Garden of Your Life   223

Highlighting small decisions that lead to super character transformation

EPILOGUE   241

SPECIAL FEATURE: IN-PERSON VISITS   243

The Jim Stovall Story   245

The Mister Rogers Story   258

The Unsung Heroes of Mister Rogers   276

Unsung Hero

A person who has achieved greatly in the context of relationships and teams, rendered selfless service and support on behalf of others, and is not always recognized for their inestimable contributions. Being an unsung hero is to provide unmerited benefits toward a cause that doesn't result in accolades for what has been achieved or accomplished. An unsung hero is driven by conviction more than celebration. Common traits of unsung heroes include uncommon humility, empathy, commitment, courage, and excellence. Unsung heroes initiate benefits to worthy and notable causes. An unsung hero derives energy from friendship, and the synergy with meaning and purpose results in extraordinary heroism.

Virtue

A timeless value proactively engaged through personal volition, decision, and choice—moral excellence. Virtue is strength, bravery, and uncommon valor in everyday life. Virtue is goodness acted upon, a practical application of a moral character code, and conformity of life and behavior to make meaningful contributions toward others. A virtue is the inherent power within an individual to act. A virtue is a secret agency of the person to perform even in adversity. A virtue infuses worth in an ordinary circumstance to provide extraordinary benefits. Finally, a virtue is voluntary obedience to what is in the best interest of others, conforming to what is right, true, and fitting in the moment and the long term.

Introduction

I woke up and looked at my alarm clock. It was exactly 3:00 a.m. I was shaken by one of the most vivid and captivating of dreams. First, I had seen my dad. In the dream, he was on the other side of life, holding large white placards face down on his lap. There was a stack of them, and each had something written, but I didn't know what—except one. He had composed a song many years before that was reflective of his life experience. Somehow, I knew this had significance. Other people weren't necessarily aware that it counted in the scheme of things, but in the dream, this mattered. The content of the other placards was not revealed to me, yet I knew they symbolized what he had done through love and devotion and didn't necessarily get credit for in the eyes of others. But in the dream, they counted. Not everything worthwhile you do will receive applause.

Do it anyway.

In some sense, I knew it was none of my business. I didn't have to know what was on the other cards. There was a transition in the dream to seeing my mother. She, too, held a similar stack of large white placards and held them on her lap, also. I sensed things in her life that might be on those cards, but none of what was written was precisely revealed to me. They were personal to her, and intimate. They belonged to her as much as her hands. Like my dad, she received credit on the other side for things she'd done through love and devotion. They were unique to her, unlike anyone else on Earth. I understood that a person isn't graded by how similarly they match or measure up with someone else. Life is about being yourself and doing what you, alone, can do. Copying negates the power and potential for what you can become. I was aware that she received credit on the other side for what she had done in this life, just like my dad. Her white placards were heroes that many people didn't know anything about. You have white placards many will never know about, too. You might not get the credit you deserve for the good things that you do.

Do them anyway.

Then, the dream transitioned to my uncle. He had many white placards face down on his lap. Something was written on every one of them, but I had no idea the content. I knew these represented what he had done in this life through love and devotion. They counted on the other side of this life. I didn't have to know what was written on any of them. And my not knowing didn't diminish the essence or quality of what he had done or who he had been to others.

On the other hand, I knew he was a family man. He was devoted to his wife, kids, siblings, and grandkids in an extraordinary way. He made it his duty to go above and beyond with tender, loving care. He was their friend. It wasn't hard to imagine what might be on some of those white cards. I mention this because sometimes people make the mistake of measuring themselves by outward, extraordinary achievements. The truth is even better. You'll be more accurately judged on just being an *extraordinary person*. And that will make your accomplishments count even more. There are things you do that people may never know about.

Do stuff anyway.

With all three individuals, they held their cards in a way that didn't display pride, but instead personal ownership. There was a reverence. They were calm and peaceful. Their cards differed from one another. What they had done wasn't in vain, no matter who on Earth was unaware. I learned valuable lessons in those moments. When I awoke at 3:00 a.m., tears moistening the pillow. I was deeply moved. Not wanting to disrupt the moment, I remained still for perhaps an hour or two, mesmerized by what I'd seen. This is as vivid today as it was so many years ago.

There are things I'll do that many people will never know about, and I'm determined to do them anyway.

I don't know everything there is to know about every person I meet. They have their white placards, nonetheless. But I can treat them as if I do know—in advance—that I'm very interested in finding out. How often this has happened for me when I connect with someone's story? I can form a relationship, a friendship. I can recognize and acknowledge their strengths and aptitudes and experiences. I can learn what they do through love and devotion. Often, I'm surprised. There are things they'll get credit for on the other side. Their experience can significantly benefit your life. Never underestimate yourself or other people.

Who hasn't had someone misunderstand the reasons for your success or what makes you tick as a person? They didn't see you behind the scenes when no one else was watching. Maybe you haven't been recognized like you could have been or should have been. But you didn't do it for the credit. You didn't have to tell others. But you knew there were deeper reasons and motivations that made you who you are today.

Discovery is like a treasure hunt. Finding and increasing that treasure is the essence and purpose of life. Helping others do the same is fun and provides the greatest joy. Virtuous acts provide a thrill like none other.

While there are many books about success, they're not as interesting as learning about the unsung hero, whose success has nothing to do with money or influence.

That will last a lifetime.

What don't you know about that person next door? At work? School? What about that friend, associate, or stranger? How about that family member? What about that brand new acquaintance? What makes them tick? What carried them when the chips were down? What was it that gave that man, woman, boy, or girl the yeast to rise? You might never guess how much *love* played a major part. *Diligence* may have been the engine that influenced key decisions, instilled the will to win, drove the discipline to practice, or inspired the capacity to connect with others. Maybe they were *honest* to a fault, causing a stinging loss but acquiring priceless gains by the end of the tragic story. These character attributes are exercised with no guarantee of reward. They are their own reasons for being, growing, and living.

People are in themselves *gifts*.

Essential virtues should be practiced proactively. Put your best foot forward with the ones you rely on the most. They stay with you when you go to bed. You wake with them in the morning. You live and breathe them during the day. They are foundational and make you the person you are now and will become over time. They shape how you will make yourself accessible to others. They touch everything you do. It's the Midas touch of *meaning*. They make all the difference.

At the end of your life when you look back, you will realize that what you did and who you were counted more than you ever imagined or understood. You really did positively influence the lives of others—some of whom you influenced that you didn't fully realize at the time. When the rewards are passed out, you'll be surprised at things you thought passed under the radar but will come to light as having been profoundly significant.

Like Clark Kent, you might not look the part of the superhero. But when times get tough and the need is great, enter the phone booth and clothe yourself with the superpowers at your disposal to serve. That's why characters like Superman, Batman, and Spiderman resonate with young and old alike. I've never seen Superman come out of the phone booth except with a cut-above disposition to help someone in distress. There lies your superpower, too. When you come out of that place of dedication, you're changed—because you determined within yourself to serve others. You're not mild-mannered, but bold. Take any crisis you may be facing and begin the hero's journey—that of your own.

When I was fired from my job in 2012, I lost a lot. Outwardly, I lost nearly everything. But what remained were the essential virtues discussed at length in this book. I passed through the dark waters of that loss—pain, humiliation, financial blows, reputation. What was I going to do? There were people that were for me; friends that provided love, courage, and mercy. Life was reduced to the lowest common denominator—humanity. I engaged the essential character virtues within; the ones that helped me achieve my success before. But now, they were all I had left. They became the character traits I couldn't do without. This set the tone for my future—new relationships, out-standing opportunities as a writer and speaker, and an educational path—all of which helped me focus on becoming an *extraordinary person* even when the going got tough.

Someone helped you get to where you are today. Be sure to thank them. Don't take people in your life for granted. You have unsung heroes in your life to credit. Come away better than before, committed to the well-being and success of people around you. Set new goals for how you will be a positive influence. Target someone in a good way with love. Be prepared for that person directly in your path or even outside your comfort zone. It may be someone you least expect that you'll freely pour into.

How unselfish can you be? Will you receive the credit? *Maybe or maybe not.* You're good either way. You'll place emphasis on *friend-ship* and seize more opportunities than you would have otherwise. You're going to be *extraordinary* by enlarging small moments with a magnificent view. You're a genuine helper for all the right reasons, and you're fully equipped with all the tools that will be necessary. You're attaching who you are to the highest virtues and values in the universe and making them uniquely your own.

I've held positions of leadership and service in a wide variety of contexts for many decades. I've been a teacher and a caregiver for young and old alike. My educational path has spanned twelve years. Yet, my meaningful relationships have stretched over the course of a lifetime. I'm so grateful for those—an education you can't obtain any other way. I've learned profound lessons through every means possible. I'm a listener and naturally empathic. I value people and experiences equally. All roads have led to this moment of publishing an encompassing book to highlight virtues that make a profound difference in the lives of those who desire to make a difference.

As an award-winning writer, I've taken the opportunity to explore the concept of what it means to be a helper of others. I've woven the unique privileges I've had in journalism to interview people with fascinating stories. I maintain that everyone is capable of being an *unsung hero* with a little inspiration and direction, using the character virtues we each possess. In some way, this can be practiced every day and personal growth becomes exponential. I'm an encourager by nature and hope to spur you to greater achievement in any realm of life with these *exhortations to excellence*. Maybe it's personal, academic, social, or professional—yet hopefully this book will help to raise the level of every area.

Open your life like a canvas to new possibilities. I wasn't always a *grateful* person, but I've learned it's never too late to express appreciation to those who influenced me—even, at times, beneath the radar. The act of bringing those to the surface will catapult you into a better future than you dreamed possible—by the power of acknowledgment.

In this book, I explore twelve essential virtues:

- ◆ Love
- ◆ Courage
- ◆ Honesty
- ◆ Friendship
- ◆ Optimism
- ◆ Hope

- ◆ Diligence
- ◆ Creativity
- ◆ Gratitude
- ◆ Faithfulness
- ◆ Mercy
- ◆ Growth

Each chapter begins with an unsung hero story that personifies one of the twelve. The fact is that many of these character traits overlap. Generally, there are multiple virtues being practiced at the same time. Many unsung heroes have changed me for the better when I entered their story and made it my own—or by their entering into mine to make it theirs. Consider each lead story a gateway into that chapter's subject matter. By the conclusion of the chapter, you'll think of stories along that vein that have shaped you. You'll consider with a renewed optimism who you intend to help, even those you haven't met yet. It all lies in your dedication and resolve.

You're looking toward that already.

The main chapters are exhortations and explorations of virtues—defined as moral excellence. Throughout each chapter, timeless quotes demonstrate that virtues have always been keys to an extraordinary life. At the close of the chapter appear reflections to reinforce the main ideas. Review them often to light your fire all over again. The challenge is to raise the level of life through increased dedication to others. Help make other lives extraordinary, and inevitably that disposition and attitude will boomerang.

The time for super-growth and change is now.

Included in this book are interviews I conducted over a period of years to bring these virtues to life. Real people provide unique insight into their journeys. The following is a list of fascinating people I interviewed—plus many other stories based on meaningful experiences or targeted research. I've learned that understanding someone else's story will double your life—at least. Not by mental assent, but by making it your own.

Become an advocate.

Learn about:

> Renee (theater student in two Black Friday car crashes)
>
> Jack Shadwick (Ambassador to the Modoc Nation)
>
> Hedda Sharapan (Mister Rogers story)
>
> Jim Stovall (Founder of the Narrative Television Network for the blind)
>
> Kevin Matthews (Oklahoma senator from Greenwood on the Black Wall Street story)
>
> Nir Sarussi (World-class violinist from Jerusalem)
>
> Douglas Lankford (Chief of the Miami Nation)
>
> Gene Hughes (Founder of Nature's Sunshine health products)
>
> Mark Frank (theater coordinator, director, and playwright)
>
> . . . and many more

At the end of the book are in-depth conversations I've titled 'Special Feature: In-person Visits' with Jim Stovall and Hedda Sharapan. Brief capsules of their stories are the lead unsung hero stories at the beginning of the chapters on Friendship, Optimism, and Faithfulness. The 'Visits' are in-depth conversations and explorations of their intriguing and fascinating stories.

Love, the master gift, touches all virtues and gives them the energy to flourish. Growth is the primary goal of the book; an arc of individual transformation. With every step, one foot is planted in the meaningful past and the other striding toward a bright, promising future. We're sure to get there. This is a brainstorming opportunity for new possibilities. You can elevate your unsung hero status by being a super-helper of others—the safest, surest, most reliable path to an extraordinary life.

Get ready for liftoff.

- Embrace the superpowers within and multiply the extraordinary
- Scale your purpose with twelve essential virtues to be an exponential influence
- Recognize small moments as magnificent opportunities—and be the unsung hero
- Open your life to creative possibilities and be grateful for every experience
- Synergize and transform leadership and teams with timeless building blocks
- Take personal character development to new heights, inspiring others to do the same

What's essential in life is what's invisible to the eye.
-Fred Rogers

VIRTUE #1

Love: The Master Key
What's behind the doorway of unlimited inner wealth

Unsung Hero Story

The waters of the river were dark, churning, turbulent. I watched through a plexiglass window to see it from a close distance, yet there was a separation between me and the vivid scene. I believed that to be a symbolic forewarning of what was to come. This served as mental and spiritual preparation for adversity. These were formative moments. I remember bracing myself on the inside. Out in the center of the river, there was a person treading water amid the swift current. She was so relaxed; the look on her face was calm and peaceful despite the adverse conditions.

The waters were intimidating, threatening, swelling. The sky grew black along with the water. They mirrored one another, fed off each other. I've never witnessed a darker scene. It was threatening, foreboding, ominous. The feeling was overwhelming. There were many beats in time while I took it all in, contemplating the inevitability of what was about to happen. Suddenly, I was sucked into the dark flow, carried along by the tremendous current.

I became one with that river of adversity.

There was a transition as I was suddenly transferred to a completely new scene of a much brighter, hopeful day. The waters had receded and returned to a beautiful aqua color. The skies were clear and blue. The sun was shining. People splashed and played in the shallower waters of that river. I couldn't help but notice the demeanor of the people gathered was happy and joyous. Whereas it took only one to help, many benefited from that victory.

In the dream, the storm had passed.

Not long after, the trial that had been figurative became a harsh reality.

After I was fired from my long-held job, I realized the dream had prepared me for what became one of the most excruciating trials of my life. The inevitability of my termination was apparent for some time. It took five weeks for it all to unfold. It was torturous knowing it was going to happen but not aware of when or how. At the crisis point, I broke down sobbing uncontrollably in the conference room, alone with a human resources person. Everyone else had filed out of the room one-by-one. I was inconsolable. I went home that afternoon and broke the devastating news to my wife. Within a few days, I received the dreaded phone call of an ultimate dismissal.

I asked for clarification. "Are you saying I'm fired?"

"Yes, that's what I'm saying."

The financial ramifications for my household were far-reaching. What was I going to do for income? What about the house payment? The car payment? I dreamt for many years of picking up my schooling again and returning to college. Things had gotten in the way before. There was always a more pressing priority, and when you're raising a family, it's not easy to do. But I wanted the clear focus, the undivided attention. I said, "You know, I just wish I had five years to devote to my studies without distractions."

I verbalized this again to my wife after I was terminated. It felt good to be daydreaming once again. My enthusiasm was high, yet the pressure of paying the bills took over and a wet blanket came settling back down. I started looking for a place where I could get back to work, met a sales manager for an interview, and was to report to a furniture store that Thursday for a brand-new sales position.

Without hesitation, my wife asked, "I thought you were going to pursue your education?"

That kind of shocked me. I wasn't expecting that response because I was feeling nothing but pressure. That was all I needed, to know she approved of the idea. I notified the would-be employer that I wasn't going to take the job after all. In short order, I learned that the first two years of my schooling would be funded due to the circumstances surrounding my dismissal. Yeah, there was unfairness about it. I received unemployment benefits for the first time in my life. I marched myself over to the local college, enrolled in classes immediately, and didn't look back. All I needed was that vote of confidence from my wife. My dream started coming true and the positive experiences began stacking up. To date, they've never stopped. The achievements, experiences, relationships, opportunities, and learning were more than I even had dreamed. All of that said, I finished multiple degrees debt-free with as close to a 4.0 GPA as you can get—nearly straight As.

My wife didn't ask for the credit, but her encouragement was key. She was also significantly supportive of me writing this book. She has always recognized my gifts and believes the themes of the book are needed in the world today. Her belief added to mine. She's a consummate *unsung hero*, a super-helper for all the best reasons. Her selfless love gave the unswerving support I needed to forge a new and better path ahead.

Who in your own life can you highlight in a similar way? Equally important, who can you be that person for going forward? Be in the river for someone in advance. Let them know you're there. That is the best way to the highest kind of fulfillment. You can make someone's day, week, month, year—and life. There will be many beneficiaries of your commitments going forward; more than you could have dreamed of. You'll revel in the light of a new day, a new scene, a bright and beautiful environment where the storms of life have passed by. Everyone's happy, free, and connected—better through adversity. My wife and I have not had an easy go of it, but without the essential virtue of love, we wouldn't have made it through the innumerable tough spots.

You're never alone, and I think that's important to understand. When you feel isolated, shun the thinking that no one cares. You don't always know who is going to help. You don't always know who will identify with your suffering. They are not always visible. Sometimes, they're behind the scenes, working on your behalf while you're not looking. They have your back. They're unsung heroes. And they don't care if they get credit or not. Or, if they do, they take it in stride. Love is unselfish, focused on the needs of others—especially in their dark hours.

Someone told me they thought that person in the center of the river might have been my wife—which I can't dispute. We all have people who believe in us. They may be closer than you think. Perhaps it's a spouse, a parent, a child, a friend, or a colleague. While some have no idea what you're going through, don't forget that there are others who do. Put your finger on any adversity and mark the beginning point. You're going to come out on the other side transformed—on a new and improved, more dedicated than ever before mission to serve others—and you're not asking for the credit. This makes the fulfillment sweeter.

I've never known of a more selfless helper than my wife—and helpers are heroes. The gift of recognition will lead you to appreciate more and proudly acknowledge your own unsung heroes of love, too.

Exhortations to Excellence on Love

> Love is like infinity. You can't have more or less infinity,
> and you can't compare two things to see if they're equally
> infinite. Infinity just is, and that's the way I think love is, too.
> –Fred Rogers

Love is the greatest, most adaptable gift ever given to human beings. It fits like a glove and equips you for the hardest circumstances. The applications are infinite, according to the need. Got problems? Love has answers.

You can't control what goes on around you or the degree of adversities you will face. But love is a power that will see you through the grind. This gift has the versatility and adaptability to treat others in the same manner; as mighty overcomers against the odds. It's a *pearl* of great value. It can't be kept and hoarded, but instead demands to be given and shared. If there was one acquisition in life worth the giving up of lesser commodities, it would be the priceless jewel called love.

**Turned loose, love will give until exhausted.
Then it miraculously replenishes all over again.**

Love isn't a concept. Love demands engagement and involvement. Words alone are empty. Love holds the power to move mountains and makes all things possible—nothing leaps obstacles in a single bound like this superhero—a sleeping giant that finds expression in the hearts of ordinary people like you and me. Love can be characterized as the essential character virtue of the ages and stands the test of time.

THE TRIUMPH OF LOVE

Are you welcoming love showing up to the table in every small thing? Make the allowance and take the deep breath, the brief pause. Love should never be overlooked as the dark horse to win in times of trouble. Stake the odds on the winner with a perfect track record. Think of how this gift is within your grasp and at your fingertips. At any time, you can alter your circumstances by changing *yourself*. When you change your disposition, you change the perception of what you're dealing with and how it affects you, positive or negative—and those around you. Love is the key to happiness and fulfillment. It doesn't depend on others for initiation. Love has staying power. It has been said that every step out of love is a step into trouble. Considering these factors, to say love is the essence of wisdom seems fitting.

> **A loving heart is the truest wisdom.**
> **–Charles Dickens**

You can be internally happy and prepared for any adversity. The boundaries of your life may shrink and still not keep you from making the most of your circumstances. Love functions equally well on small fields as it does on large ones. Love can be equated with *light* and *life*. Hate can be equated with *darkness* and *death*. There's only one person who can flip the switch from one world to the other. That's you and that's me. There's something empowering about that knowledge. This takes you out of the victim mentality and makes you the sole proprietor of your own personal well-being. No one can take that away from you.

Love makes you a free person.

Death is a condition of the heart, not the mere cessation of life. Rejections from other people can be forms of death. What are you going to do when you feel opposing forces? Because they're coming. Have you been tempted to be overtaken by bitterness, revenge, or anger? Such emotions can eclipse the true potential of love. Even though you experience these at times, don't let them take root. Stay in charge and find a place of repose you wouldn't trade for anything. Consequently, the love you follow will find that place in you. You can feel the inward depth this brings, the authenticity. As you project that to others, you feel the *miracle power* of love. If this was in capsule form, you'd take it multiple times per day to cure every woe.

A WORTHY EXPEDITION

So many have wanted to scale Mt. Everest in the Himalayas. Bordering Nepal and China, this is the highest peak on Earth. Thousands have been successful, though hundreds more have died. But there's something about the intrigue, mystery, and adventure of doing something so few have attempted, let alone finished. There is high risk and reward. It must be an exhilarating feeling to reach the top; such a sense of victory. There are notions to battle in one's mind during the journey: the desire to give up, to turn back, the fear of death, the physical trauma, and the torture of the elements. The conquering has to do with the battle raging between one's ears as much as anything. Lose there and you lose your mountain. Win there and you've partially arrived. Those who aren't equipped and prepared mentally don't make it to the top.

Have you ever asked yourself what difference it would make to summit the highest mountain of the unseen world called *love?* The high risk, the high reward, the exciting adventure, the beckoning call, the greater good, and the inestimable benefit toward others? There are many beneficiaries along the path of your quality decisions.

What if you risked all for love? I, myself, have tasted this cool, refreshing fountain of youth, but I have also left a lot on the table.

I haven't risked enough over the span of time. But when I've been successful, it was due to leaning hard on love. Love sustains the weight of belief and actions. Love purifies motives and sets them in order. What is most important?

I'll do that.

> Till I loved I never lived.
> -Emily Dickinson

There are untapped benefits that you miss out on by fearing to step out on the relationship limb. Nothing ventured, nothing gained, goes the saying. Love is a daily journey, a thrilling adventure. I've heard it said before that a single day is a miniature lifetime. Break down larger love aspirations into small achievable goals.

One day at a time.

No one gets all the answers in advance. No one gets all the assurances up front. No one has foreknowledge of every trapping in living this higher life. What about the rejection, conflicts, misunderstandings, misinterpretation of motives, or opposition? They're sure to come. Yet there is a fulfillment in risking to embrace this virtue like none other.

GO THE DISTANCE IN LOVE

As an avid runner, I get the proverbial runner's high only after having gone the distance, not before. The process can be rigorous and tough, taking a toll on the muscles and joints, but the results are beyond comparison. The thrill comes with the accomplishment. The work is in the process. Afterward, there's a blissful rest. The same holds true with love.

The only rest in life comes through the avenue of love.

Experience the fulfillment of seeing love to completion. Be the finisher. Leave it all on the court. Even your sleep will be sweeter. Nothing replaces the sense of spending oneself for a noble cause, because you risked something for love's sake and won. Sometimes, that love is rejected. There are no guarantees. Yet you did what you could and benefited for having placed a wager on the world champion of all essential virtues.

You don't win every battle. Love picks up another day and never quits. You pick up where you left off, whether it's after a disappointment, discouragement, or setback. No one else can take aim and shoot at life's lofty goals for you. Keep reaching for a great cause; better still, for another person. Be involved in the well-being and success of others. The beneficiaries of your love lifestyle are those individuals you serve every day of the week.

Love is a two-way street. No one goes it alone. You'll have help along the way. It's going to come up beside and overtake you when you are actively engaged. Be open and vulnerable. Stay connected with others and your timely hero will appear, sometimes in a way that you least expected. Remember that famous line in the *Wizard of Oz* when the wizard was passing out the promised gifts to Dorothy and her friends: *the true measure of love is not in how much we love but how much we are loved by others.*

ASPIRE TO GIVE WHAT YOU RECEIVE

The burden of love does not always fall on the giver. Perhaps it could be said that a person who understands love also avails themselves of what others have to offer. Receive what others give and be a sponge for positive influences all around. Observe and learn.

Have you met that person who would give the shirt off their back, but are red-faced embarrassed when others give to them? They don't know how to receive. They seem incapable, too insecure to put themselves in the weaker position. Avail yourself to others. Granted, this implies great risk, because not everyone has your best interest at heart. This can make you susceptible to hurt from trusting too much. There's a balance to strike. Wisdom is understanding the difference between extremes.

> Once in an age God sends to some of us a friend who loves in us, not a false-imagining, an unreal character, but looking through the rubbish of our imperfections, loves in us the divine ideal of our nature—loves, not the man that we are, but the angel that we may be.
> -Harriet Beecher Stowe

Discern what is in your own best interest and in the best interest of those you have pledged to help. Discard the remainder. When you stumble, get back up to try again. For every bad decision or judgment, try to make it pay dividends by stringing good decisions together in succession to make up for a bad one. This is a good habit to get back on the up and up. Never let a bad decision rule your day. Put things on the better track. The route is in front of you, not behind. The wheels may have come off, but there's something you can do to regroup. Dictate your new direction by using your moral compass. This is your power. Don't stew long over a setback. Glean the learning, wisdom, and understanding, then move onward and upward. An extraordinary life awaits the seekers.

The power to change is yours. Love yourself, not abusing yourself over a failure or setback. Paying attention to your gut instincts: intuition, perception, discernment, and judgment, for they are your most reliable navigations system. There's nothing wrong with common sense, either. Sense is your friend. Make it a point to be a receiver as much as a giver. Receiving from others in the right spirit will make you a more focused and effective giver. Never give what is not appropriate for the common good—and be willing to reciprocate all benefits awarded to you.

You wouldn't be the person you are if not for what other people have invested in you. Learn from others, grow from others, benefit from others' lives. That no man or woman is an island can't be overstated. You were born for positive relationships. Pass on what you learn to someone down the line. You're a blessing waiting to happen. Like the famous line in *The Lion King*, it's a *circle of life*. Your goal is completion in all things. You're part of something bigger than yourself. Be oriented toward others in order to find your unique place.

Be a lover of life. A lover of people. A lover of learning. A lover of growing. And you'll never lose your way.

LOVE IS YOUR STRONG SUIT

Love has a rhythm and a pace. Be sure it connects to others but never leave yourself out of the mix. It's a destination and a journey. Don't come up short by hindering others. No one who causes harm to others ultimately benefits themselves. Better to be a small part of another person's accomplishments than to center too much on self and become paralyzed. You don't need the credit for the good you do unto others. Love is bigger than all people combined. There's more than enough to go around. You have the high privilege of making a difference here and there. Think of the accumulation over time as a *wow* factor.

Love is the symbol of eternity.
-Madame de Stael

The mountain of love looms in the distance. Something ignites within the climber that assures them that they can get to the top. No one wants to stop halfway there. Want it more than life itself. Love is a worthwhile goal that shows you that you can do what was impossible before. Love inspires boldness and a commitment to scale the highest calling anywhere. It travels with you and supports you like a best friend. Those who betray the kinship pay dearly. In those cases, love didn't fail them.

They failed love.

Love is an ally. How do you get to the top of that metaphorical mountain? The answer lies with intention and the predisposition to arrive. No one gets to the top of Mt. Everest by accident. They don't suddenly find themselves at the summit. And no one experiences all love has to offer by accident, either. There must be a firm resolve, understanding the essence of the conquest. *Go ahead and make as many expeditions as you will.*

In business, it's called *due diligence*. Shouldn't the aspiration and study of love be given the same? This beats the careless, haphazard living that comes from letting the chips fall where they may mentality. Spreadsheets show detail and data in business. You know every logistical item that will be needed for a great ambition or project. Every contingency is accounted for and fully considered. Understand the enemies of a love lifestyle. Never throw in the towel and say the proposition wasn't worth the effort. You're developing thorough habits that will build upon each other. Keep going. When adverse circumstances come knocking at the door, there should be contingency plans in place. Make a decision that love is the ultimate end; that you won't be denied. Make a plan to do what works toward your overall goal and eliminate everything that doesn't contribute to that goal.

LOVE EQUALS FULFILLMENT

Be steadfast in the knowledge that no matter how many times you get knocked down, you will rise. For every rejection love takes to the chin, you know positive experiences are around the bend if you hold fast. Believe in love and it will carry you. It will also carry others that you know. This becomes a lifelong mission—to keep from stumbling and to help lift others after a fall. The last word always belongs to the essential virtue called love.

Don't try to write the script, rather live the life. Don't look for the massive windfalls. Look for the small moments. Make those count. Treasure them. Find love in the little things and it will create a large tapestry over time. Go out on a limb in a positive way instead of a negative one. The lasting fruit is hanging out on those branches.

What is inside a person is a treasure greater than all the opposition in the world combined. Most people know that Thomas Alva Edison failed a thousand times before inventing the incandescent light bulb. He found those ways that didn't work first. It was a steady, methodical, calculated process of elimination. It was a conquest, but one he enjoyed, a *magnificent obsession,* if you will.

Do the same with this character diamond called love. Make mental notes of what doesn't work and don't repeat your negative history. Cross that off your list. You're not tied to failure, defeat, or the darker past. All the while be sincere, genuine, kind, honest, and truthful. These are failproof assists in life's fight that pay off with results, both now and later.

Live on the breadcrumbs of previous successes. Follow what works and toss out what doesn't. Chip away at goals, one step at a time. "Accentuate the positive, eliminate the negative," state the lyrics of an old song. Believe in love's ability. Love believes in you—your goals, relationships, endeavors—large and small. You were born for the exhilaration and affirmation love provides. You are love's hero, a supreme object of her enduring affection.

There is only one happiness in life, to love and be loved.
-George Sand

Love has its own ambitions where you're concerned—toward health and fitness, education, business, family, vocation, friendships, community service, and more. This requires an integrated lifestyle to experience and find those secrets out. One area of life doesn't have to suffer at the expense of another. Giving all the importance to finances, for example, at the expense of personal health, is unnecessary. Enjoy both. Concentrate on one character attribute and the others will follow in short order behind the steady, faithful leader of love. All essential virtues are part of the same tight-knit family.

Mountain climbers crest the top and enjoy the view for a while. Conversely, love is for the climbers, adventure lovers, thrill seekers—and those who love mysteries. You never know what amazing things can happen on any given day because you were willing to take a chance on this essential virtue called love. It's the best and most reliable guide in history.

SPECIAL DELIVERY

I heard a giant heartbeat like it was a percussion instrument. It was distinct, so real, so alive. What I knew in theory became reality in that unique moment of time. The practitioner rubbed gel on a medical instrument and stroked it across my wife's abdomen. Before long, she pointed out the faint image of my first daughter on the screen. I heard her heart for the first time. In time, that love *kicked* me. I'll never forget how cool that was in the moment.

The name came to me before I met my wife. It was as clear as a bell when it slipped into my consciousness as a young twenty-year-old. I turned to a friend in the living room where I sat on a piano bench and proclaimed that if I ever had a daughter, exactly what her name would be. A couple of years later, I shared this experience with my wife after we married. We agreed to follow through with that inspiration. By the time our baby was born at Hillcrest Hospital in Tulsa, there was no question. I said to the nurse, "Her name is Phoebe."

One of love's avenues opened and returned simultaneously that day, and many others have benefitted from her life since. She wasn't a blessing we got to keep just for ourselves. She was such a flower—a tender, beautiful flower—still her personality today. She's an unsung hero in many ways, not asking for any credit. Her life is filled with essential virtues that she gives to others every day.

I didn't realize that when my daughter was born that the gift would return more than we gave. It's easy to underestimate at times its power to perpetuate, grow, and deliver lifelong benefits. There are many facets of love to experience, which is why it behooves people to grow and adapt with this masterful teacher. Love should increase over time, and I've determined to grow connected to that fruitful vine.

Love should be more precious than yesterday. Love *appreciates* in value more than material goods or real estate, more than silver and gold. Love doesn't stand still or retreat. It moves forward. Enter its current, which has the remarkable ability to usher people into brighter futures, building them into people they weren't yesterday. There is *transformative* power to love, creating a distinct arc of change. Nothing will do quite like this virtue. It's more than the mind can conceive, but it can be imagined, dreamed, and eagerly anticipated. Go somewhere to make love happen. Someone will be thrilled that you did. Love's victories throughout the ages cannot possibly be numbered. But go ahead and add your story to the mix.

All these years later, Phoebe is grown and married to a wonderful spouse with two children of their own. Love has compounded many times over with interest. The first words that come out of a baby's mouth can melt your heart. I'll never forget when my first grandchild uttered the word, "Papa."

Every love expression from birth to death resonates and makes us feel something other-worldly. That's love worth living for, striving for, and sharing with others. Phoebe means *bright*. She's such a light. Someone commented, "What a beautiful child."

Another man said, "Don't ever forget the blessing God has put in your care," and I haven't.

Still, another gasped at the first sight of her when she was but two or three years old.

Love multiplied again with the birth of our second daughter, Evie, and yet again with the birth of our youngest, Jason—each with their own remarkable stories. Love grows exponentially.

THE GIFT OF INFLUENCE

Blessed is the influence of one true,
loving human soul on another.
–Mary Ann Evans, aka George Eliot

Taking people for granted is lessened with the character essential of love engaged. Your objective is to make this virtue sing. Place infinite value on children, parents, siblings, friends, and associates. I've heard it said that you can't just look at the apple, you must count the seeds if you want to know its true potential. Relationships make us richer by counting the inherent seeds within them and allowing them to blossom over time. Maximum love makes you the most successful individual on Earth. Who are you helping? Whose talents are you recognizing? How are you helping others achieve their full potential?

Love is at your disposal but must be engaged by a voluntary decision. The lack of love produces a void that can't be filled in any other way. Conversely, hate withers the branches and causes death to the flourishing tree of an extraordinary life. It's easy to note great financial successes. Everyone understands influence, fame, and power as status symbols. But if those are achieved without love, those statuses become hollow and empty.

Love makes you a better parent, son, daughter, spouse, sibling, friend, teacher, student, entrepreneur, employer, and employee—but most of all a better person. What if you gained the whole world but lost this unseen gem of the soul? The result would be a catastrophic relational bankruptcy. This is a heartache you can't afford. Walk in love and you can live even while dying. Forfeit love and you die inwardly, even while living. The failure to make that distinction leads to many unfulfilled lives.

Perhaps the least heralded essential virtue is the one that counts the most. Anything you do can have this dynamo at the center. Be sincere, genuine, and believable. No one likes the faker who mouths the words, "I love you," but lacks the feeling and depth to make you believe it when they speak.

UNSUNG HERO AWARDS

Bernie Madoff was an investor who bilked thousands of people out of their lifetime of savings. It took a long time for the dishonesty to catch up, but it usually does in one way or another. Bernie had fame. He had great wealth. But he didn't have his investors' benefits in mind, which constituted an epic failure of love. He died in prison with regrets. If he could do it all over, he probably would have chosen differently. It would be better to make less money and be content, than to be greedy by gaining more than what would be obtained through honest, upright means. The character diamond of love wasn't activated in this case, though it was a sleeping giant all the while.

Have you thought about taking the time to rewrite your life's resume with a whole new bent? What's important that others haven't noticed or given you proper credit for? Just because others haven't noticed doesn't mean it doesn't count on a grand scale.

For example, if you're a parent and have equipped your children to succeed in life with love at their helm, you're an unsung hero. It should be recorded on your resume. You've set the example that your kids should never settle for what doesn't contribute to their integrity as people. This pays rich dividends that will last the rest of their lives. They're rich because of what you invested—even if you never get the credit. You were an integral part of who and what they became. And if you're the best child of a parent that you can be, that qualifies too— not to mention if you're an unheralded friend, sibling, or coworker. Find the worth in relationships all around. Don't focus on the fake superheroes of fame, money, prestige, or a superficial image.

You have the real deal. The original. The indispensable. The miracle worker.

You have love.

Whoso loves, believes in the impossible.
–Elizabeth Barrett Browning

GEMSTONES

- Love is the greatest, most adaptable gift ever given to human beings.

- Be involved in the well-being and success of others. The beneficiaries are those individuals you serve every day of the week.

- Be open and vulnerable. Be connective with others and your timely hero will appear; sometimes in a way that is least expected.

- Paying attention to gut instincts is reliable: intuition, perception, discernment, and judgment. There's nothing wrong with common sense, either.

- Be a lover of life. A lover of people. A lover of learning. A lover of growing. And you'll never lose your way.

- Those who betray the kinship of love pay dearly. In those cases, love didn't fail them. They failed love.

- Be steadfast in the knowledge that no matter how many times you get knocked down, you will rise. For every rejection love takes to the chin, know that positive experiences are around the bend if you hold fast.

- Find love in the little things and it will create a large tapestry over time. Go out on a limb in a positive way instead of a negative one. The lasting fruit is hanging out on those branches.

- Love doesn't stand still or retreat. It moves forward. Enter its current, which has the remarkable ability to usher people into brighter futures, building them into people they weren't yesterday.

- Relationships make you richer by counting the inherent seeds within them and allowing them to blossom over time.

REFLECTIONS
LOVE: THE MASTER KEY

Identify what lies behind the doorway of unlimited inner wealth through love and devotion.

PROMPT: Reflect on moments when love has made a powerful impact in your life.

ACTION: List ways to show love to yourself and others.

PROMPT: Remember a moment when someone showed you kindness and how it impacted your day.

ACTION: Write down one act of kindness you can do or have done for someone today to pay it forward.

Notes:

_____

_____

_____

_____

_____

_____

_____

_____

_____

_____

_____

_____

VIRTUE #2

COURAGE: LIGHT IN THE DARK

Highlighting benefits of a commodity
that conquers in every battle

Unsung Hero Story

When I heard about Renee's heartbreaking journey, I wanted to know more. So, I arranged for us to have a conversation at her home. What I didn't expect was the wisdom that was wrapped in this young twenty-something. She was honest, transparent, and genuine. I didn't expect the depth of maturity and authenticity beyond her years. Her story became my story. I published an article and it became an award-winner for me as a journalist. But the life lessons about the essential virtue of courage went far deeper.

Renee was in a horrifying car crash at the age of sixteen, effectively ending her fast track to a college scholarship in volleyball. This occurred in 2011 on Black Friday. The crushed vehicle resembled an accordion, and a machine called the jaws of life was used to rip the roof open to get her out. Her femur bone was forced through her pelvis, totally shattering it—not to mention her broken ankle, right foot, ruptured spleen, and fractured tailbone.

She was life-flighted to an area hospital, where she remained for two weeks. It took several months of rehabilitation, including wheelchairs, crutches, and walking canes, but she survived. Though suffering the loss of a volleyball scholarship, she bounced back, viewing the experience as a second chance at life, enrolling in a theatre class at a local community college.

There she met fellow theatre students who became close friends through mutual involvement in college productions. In 2014, they planned a trip together for the Thanksgiving break, traveling through Illinois to Michigan. There was a second car crash, again on Black Friday, three years after the first one. Renee was ejected from the vehicle. She lay motionless on her right side, unable to move her body at all. Renee described to me the light snow on the street and the frigid temperature outside. Her life was reduced to small moments of time where choices, as well as timely helpers, played a role in her outcome. She remembers the dead quiet after the crash. She recalled playing with the snow in the palm of her hand.

The first thing she thought about was her friends. She prayed out loud, "Dear God, please don't let my friends die."

Renee's own injuries were horrific. She was in shock yet found the ability to utter those selfless prayers.

A nurse happened by the scene and stopped to tend to her immediate needs. She urged Renee to stay awake as she fought drifting off to sleep. "But I don't want to stay awake."

"Renee, you have to," came the reply.

This unsung hero stranger may have saved her life. Renee's pelvis was broken in half and both parts overlapped. This time, she fractured five vertebrae and suffered severe spinal injuries. After being transported to an area hospital, a rod was inserted into her pelvis. Months of rehab followed, with Renee at times questioning her will to live.

"I felt robbed. I felt robbed of relationships and opportunities. Everybody has their own breaking point; everyone at some point has something taken away from them," she recalled.

People encouraged her and told her that she was strong, but she pondered the meaning. "I started thinking about what it meant to be strong. They called me strong because I'd been dealt a difficult hand."

Renee's pain was 24/7 and didn't stop for months. She credits her mother for being her personal nurse full-time, around the clock at home during the recovery process, while simultaneously working a job. Having the rod eventually removed was like a weight had been lifted from her, both emotionally and physically.

Renee had many unsung heroes who assisted during the crisis, including her mother, sister, best friend, and stepdad. Family was central to her survival and ultimate recovery. She could not have endured the hardship without a lot of love and support. There were days so difficult that Renee wanted to give up hope. She had had enough and felt done. There were times she wished she hadn't lived at all. Yet something rose inside of her to conquer the odds—the diamond of the heart called courage. "I've prayed a lot and have done a lot of soul searching. I realize now that if I've lived through something like this twice, I must have a big purpose in life. Come what may, at the end of the day, there is still something out there for me to live for."

She found it uncanny that both crashes occurred on Black Friday and that she was wearing her sister's clothing on both occasions. One of her boots came off each time. The lessons she learned shaped how she viewed life. She shifted her focus to others, instead of her own needs. "What an experience it is to be around people less fortunate than you, and to see them overcome adversity. What a grateful opportunity I have to be around people so optimistic," she said. "Every day is a challenge. But for me, the courage and strength to get up and face the day, tasks, and obstacles all come from my faith."

Renee's heroes helped her through impossibilities where there appeared to be no way forward, yet courage surmounted her physical and emotional limitations. Renee took an opportunity to help a puppet team serve children in a local community theater to keep the essential virtue of courage alive and well. She determined to be a helper, even during her personal trauma.

Renee's friends survived the crash. The theater department and fellow students held a fundraiser to help all four victims of the crash, which she credits as being a huge contribution to help her get home. The personal injuries were so severe that she was not permitted to fly but instead was transported in a medical van. Renee is quick to point out that the community gave her a gift of courage she wasn't expecting and she's grateful for the overwhelming amount of support they provided. Conversely, she converted the gift of unfailing courage after her rehabilitation by extending hope and encouragement to others when all seemed lost.

The gift of courage is transferable.

Exhortations to Excellence on Courage

The secret of freedom, courage.
–Thucydides

When the chips are down, you need a megadose of this virtue. It's a bubbling fountain rising to the occasion when you need it most. If there wasn't a backdrop of trials pressing all about, such a gift wouldn't be necessary. Yet the role of *courage* becomes an indispensable diamond of the human spirit. How it glistens in the light. You can't lead the quality of life you aspire to live without it. It's a calling and a responsibility. Mounting threats don't diminish its ability, but only fan the flame to burn its brightest. Courage gives triumph in the dark hour. And love is the mother of all courage.

Have the magnificent view of: *What people will benefit tomorrow from the courage you show today?*

The first image that comes to my mind when I hear this word is one of my favorite movies of all time, *The Wizard of Oz*. I must admit, the cowardly lion was my least favorite character. He annoyed me. Maybe it was that he was more antagonistic than the rest of the friends. They were less selfish. Dorothy wanted to go home. Scarecrow wanted a brain. Tin Man wanted a heart. They each had their own set of problems. But they were caring toward each other. Lion was stuck in his own world of fear and let everybody know. His misery wanted company. To his credit, maybe his Achilles heel of fear was more binding and debilitating than the rest.

All he wished for every day of his life was courage, yet it was in his grasp all along. His mind was unfocused and disorganized, to the extent that it paralyzed his personal productivity. I've heard it said that pressure can be turned around and viewed as *privilege*. But Lion's courage was trapped away, inaccessible. Why? He didn't believe. He chose an inferior way to express his deepest need by the intimidation and harassment of others. He preyed on anyone he perceived as the weaker entity. But it was all bluster. He derived superficial energy from the sense of foreboding telegraphed by others.

ALL TRUTH IS PARALLEL

I've experienced this in many settings—workplace and social situations included. It's difficult for anyone to be mocked, shamed, and ridiculed. Perhaps the worst way to hide insecurity is by overcompensating and behaving like a bully. That approach is short-lived until it meets its match down the line. Lion jumped out of the trees while Dorothy, Tin Man, and Scarecrow were picking up the apples thrown at them by the talking trees. Lion was aggressive to her dog, Toto. You'd never know he had a fear problem by the way he was acting. He pushed and pushed until Dorothy had enough and swatted him on the nose.

Then his demeanor changed. *Curtains.* Lion broke down and started sobbing, People sometimes do the same thing until a line is drawn in the sand for them. "I didn't bite 'im!"

Dorothy replied by pulling out a handkerchief to dry his tears. Lion sheepishly grabbed his tail and used it as a security blanket. In came wallowing self-pity, which loved its own company just like misery did.

It's interesting that the characters called alongside to help Dorothy didn't have proper names. They can represent character traits present in individuals. They are sleeping giants waiting to be activated and turned loose on our problems. When they are awakened, watch out. How much those are accentuated during crises is up to you.

> **Nothing will come of nothing; we must dare mighty things.**
> **–William Shakespeare**

Whereas the movie is fiction, parallels of truth and life lessons can be drawn from the themes. These were fragmented individuals. Their full potential wasn't realized until they were able to give the squeaky wheel the grease, so to speak. Everyone has problems, yet how they are processed and handled in the moment can determine opposite outcomes. Don't allow circumstances to overwhelm you. Courage is necessary to shed any and every handicap.

BELIEVING AGAINST THE ODDS

Fear can take a person down for the count. At some point, you must say enough is enough. Fear retreats and subsides at the point that you take courage. Something must stop the slide—and that's what this essential virtue does. There is something within that says you can combat your fears by a firm resolve against the impossibility imposed by the situation. The initial decision is the beginning point of something better. But it must be a heartfelt one, not superficial. Are you persuaded enough to act? This has true igniting power. That's when enthusiasm kicks in and takes the decision to a new level. Nothing worthwhile is accomplished without taking the first step, and courage pours it from the bottle. That's when you've hit your stride and you know you're on the right path. You're confident, striking while the iron is hot.

To what extent you dwell on fear provides the potential for its conquering of you. But damaged courage can heal in a moment to become your biggest asset, especially in times of trouble. It doesn't necessarily change your circumstances right away, but it does affect your disposition and demeanor instantaneously, which is half or more of the battle. Conversely, to what extent you dwell on courage will be the edge to conquer the fear nagging at you.

> **We could never learn to be brave and patient**
> **if there were only joy in the world.**
> **–Helen Keller**

MOTHER OF INVENTION

To his credit, Lion showed flashes of courage during the rescue operation. He acted out of gut instinct, which is a reminder that you can do the same. Lion helped break the door down with a battering ram to get Dorothy out of the dungeon where she was being held captive. If it weren't for love, he wouldn't have had the gumption to put himself in harm's way. Love provided the courage to do what he did and became his superpower.

You've shown flashes of courage in many areas of life. You act out of gut instinct and feel energized when you step out on a limb. Love inspires courage, which is the *doing* aspect of the equation. Love is the seed of courage and the parent of all essential virtues. If you focus on love, you'll never be short on the courage it takes to get you through that trial or hardship. It will also be the biggest asset you have to live a life of service and help others.

Courage is an essential virtue for every person who wants to excel, achieve, and be extraordinary. Without thinking, you act out of the best interest of others, and it brings out the best in you. This is a good lesson to lock in—when you help others, you help yourself. Even the Cowardly Lion was born for *connection*. Life is about meaningful relationships. Have the courage to build them and you will have found a great wealth against times to come.

Your real quest is to become an integrated, harmonious person— and that's not possible without the essential virtue called courage. Conquer the mental and spiritual handicaps on your quest to becoming more than you dreamed to others. This is your journey. Every day you should strive for wholeness. And that can't be done apart from others, which is one of the most intriguing and fascinating mysteries of our world.

Dorothy's friends were unsung heroes, as was Dorothy for them. They were willing to help each other. And what each thought they lacked was in essence a gold mine within, like the essential virtues mined in you. Each of the friends underestimated themselves. They weren't the likely ones to rise to the occasion and send Dorothy home. But they were determined, and it caused them to turn the tables on a whole army of fears. Uncommon valor took the place of their deepest insecurities. The underlying message is: Don't wait until they are all vanquished to muster courage.

Take it now and turn the tide.

Everyday courage has few witnesses.
But yours is no less noble because no drum
beats for you and no crowds shout your name.
–Robert Louis Stevenson

FOCUS ON SMALL SEEDS OF DECISION

At the end of the day, Dorothy was only in charge of herself. The ruby slippers were symbolic of her personal volition, which you possess, too. She proactively *chose* courage, which prompted a sequence of corresponding actions. She then moved toward that light, even without all the answers.

Sometimes it's sobering when the weight of decisions falls on you until you realize there's more available than you ever imagined at your fingertips. You are the affecter of the change you seek. There is a transformation, and it becomes the best news. "Why didn't I think of that sooner?" you might ask.

Courage inspires you to take control of your destiny. And that begins with the first step, reordering everything that follows. That's the beauty of this essential virtue. Don't wait until everything is just right. That day will never come. Courage is a sleeping giant, vying for a fighting chance at the gate of your most threatening problems.

I imagine walking in a dark place. It's getting darker, pitch black. I can't see a thing. I can't find the light switch soon enough. No matter how dark it is, when I turn on the light, it expels the dark. Any of us would flip that switch right away to overcome the darkness, rather than continue aimlessly. Who would say, "Let me walk in this darkness a little while longer?"

Courage is that light always shining in the darkness. It doesn't require a laundry list of assurances in advance but equips us for the unknowns we will encounter around the bend. It changes the chemistry of your emotional makeup and provides a needed sense of well-being. Enter *composure*. Like those professional athletes many admire, they maintain their composure under pressure. Without courage, things would go from bad to worse. With it, you're a champion in your domain and a helper of others just the same.

THE VITAMIN C OF COURAGE

By the end of the story, Dorothy's unsung heroes have found what they've been seeking all their lives. As she prepares to go home, she hugs each hero. She sings of their friendship, their loyalty, their kindness, their courage. She knows she couldn't have made it without them. They're grateful to have played an important role in her life. They've all been changed for the better. They used the very qualities they thought they lacked to ultimately succeed. *Memo: You will too.* Courage is an essential virtue that makes all things possible.

> **Have the courage to face a difficulty lest it kick you harder than you bargain for.**
> **–Leszczynski Stanislaus**

When people cross the finish lines of life together, everyone wins. Each is happy for the other person's success. There's no need to selfishly gloat because no one was a cookie-cutter to start with. This is comparing apples to oranges. Don't do it. Each one of us has a battle, and the victory is tailored to our unique personalities, talents, and needs. The lessons courage teaches you will endure for a lifetime. You can't unlearn what you've been taught. You don't have to take that test again. It's now in your tool belt of valued transformational experiences.

Courage sees you through and becomes a permanent asset, on tap whenever needed. When you take a personal inventory, stock up this resource for your personalized road to wholeness. You have new opportunities awaiting—brought to you by the character virtue called courage. Having the boldness to begin allows the how and why to materialize. You're truly living when you step into what your heart yearns for and aspires to the most.

Trials can crush and grind or prove and refine. The outcome depends on the attitude you've set at the beginning or implemented along the way. It's never too late to change. The smallest pebble can become an enormous weight of burden. Conversely, the heaviest trial can become as light as a feather. What is your proximity to the difficulty? It's the old glass half full or half empty analogy. It depends on what you believe. It's not so much the gravity of events that spell victory or defeat, but how they are processed in the moment. Overcoming is a matter of climbing into the vehicle and driving in the right direction. You'll feel better once you're on the open road to a destination, however far away it may be. Beat the odds by choosing one of the best buddies you've ever hung around—courage.

> He who loses wealth loses much; he who loses a friend
> loses more; but he that loses courage loses all.
> –Cervantes

BENEFICIARY OF COURAGE

As a young person, I listened hours on end to the music of Neil Diamond in my back bedroom. There was something about his deep, gravelly voice. He mesmerized me. "Song Sung Blue," "I Am I Said," "Sweet Caroline," and "Cracklin' Rosie" are a few of his classic titles. What a songwriter and performer. Now, decades later, I still listen to him for hours on end while I run. Neil Diamond is timeless. His career has spanned decades. Music has kept him young. I can say it has kept me youthful, too. My perspective is that every year I grow older, I grow a year younger at heart. I thank musical artists like Neil for that—they're gifts.

What I didn't know until recently is that he attributes his amazing success as a singer/songwriter to his grandmother and mother. They were unsung heroes of his. Neil explained to one of his sold-out audiences that one hundred years before, a twelve-year-old girl boarded a train in Kiev, Russia, and made the journey of more than 1,000 miles to Holland. She then boarded a ship to make the voyage to freedom in America. That little girl, Neil said, was his grandmother. Together with her daughter Rose, Neil's mother, they both inspired him to achieve everything he has achieved in his storied professional career. He emphatically affirms that their courage will never be forgotten and lives in every song he sings.

Diamond's hit, "America," was based on his family's compelling immigration story from Kiev to Brooklyn, New York. Diamond was born to Akeeba and Rose Diamond. He attended the same high school as another Jewish musical prodigy, Barbra Streisand. Neil is proud of both his grandmother's and mother's stories, lauding their undeniable courage. They remain unsung heroes, but he chose to not let them stay that way. He's been intentional about making the stories sing. The rest, as they say, is history.

INEXHAUSTIBLE SOURCE

If you were offered all the riches of the world in exchange for courage, would you take it? I'll bet you'd turn it down in a heartbeat. You are richer with courage than without. He who has none is bankrupt. This virtue can't be faked or pretended. Those who have courage are renowned for their lofty dreams and visions of a better future. They are firm and confident. You have wisdom and understanding of the circumstance at hand. Your interpretation and adapting of those are reliable, accurate, and precise.

Attacking is the only secret. Dare and the world always yields;
or if it beats you sometimes, dare it again and it will succumb.
–William Makepeace Thackeray

You'll be remembered for your courage.

Place two letters "e-n" on the front end of the word and it converts to "encourage." Put encouragement to work on behalf of someone else. Encouragement is an art form and a gift to be distributed during any kind of crisis. Words inspire you to action, as do gestures and random acts of kindness. The encouragement you've received from others is valuable; indispensable. You might not know what another person is up against, but you observe and place yourself in another's shoes. You feel what they feel through identification. You possess this power to empathize. From somewhere within comes that fountain that can lift the spirit of the person you want to help. The prerequisite is caring sincerely. And encouragement, like other essential virtues, is born of selfless love.

To encourage is to deposit what is needed in someone else. To discourage is to withdraw; to pull something from them. There are those who take delight in the latter. Not everyone wants to take the highly specialized role of the *encourager*. But when you do, you've become an unsung hero for someone's cause, with or without the credit. Sometimes, there are those whose expertise is in finding fault and hindering progress. There can be envy, bitterness, and animosity. But take up encouragement like other duties of the day. It's a commitment and a resolve. Pressure is an opportunity to model courage, not a cause for mental or spiritual paralysis. The benefits of an encouraging lifestyle outweigh the negative repercussions of discouragement—the sure path to fulfillment. Nothing thrills like courage from head to toe.

SUPERPOWER OF ENCOURAGEMENT

Bob Goff is a bright and shining example of one who takes the specialized role of the encourager to heart. Bob is an author, speaker, and a self-described "recovering lawyer." He wrote the book titled, *Love Does*, a *New York Times* best seller. Bob has an impressive resume when it comes to showing courage on behalf of others. True to form, he's taken the virtue to great heights with his commitment and resolve to engage with others, making his own life bigger. There's room for everyone to live a life of courage that makes the world a better place.

Stories in his book include what to do with closed doors, saying yes to opportunities that turn into life-changing experiences, trading up for bigger and better, and ripping off capes to be more useful. Bob understands courage as an indispensable asset for a fulfilled life, and its counterpart of encouragement as a genuine and authentic superpower. I recommend this book to anyone looking to be a courageous thrill-seeker.

Doing the impossible is tied to a commitment to being an unsung hero for someone. Courage is about taking risks. At times it means leaning in to embrace opportunities instead of backing away. According to the whimsical book of Bob, "People who take huge risks aren't afraid to fail. In fact, they love to fail. It's because failing means they've found the edge."

As a young man, after failing the LSAT entrance exam to law school, he sat outside the dean's office at San Diego State University and asked to be admitted to their law school anyway. He was denied day after day after day. He reminded the dean that he could let Bob in if he wanted and all he had to do was tell Bob to go buy his books. A week into the semester, Bob was still positioning himself outside the dean's office every day. Prospects for admission looked bleak, but finally, the dean looked at Bob one day, giving him the green light, and told him to go buy his books. Bob describes this experience as "kicking a door down" when a door of opportunity wasn't already open.

Fast forwarding, Bob eventually became an adjunct professor of law at Pepperdine University. Through a series of events, by saying yes to unusual opportunities, he discovered children in the country of Uganda that were wrongfully imprisoned. Bob used his legal expertise to represent these children in court to secure their freedom. Eventually, the entire prison was emptied. Bob ripped the old wooden door off the hinges that held those children captive, and the door remains in the corner of his office today.

Bob has kicked impossible doors down through *courage* and ripped others off their hinges through the power of *encouragement* for people in dire need. He says that full engagement is the only way to live life and bravery has a way of expelling darkness with light. Failure is an inevitable part of the process of living full out. He thinks people should swing for the home run when they step up to the plate.

When things go wrong, there's a choice whether to be wounded or changed by a negative outcome. Which side of the experience will you dwell on? Your interpretation shapes the outcome. He says no one would refuse an open invitation to visit the White House, but people turn down the open invitation to truly live and engage every day.

Bob says you can change the course of a person's life by saying something good about them: "God made it so that ordinary people like you and me can launch each other . . . I believe it's true that the right people can say words that can change everything. And guess what? We're the ones who can say them."

**These are the ideals and words
of a truly great encourager.**

He calls it courage and bravery simply to be yourself. It will be enough, every time. He encapsulates the cut-above disposition this way: "We get to decide that people, including ourselves, are worth more than others might figure."

Bob finally sums up the adventure called *life:* "It's about doing capers without any capes. Not surprisingly, we'd get a lot more done too, because we wouldn't care who's looking or taking credit. All that energy would be funneled into awesomeness. We all get a chance to be awesome if we want to be. Not surprisingly, the way to do it best is by being secretly incredible."

Bob's book, *Love Does*, inspires its readers to take the encourager's role to another level. Go to bobgoff.com to learn more.

OPEN INVITATION

Therefore, take up encouragement like an obligation, but a joyous one. It's a resolve and a privilege. The benefit of this lifestyle outweighs the effects of its dangerous opponent—discouragement. Someone motivated you who believed in your ability, hopes, dreams, and aspirations. You can take hold of the hero of courage or sell yourself short by leaving it untouched in the vault. Those who endeavor to harm others ultimately harm themselves. When you help others, you help yourself. It only takes a spark to get a fire going, an old song says. And it only takes one person who believes in you to offset the cumulative discouragement of however many who don't.

Be that sparkling gem. Turn that timeless essential virtue of courage loose.

Dare to begin! He who postpones living rightly is like the rustic who waits for the river to run out before he crosses.
–Horace

GEMSTONES

- The role of courage becomes an indispensable diamond of the human spirit.

- Fear retreats and subsides at the point that you take courage.

- There is something within that says you can combat fears with a firm resolve against the odds. The initial decision is the beginning point of something better.

- Are you persuaded enough to act? This has true igniting power.

- Taking courage doesn't necessarily change your circumstances right away, but it does affect your disposition and demeanor instantaneously, which is half or more of the battle.

- I can't think of anyone who has won life's battles alone. People need each other.

- A good lesson—when you courageously help others, you help yourself. Life is about meaningful relationships.

- Courage inspires you to take control of your destiny. And that begins with the first step, reordering everything that follows.

- Courage is that light beckoning in the darkness. It doesn't require a laundry list of assurances in advance but equips you for the unknowns to come.

- From within comes your fountain that can lift the spirit of the person you want to help.

REFLECTIONS
COURAGE: LIGHT IN THE DARK

Think about your definition of courage and highlight the benefits of the commodity that conquers in every battle as you face challenges in your life.

PROMPT: Analyze the benefits of having courage in difficult situations. Consider times when courage has helped you achieve a goal.

ACTION: Make a list of steps to take when feeling uncertain or afraid.

PROMPT: Recall a time when you faced a fear. How did you overcome it and what did you learn from the experience?

ACTION: Write down one fear you want to face and the steps you can take to summon your courage.

Notes:

_____

_____

_____

_____

_____

_____

_____

_____

_____

_____

VIRTUE #3

Honesty: Heavyweight Champ of the World

How keeping integrity makes you a winning person

Unsung Hero Story

One way to learn about honesty is by looking at its counterpart—dishonesty—and the tragic consequences for misdealing with people.

When I was a young child, cowboy and Indian shows were a thing. Most of the time, the good guys were the cowboys, and the bad guys were the Indians. But because of the widespread mischaracterizations on the TV screen, I had dreams at night of Indians coming into our house. I hid under the bed, and what do you know, that was the first place they checked? Then I would wake up. Little did I know that I would meet so many Native Americans as an adult that broke every one of those stereotypes.

Jack Shadwick served for many years as the ambassador to the Modoc Nation in northeast Oklahoma. He is one of the kindest, gentlest souls I know. I sat down at the tribal headquarters to have a conversation about the Modoc tragedy of the latter nineteenth century. Here's a portion of the story, illustrating the highly regrettable consequences of withholding honesty from people who deserve better.

During the latter half of the nineteenth century, the Modoc people lived in five thousand square miles of California land near Tule Lake and the nearby Lava Beds. The Cascade mountains were to the west, the Sierra to the east, and the Oregon border to the north. Due to the 1849 Gold Rush, the new Oregon Trail, and the construction of the transcontinental railroad, Indians were "in the way" of modern progress.

The U.S. government funded the governor of California, Peter Burnett, to solve the Indian "problem." In 1850, Governor Burnett designated a half-million dollars from the California legislature to mount a war of extermination against the Indian tribes living there. A bounty of $25-50 per scalp was offered to the interested takers.

Eyeing a lucrative money-making opportunity, Ben Wright, a gold-mining settler from Indiana, rounded up additional men from Yreka, California, to help cash in. Under a presumed white flag of peace, Wright lured thirty unsuspecting Modoc tribal members and slaughtered them in what became known as the Ben Wright Massacre. Over the course of a year, Wright killed roughly 170 members of the tribe.

Fast forward to the 1860s, when the U.S. government pressured the chief, Captain Jack, and the tribe to cede substantial acreage and relocate to southern Oregon with the neighboring Klamath tribe based on promises outlined in the 1864 Treaty of Council Grove. Captain Jack performed his part of the treaty, hoping for a fair and equitable reciprocation of outlined benefits.

Historically, the Klamath and Modoc didn't get along. The Modoc were disadvantaged at the outset and vastly outnumbered. The 1864 treaty took many years to be ratified. In the meantime, the needs of the Modoc were not being met as detailed in the agreement. After two years, unhappy with the poor living conditions and disappointed in being misled, one-third of the tribe decided to leave the reservation and go back home to the lava beds in California, only they confined their living area to a fraction of what it was before, settling down at Lost River.

Led by Captain Jack, there were fifty-three warriors and roughly 150 citizens of the tribe. They were left alone for a time and happy to be back in their homeland, yet the prosperity was short-lived. The Treaty of Council Grove was ratified by 1870, six years after the treaty was originally signed. By 1872, under another presumed white flag of peace, the U.S. Army, led by General Edward Canby, met with the small band of Modoc to negotiate a settlement. With the disillusionment of previous "white flags of peace" lingering from the Ben Wright Massacre, suspicion was palpable. Captain Jack drove a flag in the ground upside-down, which was a symbol of Modoc distress. It became obvious to the tribe that the government was preparing to force the Modoc back to the Klamath reservation in Oregon. The pleas from the Modoc for a small portion of their homeland to live on were denied.

During November of 1873, looking closely at this momentous turning point, one journalist noted in the *Phrenological Journal of Science and Health*, "At the very time Canby was negotiating a flag of truce, he was actually bringing his men into position, violating one of the best-known rules of honorable warfare, that pushing military options under a flag of truce should not happen."

The tribe resolved not to return to the Klamath reservation in Oregon. With the impending danger of a forceable removal, Captain Jack fired a shot, killing the only U.S. General to have died in an Indian war. The Modoc War, also known as the Lava Beds War, ensued. Fifty-three Modoc men held from one to three thousand U.S. troops at bay for seven months.

Many concluded that General Canby brought the destruction on himself by his dubious dealing with the Modoc people. Captain Jack had been compliant, honoring their part of the 1864 treaty. Yet the dishonesty and lack of humanity toward the Modoc people was coming to light. Many in the East took note of the bravery of Captain Jack and his men and exalted his leadership qualities, believing he was worthy of more admiration and respect than he was being awarded.

During 1873, seven months into the war, supplies ran low for the Modoc fighting from the higher grounds, trenches, and caverns of the Lava Beds, and they were forced to finally surrender. Trials ensued for six of the tribal leaders, but the scaffolding and gallows were constructed in advance, foreshadowing the predetermined guilty verdicts. Captain Jack was sentenced to hanging along with other leaders—Schonchin John, Black Jim, and Boston Charley. Their heads were cut off and shipped to the Smithsonian Institute in Washington. Bancho and Sioux were the two other leaders tried and found guilty. They were sentenced to imprisonment on Alcatraz Island.

Conversely, the governor of California, Peter Burnett, suffered no ill consequences or criminal charges for his extermination orders in 1850. Ben Wright was not tried for his extensive murder campaign. William Tecumseh Sherman was not held accountable for ordering every Modoc to die, including women and children.

Indian reservations had essentially become internment camps. Following the executions, 153 Modoc prisoners of war, many of them shackled, were shipped in the "Iron Horse" train to Baxter Springs, Missouri. From there, they were removed once again to northeastern Oklahoma, where additional promises of provision were broken. Over time, the meager lands allotted to the tribe placed between properties belonging to other tribes already living there made it difficult for the Modoc to access and grow their own crops.

Today, there are nearly 500 tribal members. Modoc Nation is one of thirty-nine federally recognized tribes in the state of Oklahoma. The culture has revived over the years. The nearly extinct language is being restored and taught to their children. Many of their customs, practices, and traditions are thriving once again.

Rosie Jack, the daughter of the infamous Captain Jack, died at the tender age of seven in April of 1874—six short months after her father was hung. She was the first prisoner of war buried in northeast Oklahoma, far from her ancestral home in California. The cause of death is not known, but a case could legitimately be made that poor conditions were a factor—not to mention the grief of losing her father. Dishonesty and unfulfilled promises were likely contributors to the tragic outcome.

Captain Jack remains a venerated leader of the Modoc for all time. His picture hangs in the headquarters in Miami, Oklahoma. He led with integrity, endeavoring to do the right thing. Yet ultimately, he gave his life for the people he served.

Shortly after Captain Jack's death, the same *Phrenological Journal of Science and Health* journalist condemned the unjust proceedings that took place in Oregon, titling the article, *Coward or Hero: A Western estimate of Captain Jack*, writing:

> An Indian knows how to die. He fights for his freedom and his home while there is the slightest hope, then he gives up and awaits the action of his executioner. There are those who regard the Indian as being all bad, without redeeming qualities. We judge them differently and believe that proper or fair treatment would secure the same from them. At any rate, the Indian is human. God made him and he once had rights in this country. How happens that he has lost them? Will our boasted civilization please answer this?

Jack Shadwick summarized the tragic sequence of events that led to the Modoc removal from California to Oklahoma. "I think in some ways they [Modoc] were probably a very gentle tribe but once they were pushed, like many of us, past the breaking point, then they did whatever they felt like they should do in order to survive at all."

Decades before, as a young teenager growing up in Baxter Springs, Jack was working at a gas station. Cars with license plates from California came through on occasion. People asked if it was safe for them to be travelling through the area, not knowing they were looking at a Modoc tribal member, one of the kindest souls they could ever meet. Jack played along and told them they should just fill it up with gas and drive on through.

After our visit, Jack drove me out to the old Modoc cemetery. I searched for the grave of seven-year-old Rosie Jack for some time. Finally, I looked down and was surprised to be standing directly over it. The headstone was timeworn by decades of weather. Nearby stood the old Modoc church, restored so that it appeared as it had more than a century before. The cemetery, filled with marked and unmarked graves, represented the unheralded lives of unsung heroes who knew heartbreak, misunderstanding, and more than their share of dishonesty.

The Modoc story is a valuable lesson about what happens when the essential virtue of honesty is not exercised for the benefit of others. To be sure, I met and spent meaningful time with a gem of the most honest and sincere friend named Jack Shadwick.

Exhortations to Excellence on Honesty

> Honesty is the first chapter of the book wisdom.
> –Thomas Jefferson

The kindred spirits of honesty and truth can't be overestimated. They're an unbeatable tag team; requisites for a well-integrated life. These diamonds of the heart get you further down the road than other flashier character attributes. These do the grunt work, the heavy lifting. They get the job done the right way, without shortcuts. They would rather take one honest step back than two dishonest steps forward. They would rather sit in the back of the room, quietly doing their work, until the time is right for a promotion. If it's not by way of integrity, they'd rather not go at all.

Truth tellers know what makes them tick, behind the scenes, when others aren't looking. They are happy with the specialized role they occupy. Honesty and truthfulness are born for the most crucial moments when everything's at stake and on the line. This is the point when people are most tempted to fudge, but instead can turn the tables to dig into transparency, and even vulnerability—with facts and feelings.

Honesty maximizes life. To be honest no matter what requires unswerving devotion. Like other essential virtues, honesty is born of love, its underlying motivation. It's free of deceit, unpretentious, and sincere. Truthfulness is the quality of adhering to reality, thus creating strong relational bonds with others. Lying and hypocrisy break the bonds that trust builds. It's the spirit of a person that directs them toward honesty or dishonesty. This must take root in the subconscious first. This allows outward actions to correspond to what lives within. It's a lifelong proposition. Everything worthwhile follows in a timely manner.

> **You can cheat an honest man but not make a fool out of him.**
> **–Confucius**

ALL ROADS LEAD TO INTEGRITY

Many have been slain by injustice; some literally and others by way of character assault and assassination. But the perpetrator, in the process of harming others, sustains internal damage to themselves. Whatever foothold dishonesty gains in leverage is lost in the end. It's a slippery slope; a bad risk. Every false statement drives a dagger into the liar's heart. Dishonesty catches up and overtakes the perpetrator. Lying takes a toll on the conscience until it becomes seared. Once a lie is out of the bottle, it begins its malevolent mission.

No one wins.

Honesty is an inner disposition; an inclination toward being truthful. It's a moral compass; a moral code. Strive to resemble the original, like a painter does when he places his inner image on a canvas with a brush. Your outer actions should paint a picture of what is inside you. Be transparent. To be predisposed to this lifestyle is necessary for following through with appropriate, corresponding actions.

As a teenager growing up, I wasn't good at raising my right hand in the courtroom of life, swearing to tell the truth, the whole truth, and nothing but the truth. But I learned eventually, and as an adult, I've tried to make it a centerpiece. This has paid dividends. It's better than money in the bank. Your most valuable treasures lie in the heart.

When you're honest, it gives you confidence. There is an erosion of personal integrity in today's world, which means you're going against the grain. This virtue provides an advantage that can't be obtained any other way. Can you be believed every time you speak? It's a much easier road to navigate difficulties by honesty than it is by dishonesty.

HEALING AND MENDING POWER

Some individuals hope that others' truth radar is disabled to float lies by with greater ease. You can almost see it in their eyes. *Don't call me on this one.* They emphatically believe their lie and oddly expect others to buy in. They're the creator, salesperson, and consumer of the deception—all three. But it's not enough, as they are still looking for more takers. And business can be good for them sometimes. They distribute their wares to anyone who will listen. This is dishonoring to people in general. There are those who practice this lifestyle, and it doesn't faze their consciences.

> The least initial deviation from the truth
> is multiplied later thousandfold.
> –Aristotle

Consider the disaster caused by the Exxon Valdez oil spill on March 24, 1989. The famous oil tanker was en route from Prince William Sound in Alaska, bound for Long Beach, California. However, it ran across the Prince William Sound Bligh Reef before it could get far. The ship spilled nearly eleven million gallons of crude oil of its fifty-four million gallons on board. One of the largest spills in U.S. history at the time adversely affected thirteen hundred miles of coastline and the natural habitat of salmon, sea otters, seals, sea birds, and other wildlife. Eight out of eleven Exxon Valdez cargo holds punctured. The ship lost five million gallons of oil within three hours of time. The cleanup effort took years, and, in some sense, the damage was insurmountable. The toll may never be quantified, as the environment bears vivid and lasting reminders of the catastrophe.

The cause was small, but the damage was great.

The effects of a singular event can be far-reaching. In a similar manner, the tongue is a lethal instrument that can cause irreparable harm. There is a part of life that can never recoup through dishonesty—a tragic loss of epic proportions. Things may never restore to their original condition. The essential virtue of honesty prevents many relational calamities before they occur. You don't control the outcomes in every situation, but truth gives you the best chance. Honesty in your corner will help you come out on the better side. Your integrity remains intact in every case, even when you're dealing with dishonesty.

THE HABITS OF HONESTY AND DISHONESTY

I've heard of cases where a witness lied to put another person in jail for the rest of their lives—or someone was accused of stealing when they were innocent. Many have been framed for crimes or deeds they never committed. This has affected families, livelihoods, bright futures, and lofty hopes. Misdeeds of the tongue are difficult to overcome. People can be susceptible to believing testimony when it's false. It depends how good and persuasive liars may be at their game. Even as a small kid, you knew lying was wrong.

Lies spawn more lies. Small ones lead to greater ones. It catches up down the line in ways you can never script. Whatever is gained by lying can't endure forever. There's the *ring* of truth and the *gong* of a lie. Liars seldom budge when confronted. Lies are abusive toward the object and dishonoring of relationships in general. Promoters of lies are self-serving in nature and lurk in the dark. They gather in the bushes but peddle in the streets.

> The truth is the kindest thing we can give folks in the end.
> -Harriet Beecher Stowe

It's been my experience that when you tell a person they lied, they think you're lying. They can't believe it. They can't endure the spotlight. Unfortunately, lying to one is precedent for lying to anyone. Call them serial liars. This character diamond of honesty makes you trustworthy and reliable in all circumstances. You cut to the chase and there are no side journeys or back roads to confuse the clear path of your most honest intentions.

Stay in your lane. It's less crowded.

Honesty and reliability set you apart. You're different. Not everyone embarks on this remarkable journey. Honesty is your main feature.

You're not looking over the rainbow for fantasy, because the green grass of truth is growing in your own backyard. You carry that tried-and-true disposition into every endeavor. The truth adapts to any circumstance. I place a wager on your faithfulness because you deal honesty in everything you do. Your words don't differ from who you are at heart. Honesty is the wiring to connect your worlds. Who you are, what you say, and what you do synchronize when you remain honest.

NOTHING TO HIDE

You are trustworthy because your behavior supports the weight of scrutiny. And when you make a mistake, you don't run and hide. You stay true and own it. Honesty propels you forward unencumbered, not weighed down by the past.

Honest people do their utmost not to flatter. They represent people and circumstances accurately and sincerely. When you tell people only what they want to hear, it doesn't have the same effect as when you're sincere and truthful. A negative can become positive through honesty, and a positive can become negative through dishonesty. Reputations are authentically built over time, not selfishly contrived or manipulated. They leave a steady track record, one word and deed at a time. The accumulation is exponential. At the same time, you are building an immunity to deception.

When you practice telling the truth, it's easier to discern when someone else might not be. Always be a student of life in every kind of circumstance. If someone tells the truth, you learn from that. If someone lies, you learn from that what not to do. Teach others to be honest by being honest. "If a man deceives me once, shame on him; if he deceives me twice, shame on me," Edgar Allan Poe said.

ACTIONS FORM BEHAVIORS

Honesty sets the tone for how you deal with others' difficulties. Recall the stories of Jews being sought out during the Holocaust. Families in Germany would hide people in their homes to protect them from death or imprisonment. They might lie to the searchers, telling them they hadn't seen anyone when they were literally under their roof. They were true to the victims and not the aggressors.

Other exceptions include instances where a person not telling the truth did so on behalf of someone they were protecting from an abusive spouse—or to shield an innocent child. No one would be considered a liar for diverting attention to save them. It didn't form negative behavior. It was out of character. *It was acting.* The aggressors were violent, not trustworthy. They weren't deserving of the honesty preferred to be exercised in the moment. Helping people is superior to saying something wrong under pressure in the moment.

If you want to be an unsung hero for someone, loan them your honesty. If you want to be an extraordinary person, practice it every single day of your life. Your positive steps forward will cancel out many negative mistakes made in your past.

> When one realizes that his words are the coin of his kingdom, and that his words can be a cursing influence, or a blessing, he will learn to value the gift of speech.
> –E.W. Kenyon

When I was a young dad, someone banged on my front screen door at midnight. I knew it was trouble. Everything was black in the house, no lights on. I felt chills run up and down my spine as I walked slowly to the front door. I didn't have a weapon for protection. My wife and kids were in bed. The only thing I knew was to act bolder than I was and yell loudly through the locked door, "What do you want?"

I mean, really, loud. Like I was angry. The man pretended to be asking for directions to a nearby street. I was boisterous and audacious, yelling again through the darkness that we were in bed.

I left all the lights off, waiting with bated breath.

Nothing but silence.

This wasn't my nature, but it worked. I intimidated him. My over-the-top boldness made him go away. Maybe he thought I had a gun. I was acting like something I wasn't—but for a good cause—the protection of my family. I didn't know how to fight. Who I was in word that night did not connect to who I was in deed. I knew this was the only way to behave in the moment. And it likely averted a terrible family disaster. I didn't trust the man on the other side of my front door.

A STRONG OATH OR VOW

Honesty is not just a building block, it's the cornerstone of an extraordinary life. To swear means to vow; to give one's solemn oath. If you can raise your right hand in the courtroom of daily living and swear to be telling the truth, that's great. Develop a habit of not saying anything you don't mean or fully intend to come to pass. To not do what you promised is out of the question. Honesty is a diamond of the human spirit with wonderful facets.

To swear is to pledge one's personal honor and proves genuineness and authenticity. No one likes fake, empty promises. I heard a friend once say, "I don't do fake."

Your word and heart agree. You are grounded and connected to reality, not fantasy. The past, present, and future have merged into one grounded perspective. You look at all facets of your life squarely.

You're introspective about the past and more decisive moving forward. This builds your life on a rock, not the sinking or shifting sands.

Lies are difficult to refute, and at times powerful. They can get a stranglehold on you. It's been my experience that when you try to set truth in order, it may not be believed or accepted. Lying has a long-term effect on relationships that can exceed what is repaired after the fact. The ripple effects can last for years, decades, even lifetimes. Being honest and true in adverse circumstances is a worthwhile goal, far worthier than the person who vows to be a millionaire by the age of thirty. Treating others with honesty is like doing others the favor you wish upon a star for yourself.

> **Honesty: The best of all the lost arts.**
> **–Mark Twain**

Honesty is the best policy, according to one of America's framers, Benjamin Franklin. To honor is to show respect and to give appreciation where it's due. Perhaps it can be said that truth is communicated, while honesty lives inside a person through disposition. Truth can't be spoken out of a dishonest heart, therefore the latter precedes the former. So, change the heart first and the tongue next. That's the order.

YOUR WEALTH IN CHARACTER

No one can make you honest in every situation. *But you can.* No one can make you dishonest, no matter how much pressure they exert. It is both responsible and necessary that words accurately reflect what is inside of you. Connect sincerely and genuinely to people, places, and things all around.

There must be deposits laid up for the truthful tongue to draw on. This is a 24/7 proposition, not a do-it-when-it's-convenient scenario.

I think we've all heard it said at one time or another that truth tellers have far less to keep track of than those who don't.

I heard a great man once say that the best definition of success is looking at people, places, and things as they are, not as I want them to be. This is an objective way of looking at life and takes in the good, the bad, and the ugly. Things aren't always as they appear.

Prepare for the unexpected. Be resilient. Be true. There are no good reasons to fudge the truth or to tell little white lies. Maybe no one notices your commitment to truth right away. But you're not honest for the applause. You do it because it's the right way, the only way, to live an extraordinary life.

To be an unsung hero for someone, use this virtue in your toolbelt. Flattery never helps anyone in the long run. History is littered by the tragedy of those who demanded the blind following of others. Ultimately, there is no difference between the tyrant who forced an unhealthy allegiance and the dishonest person who was the accomplice for an empty cause.

THE CUTTING EDGE

Honesty is a habit, and so is dishonesty. Make your repetition work for you, not against you. *The latter makes you tired. The former makes you alive.* Honesty and truth allow for maximum potential. Your business will be better. Your organization will run better. Your team will play better. Your family will live better. Your marriage and significant relationships will thrive. Friendships will flourish rather than die on the vine.

Deception has no benefits. The essential virtues of honesty and truth have depth, meaning, and veracity. A statement rings true or it doesn't. There is resonance with truth tellers. It makes you happy to tell the truth. There's a lightness and an affirmation you sense, like an inward pat on the back, which can be felt, adding to your sense of well-being. Yes, this is a built-in navigation system. The trick is not to override when it speaks. Pay close attention. Be introspective. Listen to the still, small voice. Pause for a beat or two, if necessary. Then state what you mean and mean what you say. Speak what you won't be sorry for later.

> I am not bound to win, but I am bound to be true.
> I am not bound to succeed, but I am bound
> to live up to what light I have.
> –Abraham Lincoln

If you look back in hindsight and realize you owe someone a clear explanation of what you previously provided, follow up with that person to make an adjustment. It's never too late to set things in order. Be as thorough and reasonable as necessary. That doesn't mean you have to go down every single rabbit hole. Pay attention to what your conscience dictates. What is right and wrong? Be reflective, considerate, and kind. You're looking out for the best interest of others. You're not out to cause harm. You're committed to doing good. In the process, the truth sets you free. You're going to know people better and they're going to know you. Honest exchange is worth its weight in gold.

ORGANIZED THINKING

You betray yourself when you don't tell the truth. It should nag you if you don't. It should feel like there's something scratching the subconscious. You were born with a tender conscience, and it is best to keep it that way. Never betray the virtue of honesty. People are going to be grateful for what you bring to the table.

One of the results of violating the dictates of the conscience is that deception stacks up like the house of a hoarder. Hoarders don't throw anything away, not even things that are bad for them. This is a commodity best not acquired, so kick it out before it grows larger, becoming an addiction. Dishonesty can spiral out of control. Keep a tidy and orderly house. Take out the trash every day. Discern the true from the false. Be a sorter, not a hoarder.

It's better to admit your errors than to push through and make people believe something untrue. I've seen people work tirelessly to hold up a lie like Atlas holding up the world—or tell another lie to mend a previous one. It takes an immense amount of effort to perpetuate falsehood. It messes people up who are not designed to be this way. Bad character is comprised of bad habits. Break the dishonesty habit early in the game. Yet it's never too late, either. Honesty can deliver immeasurable benefits if you're willing to make it a top priority. You need it like flowers need soil, water, sunshine, and air.

No one summits an extraordinary life without elevating the essential virtue of honesty to its rightful position. If you place it on a pedestal, you'll never need to exalt yourself. It will place you in the highest position possible—whether anyone notices or not. There are times you may not see tangible rewards right away, but you can rest assured that the ripple effects of honesty and truth will continue well beyond your lifetime. *This lifestyle will leave the richest deposit for friends, loved ones, and associates—one that won't bend, break, or mutilate—an honest and truthful reputation.*

No legacy is so rich as honesty.
-William Shakespeare

GEMSTONES

- Like other essential virtues, honesty is born of love.

- Honesty is an inner disposition, an inclination toward being truthful. It's a moral compass, a moral code.

- The essential virtue of honesty prevents relational calamities before they occur.

- Lies spawn more lies. Small ones lead to greater ones. It catches up down the line in ways you can never script.

- Lying to one is precedent for lying to anyone.

- Honesty and reliability set you apart. You're different. Not everyone embarks on this remarkable journey.

- Who you are, what you say, and what you do synchronize.

- Being honest and true in adverse circumstances is a worthwhile goal; far worthier than the person who vows to be a millionaire by the age of thirty.

- Perhaps it can be said that truth is communicated, while honesty lives inside a person through disposition.

- Honesty is a habit, and so is dishonesty. Make your repetition work for you, not against you.

REFLECTIONS
HONESTY: HEAVYWEIGHT CHAMPION
OF THE WORLD

Honesty and truth may not always be easy, but they are the best way to live a life of integrity and self-respect. How does keeping integrity make you a winning person?

PROMPT: Examine the value of keeping integrity in all areas of life and reflect on a time when you took responsibility for your actions.

ACTION: Make a list of ways to practice honest communication. Reflect on the positive outcomes that resulted from being honest.

PROMPT: Recall a time when being truthful was difficult. How did you handle the situation and what was the outcome?

ACTION: Write down one truth you have been avoiding and plan steps to address it.

Notes:

_____

_____

_____

_____

_____

_____

_____

_____

_____

_____

VIRTUE #4

Friendship: Armor for Life's Good Fight

Examining standard equipment that multiplies superpower

Begin Unsung Hero Story

When I think about friendship, I can't help but think about the legacy of Mister Rogers and his team. So much is accomplished by consistently modeled loyalty. Children and adults alike became so familiar with this kind man who devoted his life to serving families through the television series, *Mister Rogers' Neighborhood*. Fred spoke to children as if he was talking directly to them—and they felt like he cared about them.

"Won't you be my neighbor?" Fred asked in his welcoming song for each episode. It was a direct appeal to children who in turn gravitated toward unconditional love. Fred's mission was making *goodness attractive,* and he taught that caring for others is what in turn can change the world. He was an unsung hero to many, yet he had heroes, too. Dr. Margaret McFarland was one of them. Behind the scenes, she was helping him understand the complexities of child development to create a television experience that would be meaningful to young children.

Hedda Sharapan, who worked with Fred Rogers from the program's inception until he passed away, explains how their professional relationship developed:

> With her [Dr. McFarland's] background in child psychology, she would occasionally be asked to speak at courses for the seminary students. So that's how he [Fred] connected with her, through the advice of one of his seminary professors because his interest in the ministry was with children through television. He then went on to take graduate classes in child development at the University of Pittsburgh, spending a great deal of time observing young children under her guidance. When Fred got funding for Mister Rogers' Neighborhood, he asked Dr. McFarland to be his chief consultant. They met every week so that he could continue to learn from her what is essential for young children. With that deep understanding, he was able to work on constructing a meaningful television experience for his viewers.

The concepts of neighbors, visits, friendship, kindness, and love were discussed at length during those private, one-on-one sessions. Dr. McFarland once stated that no child can learn apart from love, and in turn, Fred manifested that principle in his programming.

"She was central to his work," Hedda said. "I would say she was the guiding light who helped him know what was important to help children grow and develop in healthy ways."

Fred once stated that a single suggestion from Dr. McFarland raised the potential of any creative idea. He characterized her as a true *gift*, yet at the same time, she embraced her unique role of being counterpart to Fred's creativity.

From the beginning, Fred called the program a television visit. Visits imply friendship, and Fred spoke to each child as if they were the most important person in the world. There were times he emphasized on the program that he could not see or hear the children through the camera and could only be a television friend, but that he thought about them whenever he made his television visits. He always felt that was an important distinction to make. Consequently, there was an intimacy and care extended through the ongoing programming into living rooms across the country.

Mister Rogers described neighborhood as "a place where friends help each other find within themselves the courage to grow."

This theme resonated with young and old alike. Fred not only hosted the *Mister Rogers' Neighborhood* program, but wrote the 900 scripts, as well as the melodies and lyrics of 200 songs for the episodes over the years.

Regarding friendship, Fred understood that there are often conflicts or misunderstandings in friendships and in life. Many of the *Neighborhood of Make-Believe* stories were parables to help children work their way through the ups and downs that often occur in friendships. From 1979 on, Fred deliberately wrote the *Neighborhood of Make-Believe* stories with the beginning seed of a conflict or misunderstanding. The puppets and other neighbors worked though the situation, and it often took a full week to resolve the tension or conflict—as in real-life situations where it takes a while to find a way to make things better.

Fred recognized the value of heroes in his own life. He said:

> I'll never forget the sense of wholeness I felt when I finally realized after a lot of help from a lot of people, what in fact, I really was not. I was not just a songwriter, or a language buff, or a student of human development, or a telecommunicator, but someone who could use every talent that had ever been given to me in the service of children and their families.
>
> Anyone who has ever been able to sustain good work has had at least one person—and often many—who believed in him or her. We just don't get to be competent human beings without a lot of different investments from others. From the

time you were very little, you've had people who have smiled you into smiling, people who have talked you into talking, sung you into singing, loved you into loving.

Hedda considered Fred to be her mentor, describing what it was like to work with him. Within the professional relationship, there was respect for what she and others on their small staff brought to their work environment. He was always supportive, kind, and thoughtful.

"Fred used to say that it's through relationships that we learn and grow best," she said.

She also described the culture Fred created with the people surrounding him—both in the office and in the studio:

He recognized that each of us brought something of our own gifts. When you work with a team, it can make such a difference when you tell people that you appreciate them. Fred was a great appreciator, and I've learned from him how important that is. We never had arguments in the studio. There was no blaming or shaming . . . many of the crew in the studio had worked together for decades and they all cared about Fred's mission. He cared about what the rest of our lives were like outside of work. There was also a lot of humor, warm humor. It was never snappy humor, or sarcastic. The crew, the staff, we were all like a family. We were only twelve or fourteen. And each of us came with different kinds of backgrounds and different understandings of how to deal with things, something like a neighborhood. We essentially worked together in the office and in the studio as a neighborhood.

There was a uniqueness in Fred's approach to the children watching at home. "You are special. What does that really mean? That's a powerful phrase. It means you are unique," Fred used to say. "There's only one person in the whole world exactly like you. There never has been, and there never will be, another person in the history of the earth just like you."

But it also means that your ideas, thoughts, and feelings matter. It's empathy. It's appreciation. It's getting to know somebody . . . getting to know each other helped us respect each other and understand when there were differences and find ways to work things through.

It was equally important to Fred to offer children a diverse neighborhood. He introduced them to an African singing group, an Asian ballerina, a Metropolitan Opera star, a Russian visitor, a plumber, a shoe store salesman, the young boy with a disability, a world-famous cellist, Native American dancers, and on and on—a neighborhood.

Fred used to say even though the outsides of children's lives may have changed, their insides have not changed. The things that were essential are still essential, like basic trust. That's key in relationship-building. So, you have to establish trust as the foundation. And how do you do that? You know, through structure where things happen in a predictable way, through rituals and routines that help you feel safe and develop a sense of trust. Through careful transitions so you know what's coming next . . . through all those verbal and non-verbal ways that we have of saying, 'I care about you.' When you know people care about you, you can move forward, you can grow from there.

The amazing thing is that this legacy has lived on. It is even more highly regarded now than it was in the earlier decades of 1990 and 2000, which is really fascinating. Maybe because of what we're living in now, people are saying we need this kind of caring about each other, a sense of neighborliness, listening, authenticity, helping, kindness—we need that more than ever in our world," Hedda concludes.

Exhortations to Excellence on Friendship

> There is nothing on this earth more to
> be prized than true friendship.
> –Thomas Aquinas

There's a mutual chemistry you can feel—and the trust is palpable. Friendship changes the atmosphere around you, raising the emotional temperature in any setting, as opposed to an adversarial relationship which has an equal but opposite effect. Let's call friendship an essential virtue that makes not only a great day—but an extraordinary life.

The benefits are more than can be even measured. Friendship lights the eyes and lifts the burdens. It's a *miracle*. You don't need tons of friends in a crisis. Often, it's a few or even one that make the difference. The essence of it is unexplainable, but you know when it's there or not. Friendship has a pulse, elevating relationships to a new level. A friend isn't going to betray you when we're not looking. A friend has your best interests in mind, caring about your needs like their own.

You're at home with a friend no matter where you are. You are favorable toward one another, having each other's backs. You're protective and hospitable, not grieving each other by unfeeling, callous behaviors. Friends don't taunt one another or make fun at the other's expense. Nothing will destroy friendship quicker. It takes a long time to build a friendship but not nearly so long to destroy one—just a brief, careless moment.

Contents are fragile: handle with care.

THE KINSHIP TO FRIENDSHIP

Friendship is *neighborly*. I've heard the analogy that it's love with skin on. Friends don't just say what they're going to do, they follow through. It's a blessing to have another person identify with the difficulties and joys you are experiencing. In the positive or negative, it's a bust to go it alone. Listen to friends as advisers and make decisions with all things considered. Reap the benefit of another set of eyes or ears on the situation. Others can see what you can't at crucial times. Friends are willing to offer constructive feedback but are careful not to destroy the foundations they've built over time. The gift of a friend is a trusted advisor at critical junctures of your life—and just as important, you are there as a gifting for others.

> True friendship is a plant of slow growth.
> –George Washington

The qualities of friendship are cultivated toward all people you interact with. Every friendship doesn't grow equally, but you can practice those qualities with everyone. You don't know what may come of that relationship. People are worth the expenditures—all the time. Be reliable, go the extra mile, and identify with their pain and suffering whenever possible. You're not wasting the moment when you sow incorruptible, timeless seeds.

Friendships can be considered the footsteps of love.

There are heartwarming stories of those who have excelled and exceeded all expectations—that includes what they thought possible or what others believed to be possible. They thank their families, coaches, influences, mentors, teammates, teachers, siblings, and more. The acknowledgments go on and on. They didn't arrive alone. There were unsung heroes and helpers along the way. There were genuine friendships that enabled them to rise to the top.

TAKING PERSONAL INVENTORY

Love is the fountain from which this asset flows. When you hear about a person's life goals, most often the financial, educational, or professional goals top the charts, getting the most attention. But it's rare that a person lists friendship on their goal chart, even though it has a higher ceiling than you've ever dreamed or imagined. When you think about what might position you for the achievement of your dreams, or what will provide an extraordinary life, I can't think of anything comparable to *friends*—true unsung heroes. They're a rich mine of inspiration, a great wealth, and can never be exhausted. Nothing crowns your life like a loyal friend. He that would have a wonderful friend is equally committed to being one.

Friends go the extra mile. There's a uniqueness to each relationship valued for its merits. Each adds wealth to your life. When a person states that their whole life is in front of them, that includes a myriad of friendships waiting to happen. Spend yourself for a good cause like you were money in the bank. Invest without expecting something in return and it will come back in ways you never scripted before.

My friends have made the story of my life. In a thousand ways they have turned my limitations into beautiful privileges.
–Helen Keller

INCREASE RELATIONAL ASSETS

As a child, I had a fear of abandonment. This innate need made me rush toward relationships and friendships. While growing up, I can say I had at least one best friend in every location we lived. My family moved every two or three years, so it was difficult to pull up stakes and transplant to another town and state. I grieved when it was time to leave. My heart ached every time. I didn't think I could ever have another friend like that one. The separation was intolerable. However, a sadder story might have been if I had no friends to grieve over. I was constantly leaving the familiar and launching into the unknown. Yet, once we arrived in the new location, it didn't take long to find that new best friend and all was well again. As a teenager, I gravitated toward adults. These were unlikely friendships, but those individuals took an interest in my life and helped me in ways that I could never imagine. They took me under their wing. Even though I didn't properly thank them at the time, I have made up the difference in recent years.

As an adult, I've learned to treasure multiple friendships at the same time. Capacity for friendship, trust, and loyalty grows. You increase in relational ability like any other ability. Use it or lose it, they say. An athlete who isn't better than they were five years ago hasn't worked hard enough. A person who isn't a better friend than they were five years ago hasn't either. The skills of loyalty are developed, enhanced, and elevated over time.

Some friends serve as mentors, educators, professionals, family members, and more. Never prejudge what a relationship can become given the chance. Your relational bank enriches over time, like your 401k retirement plan. Review your friendship assets. Never stop developing the ones you have. They improve. Accept them as they are—in different stages. Care for them like your most valuable possessions. They make you a rich person. And the more time that passes, the sweeter those become.

> My friends are my estate.
> —Emily Dickinson

SECRET INGREDIENTS

One of the most endearing and enduring characteristics of friendship is loyalty. No matter how old you are, it means the world. Perhaps the best illustration I can give is the need of older people who have felt abandoned. I've heard that age discrimination is the modern-day kind that has become socially acceptable. Yet in my experience, the need for loyalty becomes greater in the twilight years—and the ability to *show* friendship doesn't diminish.

I visited an Alzheimer's/dementia home for assisted living, where my mother-in-law was a resident. I discovered that these people find ways to demonstrate this essential virtue of friendship, even without all the verbal cues. Being a friend takes on a new meaning in the context of loneliness, sorrow, grief, and solitude.

One lady named Patrice was holding a doll in her arms. She believed that the baby was real. She approached an older man and asked him if he was the father. He denied the allegation and pointed across the room toward me, like I was the dad. I shrugged it off like it couldn't have been me. This showed me the innate desire that woman had to being a caregiver and friend. Even though the doll was inanimate, the love of this elderly person was alive and well. Patrice was a nurturing person. She handed the baby to my mother-in-law, and I was surprised that she cradled the doll in her arms also.

Nancy was the outspoken one. She was sitting with her friend, Susan. Across the way was my wife's mother, Betty. Nancy had a way of speaking up for others like a loyal advocate. She knew who in the room showed friendship and who didn't. She was more than willing to let anyone know exactly where she stood. She was brutally honest, but kind and caring in her own way. But if she was betrayed by someone, watch out. She would let you know.

Nancy stressed when I sat down with her and Susan that she didn't ever lie. "I don't stretch things," she said. "Why not be honest? Tell the truth or it will bite you."

Nancy was teaching, and I have to say I enjoyed the lessons from a person who had lived her dream and experienced an abundance of hard knocks. She was more than willing to share the essentials that make you an extraordinary person.

As my wife was conversing with her mom across the way, Nancy filled me in on Betty. "Don't tell her I said so, but she is going through it. I already asked that lady to be my friend. She said, 'we'll see.' We are friends. Her nature shows in her face. I examined her face real close because I love that lady. She just didn't make friends with people. I said, 'Well, I've been watching her. She needs a friend.' When she asked me what I wanted, I said, 'I don't need anything from you, just to be your friend.' She's just not forward with most people. She's been hurt. Please, take it from an old lady that understands. Anybody who hurts her is going to find my foot right in the middle of their rear end. You think I'm fooling?"

THERAPEUTIC BENEFITS

Susan spoke up, saying how she met Nancy. She wasn't as confident or outspoken as her friend, but the loyalty ran as deep. Nancy said about Susan, "She's a blessing in my life. She's taught me a lot of things. How to make things that looked impossible to me. Susan would say, 'Now, fix it like this, Nancy.' I'd fix it that way and it was just heaven."

Susan spoke up, "I'm glad I've got a good friend. You need all the friends you can get."

Nancy turned her attention back to my mother-in-law. "Yes, I've made a friend with that Betty. She's careful. Real careful. People have hurt her. They don't take time to try to understand her. They want to transform her into their way. If you can't accept people as they are, then leave them alone.

"Susan came into my life . . . she's a Godsend. I told her, 'You're gifted.' She didn't want me to tell her she was a Godsend. I said, 'You are.' I needed a friend, and God gave me Susan. She never lies to me. She tells me the truth right on top. I sure appreciate her."

My wife was still tending to her mom across the room. Nancy observed the interaction and commented, "Betty deserved those caresses. She's a good lady. I'm tired of her hurting. Yes, she does hurt. I can see it in her eyes. I love her. She never gripes, never bellyaches, never wants to fight with anybody. They take advantage of her. They do. They just do. She's worked every bit of her life. She's been a wonderful woman in her day. She needs help now, and she hates to admit it, but she does need help. The people here love her because she doesn't bellyache. She's a real lady. A real lady. I've been with her enough to know. She's earned every bit of love that I can share with her, so has Susan.

"Susan knows that I love her. She's got an education. She's a college graduate."

Another resident passed by us that had not shown loyalty to the others. Nancy was quick to point that out. "That one is the worst salt. She changes all the time. You never know. If she tells you she's your friend, then she'll go behind your back and stab you in the back. She does! She's done it to quite a few people."

Susan asked, "Is that why I never like her?"

Nancy turned Susan's question into a teaching moment. "Honey, you are not going to like everybody you meet."

Susan replied, "I know."

"Yes, that's the way God made us. There are some that we prefer more than others. They match our personality better. Do you hear me?"

Susan said, "I hear you."

Nancy concluded her thoughts on the matter. "All right, listen to me. Let it soak in. You're not going to like everybody. Anybody that says they do is lying. Under pressure, they'll admit they're lying."

Then she turned once more to my mother-in-law. "I like talking to that lady. She's receptive to the things you're saying. Later, she'll ask you about some of it. Yes, she does listen. Then she'll question you about those things. I've told her a lot of things that my mother shared with me from childhood. She said, 'That's a long time ago.' I'm ninety. I said, 'Yes, but I adored my mother.'"

That's when I thanked Nancy for talking to me.

She replied, "It was nice to blow off and to share with you, sir."

That conversation was revealing. No one outgrows the need for the timeless blessing of friendship or the need to *be* one.

THE JOURNEY OF FRIENDSHIP

Friends are companions travelling the same road arm in arm. They've bonded. There's a mutual respect and regard. Friendship is level and equal, complementary, an ultimate solution where everyone bene-fits. There's an intimate connection. Friends are tried in the fire and found true. The more time passes, the more strength is fortified—like mighty oaks.

Generally, there were trials where either could have cut and run. But they stuck together. All the while, trust grew. Love grew. They are better than they were yesterday. They don't leave communica-tion matters to chance. They have depth and authenticity. They are pleasant, well-disposed, sociable, cordial, warm, and kind. They are unsung heroes, helping you go places that wouldn't be possible in any other way.

A good friend is like a warm fire on a cold day.

Friendship is synergistic—the sum of the parts is never greater than the whole. Friends aren't competitors. They've joined forces and teamed up. They believe in one another. They never lie to or about the other. They would rather die than betray their word. Honor is at the forefront of all their dealings and interactions.

Friendship is a secret force, one that receives lesser credit but is often due the lion's share. The master mentor is love and friendship its protégé. Demonstrate the same quality of friendship you desire to elicit from others.

> **The only way to have a friend is to be one.**
> **–Ralph Waldo Emerson**

MODELING FRIENDSHIP

I had lived in Ohio for many years but had never been to the quaint, unassuming town of Ripley. I had done interesting research and vowed that the next time I was in the vicinity I would visit this historic spot on the Ohio River. I drove nearly an hour with my family from the southernmost tip of Ohio in Portsmouth, northwest toward Cincinnati, stopping about halfway. Ripley is picturesque; as beautiful as a painting. You'd never know the town had a reputation for being a hotbed for abolition during the mid-1800s.

I walked down to the boardwalk on the edge of the river and looked over to the Kentucky side. In my mind's eye, I time-travelled back to the 1830s and 1840s when it was dangerous to help slaves cross the river from Kentucky to Ohio. For a slave, the stakes were high—freedom and a chance for a new life—or recapture, torture, and sometimes death if apprehended and returned to their owners in the South.

What I wanted to see in Ripley was the John Rankin House, built on a five-hundred-foot bluff overlooking the Ohio River. Rankin purchased the home for the purpose of helping slaves from the South to the North. Over a period of years, Rankin and his family helped more than 2,000 slaves, using the essential virtue of friendship. If a slave was brave enough to cross, Rankin was brave enough to receive them into his home.

From the high vantage point on the bluff, Rankin could see across to Kentucky and at the same time survey the small town of Ripley below. There were slavecatchers in those days, combing the area by horseback. They were paid a bounty to return stray "property" to their rightful owners. They rode with torches throughout the village at night, combing the streets for runaways. But if the coast was clear, Rankin lit a lamp and placed it in his picture window as a signal that the time was right to make a break and cross over.

Once the slaves crossed the Ohio River, they climbed the steep bluff to Rankin's home. The *100 Steps to Freedom* still exist today, leading up to the front door. Once Rankin and his wife received the slaves into their home, they fed and cared for them like their own family. But slaves couldn't stay for more than two or three hours due to the danger of recapture. Rankin's sons took the slaves out back of the property and escorted them further along the Underground Railroad. Then his sons would return empty-handed and do it over again the next time.

UNEXPECTED FRIENDS

Harriet Beecher Stowe lived in nearby Cincinnati at the time. Her father was Lyman Beecher, the president of Lane College. Harriet became acquainted with John Rankin and personally visited the Rankin home in Ripley. The effect of their friendship took an interesting turn down the line. She was studying to be a writer.

During their conversation at the Rankin home, Harriet learned that there was a young Black mother from Kentucky who was being pursued by her slave owner. On the Kentucky side, a total stranger pointed her in the direction of Ripley. If she could just get across the river, she would find her freedom, he admonished. But it was the dead of winter. As the woman crossed the thin ice, it broke through. But she kept going. She waded through the cold, waist-deep water, placing her baby on whatever solid ice there was around her as she went along. She pressed through the elements, step by grueling step, falling exhausted onto the Ohio shore. When she looked up, a slavecatcher was already standing directly over her.

He marveled at the fight for life he had just witnessed. Promised a bounty for her return, he changed his mind, telling the mother that anyone who had the guts and determination to do what she did deserved her freedom. He could have collected reward money. Instead, he pointed to the top of the hill at the Rankin home and told her she could go there to get the help she needed.

There are no strangers here; only friends you haven't yet met.
–William Butler Yeats

The mother climbed the hill and the final *100 Steps to Freedom* with her baby in tow, knocking at the front door. The Rankins received them for a short time, cared for them, and helped them further along the Underground Railroad. The woman and her baby settled in another town in southern Ohio. Not satisfied to keep the blessing to herself, the mother reciprocated the benefits of freedom and returned to Kentucky to help others in her family cross the Ohio River. She risked her life to extend the friendship she had received, keeping the blessing moving forward for others.

Harriet was so enamored by the story she learned firsthand from

Rankin that later, she wrote *Uncle Tom's Cabin*, inserting this true account. Eliza is the name she ascribed to the mother who, along with her infant child, made entry into one of the best-selling books of all time; a shining example of unselfish, enduring friendship.

Rankin's demonstration of loyalty to African Americans marked his life. He was the consummate unsung hero, not seeking the credit or ever receiving his full share. Those he helped were eternally grateful for the unlikely relationship that evolved from his tireless devotion to helping others. So many would have given any amount of money for their freedom. But the essential virtue of friendship eclipsed money and social status. Those relationships became stronger than race or creed.

BUILD A LEGACY

I met Paul Mabrey for private voice lessons years ago in Tulsa. Mabrey was a vocal music professor. He passed away in 2014 but left a rich legacy when he died. Tributes filled the memorial auditorium from faculty, friends, church members, and his students. Solo vocalists and choirs performed special numbers in his honor. I didn't realize he was an unsung hero to so many. He didn't aspire to being famous, but Paul was rich in friendship, more than he or anyone else really knew.

I visited Paul when he became sick with pancreatic cancer at age sixty-six. I didn't claim to be his best friend, not even a close colleague, but I did want to be a friend in his time of trouble. He cried openly in that hospital room, lying in the bed. It wasn't because of the pain. It was because he knew the inevitable was coming—the end of a life well-lived—one he was deeply grateful for. His life was passing in front of him in those moments. He was incredibly kind, personable, and relational. He never tried to make a person feel bad for whatever level of musical talent they possessed. There was no one-upmanship. He valued relationship above the gift and privilege he was allowed to share. He didn't boast about his own talent or hold it over anyone. He placed his gifts in the context of genuine friendship and sharing.

All love that has not friendship for its base,
is like a mansion built upon the sand.
–Ella Wheeler Wilcox

If he was able to peer in on his memorial service, he would have been astonished to hear the glowing accounts, one after another. One student was impressed by the fact that this man could have chosen to entertain the world but elected to entertain them instead.

Anyone who knew him knew the genuine, caring human being he was—a bigger than life man with a bigger than life heart, one man said. He was admired and respected for his indescribable way with people. Friendship was always his first priority. Mabrey's connection with students and colleagues was more important than teaching the craft—which made the learning more valuable.

Kingsley Leggs was a protégé of Paul and became an accomplished actor and singer. Here's his poignant tribute to his mentor: "Simply put, he was one of the greatest men I have ever known. He changed so many lives. He touched everyone and everything with passion, love, and care. He was a gentle giant. More than a teacher, more than a mentor, he challenged me in ways I had never even thought about."

To be an unsung hero and lead an extraordinary life—the admonition is clear.

Be a helper of others.

Be a friend.

A friend is a gift you give yourself.
–Robert Louis Stevenson

GEMSTONES

◆ Friendship changes the atmosphere around you, raising the emotional temperature in any setting, as opposed to an adversarial relationship which has an equal but opposite effect.

◆ Friendship lights the eyes and lifts the burdens. It's a *miracle*.

◆ He that would have a wonderful friend is equally committed to being one.

◆ It's rare that a person lists friendship on their goal chart, even though it has a higher ceiling than you've ever imagined.

◆ Friendship can be considered the footsteps of love.

◆ Never prejudge what a relationship can become given the chance.

◆ Friendship is synergistic—the sum of the parts is always greater than the whole.

◆ Friendship is a secret force, one that receives lesser credit but is often due the lion's share. Demonstrate the same quality of friendship you desire to elicit from others.

◆ Place your gifts, talents, and abilities in the context of genuine friendship and sharing—watch them multiply.

◆ To be an unsung hero and to lead an extraordinary life—the admonition is clear. Be a helper of others. Be a *friend*.

REFLECTIONS
FRIENDSHIP: ARMOR FOR LIFE'S GOOD FIGHT

Investigate the standard equipment of friendship that multiplies this superpower.

PROMPT: Consider how to be a true friend to others and reflect on moments when friendship has been a source of strength or courage.

ACTION: Be a friend in your sphere of influence today, a helper. We all need one.

PROMPT: Think about a time when you put someone else's needs before your own. How did it impact your relationship and what did you learn from the experience?

ACTION: Write down one way you can be humble in your actions today.

Notes:

_____

_____

_____

_____

_____

_____

_____

_____

_____

_____

VIRTUE #5

OPTIMISM: FOCUS OF DESIRE

Reasons to choose the magnificent view
no matter the circumstance

Unsung Hero Story

When I met Jim Stovall, I knew he wrote books, produced movies, and was an extraordinary achiever. I asked to do a studio interview and discovered even more how the essential virtue of optimism was key to his extraordinary success. Then I visited one-on-one in his Tulsa office to have a sit-down conversation. As an unsung hero for millions of blind people, he also credits unsung heroes for helping him do what he does. Here are several points of interest in his *all things are possible* journey from one success to another.

Jim was born and raised in Tulsa, Oklahoma. He wanted to become a professional football player as a young adult until diagnosed with an eye condition that caused him to gradually lose his sight. Not defeated, Jim changed gears and became an Olympic weightlifter instead. By his twenties, he finished his athletic career in that sport and had another lofty vision—to develop a system whereby blind people could access television.

The Narrative Television Network (NTN) formed in 1988, and by 1990, he won an Emmy award for his first season on national television. NTN programming has appeared on ABC, NBC, CBS, and Fox, as well as top cable networks around the world.

For NTN, writers prepare a script to insert between spoken lines of dialogue, which describes a scene and helps the blind person imagine what is taking place in the movie. Concise words are selected which bring the scene to life for the hearer. The listener in turn becomes a watcher through their mind's eye. NTN produces thousands of hours of programming each year for thirteen million blind people all over North America and even more around the world.

Jim describes that breakthrough as the beginning of everything he's doing today: movies, television, books, speeches, and columns. He says he is in the message business. "Focus on your mission, not the method. Blindness is limiting to my methods. It's not limiting to my mission."

Steve Forbes has called Jim one of the most extraordinary persons of his generation. Jim has written more than fifty books and produced many motion pictures based on them. There are well over ten million of his books in print. He writes a nationally syndicated column that appears in roughly 400 major publications around the world, both in print and online.

How does a blind person write books? He dictates them to Dorothy in his office and they are captured in real time as he tells a story he doesn't know until he hears it coming out of his own mouth. *The Ultimate Gift* is one such title which was in turn developed into a movie. Other book titles include *Wisdom for Winners* and *One Season of Hope*. Find more of his material at jimstovall.com.

When I asked Jim how he became a writer, he said that he became a good reader first. Not limited by blindness, Jim personifies the essential virtue of *optimism*. He says he's read a book per day for each of the last twenty-five years. He estimates that he's read in the vicinity of 10,000 books during that time span. Yet how does a blind person read books? Jim says he listens to them at high speed, 700 to 800 words per minute, via audio recordings.

There's always a way through, over, or around obstacles for the optimist.

The secret to his success? Jim says it's not about him; it's about those he serves. That's the legacy he wants to leave. He's travelled around the world nearly 100 times. He has people that help position him onstage when he speaks. He says he couldn't do what he does without the valuable people around him. Heroes are *helpers*. Understanding this concept takes the mystery out of the success equation. Anyone can help other people. Jim doesn't know how to write, but he credits his editor as being the best in the business. "I get all these awards and accolades. I write bestselling books, but I don't know how to type."

He differentiates between sight and vision. Vision is the greater of the two and tells people where they can be and what is possible. "I believe the meaning of life is to find our gift, what it is we've been given—and the purpose of life is to give it away. The happiest people you will ever find are those who have found their gift and give it away to serve other people." He describes frustrated, unhappy people as those who haven't found their gift—or don't give it away. The irony is that a sighted person may become blind to their true gifting and potential, but a blind person can see through their inward visioning.

"My legacy would not be what I did, as much as what other people do as a result. The world belongs to the man or woman with a big dream that will take the next step and figure out what to do after that. Find the most compelling ways to give your gift away."

Jim emphasizes that he's a fellow traveler with others on the path. He doesn't have all the answers. He's not accomplished everything he talks about but believes every person can excel by acting on what they know. To fail is simply not to act.

"I always like people to remember that the biggest dream they've ever had, the biggest goal, is alive and well, and it would not have been put inside of them if they didn't have the capacity to achieve it. The question is never, 'Can we?' The question is, 'Will we?' The world belongs to the man or woman who will step out and visualize that goal and take one more step toward it, then see where you go from there. If you'll just take that next step, sooner or later, you will own your destiny and live a life very few people can imagine."

Exhortations to Excellence on Optimism

> Write it on your heart that every day
> is the best day in the year.
> –Ralph Waldo Emerson

There's something about the *upward* look.

It's powerful. It's inspiring. It's motivating. It's encouraging. It's affirming.

Step outside at night to look at the starry expanse and realize you were born for infinite possibilities. Each day is a world of its own. Each day is a personal invite to reset. You're new today—along with your most creative thoughts, dreams, goals, and vivid imagination. This is your opportunity to integrate previous experiences, positive and negative, and use them as a springboard for the future. It's a clean palette on the easel and you're the artist with fresh watercolors to freely dream with.

Make choices count. No one is exempt from disappointment. But no one can regroup like you can. You weren't born to flounder but to rise to the occasion. It may be surprising how far you've come after one month, one year, five years, or ten. It's the cumulative effect and the stacking of positive experiences one upon another that tip the scale in your favor. Stretch your wings now. It's time to fly.

You're a dreamer, so you want to order your life on what's possible. This is conceived in the heart and mind before anything. Even more than food, a life full of possibilities is your daily bread. The banquet table is spread—you get to choose what's put on your plate. You're not surviving. You're thriving. The heart guides from there, coming alongside to help, sharing the burden, the workload. You're an optimal thinker, achiever, and liver. Write down what you're striving for—it will help to inspire you all over again.

Perspective is everything. Can you envision the thing for which you are fondly hoping? That's more than half the battle. Move toward that light. Let it live inside you before it ultimately comes to pass. No one moves in a positive direction with their head down. They told me in driver's ed when I was a teenager to aim high in steering. The same is true in life; aim high. There's good reason for staying upbeat and positive. Adapt and adjust while you're in motion. You're going somewhere to make good things happen. You are resilient for a reason—respond positively to any blows you may experience. Get back up and go back at it again. You already thought this through. It's no time to quit or throw in the towel.

> Every great dream begins with the dreamer.
> Always remember, you have within you the strength,
> the patience, and the passion to reach for
> the stars to change the world.
> –Harriet Tubman

TIPPING POINT OF OPTIMISM

When I was a kid in Sunday school, I remember the teacher saying if you really believe something with all your heart, really and truly believe, it will happen. I thought, *wow, that's cool.* That struck me because I knew he believed what he was saying. It wasn't something he was cramming down our throats. He really wanted us to know. And what he shared from the heart was believable because he was genuine. All these years later, I realize he was an embodiment of a truth that all things are possible to the person who believes. Those who wholeheartedly believe are close to obtaining what they desire. Steadfast faith in unseen possibilities can become so real that others perceive your conviction and persuasion. Many will align to help you.

Optimism is an essential virtue; a diamond of the heart. Embrace what you desire in advance. Many hopes and dreams have come to pass in your life already. Others are moving through your pipeline. But there's a bigger, more thrilling climb ahead. If you could see all the marvelous things in your future, it would make your heart race with excitement. The down payment for what you desire is now.

Your objectives are rare and unique. No one else can do quite what you do. Your steps and journey toward goals is different from others. You bring something to the table sorely needed. That's why you were born. No one else could fill your shoes. When the discovery of that uniqueness and individuality is embraced, it's *gold* forever.

Your beat is of another drummer. It's freeing to realize that your biggest challenge and responsibility for achieving great potential is to authentically be yourself. If you try to be like someone else, you chop yourself off at the knees. You reduce yourself to half the person you might have been. Who you are is more important than what you do. Yet, who you are infuses an equivalent value into your work, whatever it may be.

YOUR SIGNATURE ON EVERYTHING

My wife and I watch *The Voice* and *American Idol*. The coaching from the pros on these shows is outstanding. "Make the song your own," is the admonition I've heard time and again. Just because a person has a skillful and lovely tone, doesn't mean they will adapt the song and demonstrate they've put their one-of-a-kind signature on it. Those who try to mimic the original artist perfectly don't make it to the finale. Yet they may be ultra-talented. Sooner or later, they must shed the handicap of using their gift like someone else to perfect their talent.

> Start by doing what's necessary, then what's possible; and suddenly you are doing the impossible.
> –St. Francis of Assisi

You were born to win in any endeavor when you choose to make it your own.

Possibilities are enriched by sharing your talents and abilities with others. You're letting your light shine. Your potential multiplies every time you get to know another person. If you want a bigger world, understand the stories of more people. You're richer for every relational risk you take.

Your possibilities enhance mine. I see how we can team up and be better. You inspire me to new heights. I'm bigger together with you than I am singularly. If I limit myself to what I can do—the weakening begins. If I want to run, I'm willing to walk with you first. Conversely, my strength has already begun to multiply.

There lies the richest joy and fulfillment. I've heard it said that love is *willing* to share even the half loaf. It's the disposition to share that will release the adrenaline to push you over the top. Anyone who shares their gift finds it returning in an enhanced form. Relationships multiply what you possess in talents, setting your life ablaze with greater purpose. What you have was destined to become a living will for others.

You have a destiny no one else can fulfill. When you look back, be able to say you left it all on the court. Finish what you start. Complete your circles. You have positive experiences under your belt. Every success sets you up for an opportunity you didn't dream of before. You're going from strength to strength and faith to faith. Shedding personal handicaps requires optimism. You practice the essential virtue by investing yourself completely, and when you do, your world is on a string, tied to a rainbow of promises.

LINK TO PRESENT POSSIBILITIES

How often do you hear championship teams credit belief in themselves, their teammates, and their coaches after the big win? They know it's possible to excel and reach the highest star, but never alone. Yet if they don't translate intangible belief into tangible steps, those possibilities die unborn. If they don't link arms with others, they die on the vine. There's nothing more tragic than aborted dreams and nothing more magical than keeping them alive and taking them to the next level.

Be wowed by your potential, for it is vast. There are as many possibilities for you as there are stars in the sky. You are a universe of rare talents, gifts, and abilities. Your will ignites and sets fire to that potential. As soon as you *determine* to move, you've mobilized in the direction. You gravitate toward what you aspire to the most.

You can be as happy for the progress as for the eventual arrival. It always does the heart good to *begin*. You're the choir director; the maestro. If you don't command the attention of what is in you, no one else will. Optimism keeps you from becoming unfruitful, stagnant, and unproductive. You're a goal-oriented creature. And you go after them with *love* on your hip.

> Not knowing when the dawn will come,
> I open every door.
> –Emily Dickinson

Think big. More than that, *be big*. Grow into greatness. Be willing to translate dreams into incremental steps. When someone asks after the fact if you were surprised at an outcome, you'll probably reply that you weren't. You believed. It mattered more what *you thought* than what the skeptics thought. Block out the negative noise, because there will be plenty.

Your goal is to be an extraordinary person.

Optimism is one of your closest allies.

Possibilities hinge on how grounded and connected they are. They aren't pie-in-the-sky wishes. If you can dream, there's an anchor for it somewhere in your soul. Then comes the action that derives from that fervent desire. If it doesn't excite you, forget about it. Choose winning ideas that synchronize with your personality.

THE ROOT OF INTENTION

What thrills you? What arrests you? What sticks to you and won't let go? What keeps you up late at night? What do you daydream about? What nags away at you if you don't act? These are the clues for what you should pursue. What doesn't alter you in some way isn't worth the expenditure of time or energy. A possibility that doesn't reorder priorities will wither. There's a learning curve to seeing lofty visions come to fruition.

I read a book as a teenager called *Move Ahead with Possibility Thinking*. At the time, I thought it sounded great. The concept resonated. The problem was I didn't know how to make it a reality. *Think and Grow Rich* was another title. But I was as poor as Job's turkey, as they say. All my efforts were mechanical, wishful thinking. Then there was another title, *The Magic of Thinking Big*. But that's all that ever came of it—magical thinking.

I may have been the only kid in my high school that enrolled in a multi-level marketing company. I tried to get a couple of my friends in the business. I played a cassette tape for them in my family dining room. The title of the tape was *Try or Cry*. They literally laughed out loud, acting like they were sobbing, rubbing their fingers in their eyes like they were wiping away the tears. I probably don't need to say they opted not to enroll.

Truly, this stuff was over my head, but not my heart. I was thrilled with the concept. Even hearing the master motivator Zig Ziglar when I was sixteen years old couldn't provide the drive and follow-through I needed to complete my inspirational dreaming. But I sure had the optimism. It was an important piece of the puzzle, yet I needed the flip side of the coin to make it spend. To my credit, my enthusiasm helped me sell six sets of lifetime warranty cookware to merciful friends and neighbors. I gave them a deal, even though I zeroed out my profits. However, I did win some recognition. My team was proud—and I didn't refuse their praise.

These were the beginning stages of a turning point.

My parents decided to make a move to another part of the state. My dad had a new opportunity looming on the horizon. I had graduated from high school and had no intention of going with them. But they had no intention of taking me, either.

After they packed and left, I lived in the garage for a couple of weeks. The only things I owned were my motivational books and a shelf, a mattress, a refrigerator with a gallon of milk, and the mag wheels for my car. But the wheels were stolen while I was out for the day. That left the books, the mattress, and the milk.

My dad returned, unannounced, to check on me after several days. He later told me I was in the backyard, taking a shower with a hose, belting out a song. I still wasn't short on the diamond of optimism. The problem was that it was lying dormant until I supplied additional action. I eventually found a place to call home. My first apartment cost seventy-five dollars a month. By the time I married at the age of twenty-two, my life turned around in many areas. I learned lessons about responsibility and commitment—and there were more lessons to come.

> **The possible's slow fuse is lit by the imagination.**
> **-Emily Dickinson**

FUEL TENACITY

In the years that followed, I became the top salesman in the company I worked for, combining optimism with a drive to see things through to completion. On one occasion, I set a sales goal one morning to win a fifty-dollar bonus. That meant I had to make forty-five more sales in one day to achieve the sixty sales required for the bonus. Plus, there was a commission for each of the forty-five sales—all totaled, not bad for a day's work. By the next morning, I was turning in the stack of orders, while others in the office were sitting around.

Optimism combined with hard work was fulfilling, even exhilarating. No managers in my office were inclined to set lofty sales goals. I felt able to achieve them at will, like placing my foot on the accelerator of my car. I willed my way to success consistently. I began with an objective and didn't stop until it was achieved. That attitude paid off when I received the promotion to a higher district manager position.

Over a twenty-five-year span, I was far and away the top salesperson in that company. Those motivational book titles about optimism became connected to my life. I made those timeless principles my own by incorporating them into clearly defined objectives. I learned that how I finished the race was just as important as how I began.

Positive thinking in a mechanical way produces nothing, yet you're capable of high achievement in the measure of your most dominant actions. One opportunity lends to another. Accept those as open occasions for growth. You're a better person than you were yesterday. It's not only about what the man or woman makes, but *what makes the man or woman.*

TRANSFORMING CHARACTER

How did you change?

There is ebb and flow each day, an exchange between what you give and what you receive. Optimism isn't a lottery up to chance, but a tried and proven virtue. It works time and time again. You've taken the sure way. The odds are for you and not against you. Connect to what you desire with predetermined resolve. Yet your dreams don't dump on you all at once. They evolve and develop over time. Your goal is to become a changed person. Any worthy goal will result in character transformation. That change sets you up for the next success.

Brainstorm. Dream. Anticipate.

Play small ball. Pay attention to the details and be faithful. Often, the smallest of increments can lead to the realization of huge goals. More than that, optimism makes you an *extraordinary person.* Go the extra mile. Possibilities multiply and work together, but lack of effort will diminish them—you can watch as they dwindle down.

> No pessimist ever discovered the secret of the stars
> or sailed an uncharted land or opened a new
> doorway for the human spirit.
> –Helen Keller

Change perspectives when necessary—a brand new view from another angle or vantage is beneficial. Stay on the upside. I think about the *Saturday Night Live* skits with Debbie Downer, played by comedian Rachel Dratch. No matter what good thing anyone had to say, Debbie found a negative spin. She could take any positive and turn it into a downright bummer. She was perpetually dropping negative bombs on the optimistic people all around.

Yet truth is stranger than fiction. You've probably met that person who can take the sweet and make it sour. No matter what happens, you can keep a negative from being the last word in any situation. You can turn the downside into an upside, not by burying your head in the sand, but by using adversity as a springboard to something better.

Negatives can become a launch pad for optimal thinkers. One of the nuggets in *The Magic of Thinking Big*, by Dr. David Schwartz, was that *inside of every adversity, there is the seed of an equal or greater benefit.* It all depends on you and me, the beholders. There are many sides to a problem and the angle of approach for solutions is vital.

Hail to the hero of optimism.

OPTIMISM AND DREAMS

I attended an event in Oklahoma City where I learned about a man with an unlikely journey. Beneath his amazing external achievements as an athlete, I heard the hidden back story that not everyone knew about. What made him extraordinary? The essential virtues that drove him as an individual defined how he would play the game of basketball—and how he would pay that forward as an unsung hero for kids.

Serge Ibaka grew up as a young boy in the African Congo. His dream was to play professional basketball in the NBA. He explained how far-fetched that possibility was for him at the time. After all, he didn't have any money. He didn't have a pair of tennis shoes. He didn't even own a basketball.

To others, the NBA aspiration looked like an impossibility, even laughable. One of eighteen children in his family raised in the Congo, he decided to leave his home country to pursue playing professional basketball in the United States. He resolved to do what it took to make that happen. His parents played basketball in Africa, but Serge took it to the next level. He had raw talent and ability still to be developed.

Ibaka worked hard to refine and develop his skills, which translated into difficult days of sacrifice, sweat, and training. Yet his biggest ally was the essential virtue of optimism that helped him believe he could achieve his lofty goal before he even owned a pair of tennis shoes.

Optimism: Person who travels on nothing from nowhere to happiness.
–Mark Twain

His journey culminated in his being chosen during the first round of the 2008 NBA draft as the twenty-fourth overall pick by the Seattle Supersonics. Months later, the franchise relocated to the state of Oklahoma. Ibaka played for the Oklahoma City Thunder for seven years, on the same team as Kevin Durant, James Harden, and Russell Westbrook.

From there, he went on to play for the Orlando Magic, the Toronto Raptors, the Los Angeles Clippers, and currently the Milwaukee Bucks. A three-time defensive player of the year in the NBA, and a two-time blocks leader, Ibaka also played a key role in the Toronto Raptors 2019 NBA championship title run.

THE SMALL STUFF

Ibaka said that he doesn't let anyone tell him he can't do something. He will always believe he's going to make it until he draws his last breath. He describes each day as a journey that pays tribute to his long-term goals. He encourages people that, like him, they don't have to have everything at their immediate disposal to dream.

Why not dream?

Ibaka says to start with small steps.

When enough of those small steps have strung together in succession, you will arrive at your destination. To stop moving is the only way to keep you from reaching your objective. Even so, your goals include the extraordinary person you will become as much as what you aspire to achieve in this lifetime.

Ibaka could have folded his hands and taken his leisure once he arrived at his goal. Instead, he chose to give back and pay forward what he had learned. He's determined that each day when he wakes up, he will make that day pay tribute in some way. He uses everything at his disposal to make his dreams come true. Ibaka said he wants to share his blessing with others to keep the cycle going. He helps children in orphanages, not forgetting his humble beginnings in the Congo. That's where his dream was born, and was such an integral part of his story. His desire to help children is as strong as his resolve was to play basketball.

You will go places you've never been and form relationships with people you've never met. You believe in the visions of others and observe how you can help by being an unsung hero—a sincere helper of others. You aren't doing it for the credit. You see the opportunity to make a difference. Keep an eye out for persons to whom you forward your gifts as a living legacy.

Who will that be?

You don't play the odds, you defy them. You're not the same person you were. You didn't arrive at your dreams overnight. You're an extraordinary person, making your achievements that much more significant. When others ask about how you did that, you'll explain *it was the invisible traits as a person that contributed most to your outward success.*

Optimism has you trending on the upward path— for others and yourself.

This new day is too dear, with its hopes and invitations, to waste a moment on the yesterdays.
–Ralph Waldo Emerson

GEMSTONES

◆ Step outside at night to look at the starry expanse and realize you were born for infinite possibilities.

◆ It's the cumulative effect and the stacking of positive experiences one upon another that tip the scale in your favor.

◆ Adapt and adjust while you're in motion. You're going somewhere to make good things happen.

◆ If you could see all the marvelous things in your future, it would make your heart race with excitement. What you think about those today is real. The down payment for what you desire is now.

◆ Your beat is of another drummer. It's freeing to realize that your biggest challenge and responsibility for achieving great potential is to authentically be yourself.

◆ You practice the essential virtue of optimism by investing in others. And when you do, your world is on a string, tied to a rainbow of promises.

◆ Be wowed by your potential for it is vast. There are as many possibilities for you as there are stars in the sky. You are a universe of rare talents, gifts, and abilities.

◆ Play small ball. Pay attention to the details and be faithful. Sometimes, the smallest of increments can lead to the realization of huge goals.

◆ Your goals include who you will become as much as what you achieve.

◆ Optimism has you trending on the upward path—for others and for yourself.

REFLECTIONS
OPTIMISM: FOCUS OF DESIRE

Analyze the reasons to choose the magnificent view that optimism gives you no matter the circumstance.

PROMPT: Reflect on moments when optimism has led to growth or success.

ACTION: Make a list of ways to practice optimism and positivity.

PROMPT: Think about a time when you faced a challenging situation. How did you bounce back and what did you learn from the experience?

ACTION: Write down one thing you can do to build your resilience in the face of challenges.

Notes:

_____

_____

_____

_____

_____

_____

_____

_____

_____

_____

VIRTUE #6

HOPE: WIND FOR YOUR SAILS

Methods for adjusting position to accomplish the mission

Unsung Hero Story

I lived for many years in Tulsa without knowing the story of Green-wood—until I became a journalist. Many still don't know. I was to understand later that the story was buried for decades. Once I learned, I started to dig. Through my own research and conducting interviews with individuals associated with the John Hope Franklin Center for Reconciliation, I was privileged to write stories about this relatively unknown history. Don Ross and Kevin Matthews are two unsung heroes that have been voices for the cause, though there are many others that could be mentioned.

The following is a snapshot of what Senator Matthews calls a "dark stain" on Tulsa's history, but one he also believes is an opportunity for hope.

In 1921, Greenwood was a prosperous black section of north Tulsa. Booker T. Washington was so impressed with the thriving business district that he coined the name 'Black Wall Street' to describe the prosperity, innovation, and entrepreneurship he observed while visiting there.

Racial tensions were high across America. The Red Summer of 1919 was marked by many race riots, including those in Chicago and Washington, D.C. But what happened in Tulsa was the worst of its kind. Many believe the animosity in Tulsa was linked to jealousy for the prosperity Blacks were experiencing in Greenwood.

As the story goes, Dick Rowland was a young African American shoe shiner in downtown Tulsa when he boarded the elevator one day in the Drexel Building. Sarah Page was a young white elevator operator. When the doors opened again, Page was screaming, and Rowland fled on foot. He was arrested in short order for an alleged rape, yet Page later claimed he had merely "grabbed her elbow." To date, no one knows exactly why she screamed.

On the evening of May 31, 1921, hundreds of whites swelled to a mob of 2,000 people in front of the Tulsa courthouse, demanding swift justice. Fearing a lynching that had been called for in the headline of a *Tulsa Tribune* newspaper article, about seventy-five Greenwood residents arrived at the courthouse to defend Rowland. During this gathering, a shot rang out and African Americans retreated to the Greenwood locale with the mob in hot pursuit. Many Greenwood residents were shot in their streets, others in their homes.

Meanwhile, fires were started by intruders. Airplanes were spotted overhead dropping flammable material to stoke the raging flames. By June 1, the following day, more than forty city blocks were destroyed. Hundreds of businesses and homes were leveled. Ten thousand Greenwood residents were left homeless—and by most accounts 300 lost their lives to white citizens bent on revenge and vigilante justice.

In the aftermath, many whites taunted demoralized Greenwood citizens while driving through the streets. Dead African Americans' bodies were dumped into the Arkansas River and others were thrown into unmarked graves.

Property losses exceeded four million dollars, which compared to today's economy, the damage was in the billions. The once thriving, upscale, bustling section of Tulsa became eerily quiet. No more theaters, hotels, doctors' offices, churches, stores, or shops—instead, according to the 2004 *Tulsa Race Riot Commission Report*, "What they found was a blackened landscape of vacant lots and empty streets, charred timbers and melted metal, ashes, and broken dreams."

No whites were prosecuted for crimes of arson, looting, destruction of property, or murder. Internment camps were set up like war zones at the Tulsa County Fairgrounds and at the nearby McNulty Baseball Field.

What became known as a fifty-year conspiracy of silence surrounded the event, until a handful of heroes stepped up to publish the story and draw attention to the tragedy. Don Ross was one of those heroes. Ross was a teenager in the 1950s when his high school teacher showed him pictures of burned-out Greenwood. Until that moment, he didn't believe the allegation of a race riot, believing it was all a lie. But the pictures proved otherwise. Ross became what he called a "living memorial" to the riot, now called the Tulsa Race Massacre. Ross became a journalist by profession, dedicating his life to the mission of making that tragedy known, and was the first man to break the story open in the 1970s. Others joined him, and the energy has snowballed since.

Down the line, Ross became a public servant in the Oklahoma House of Representatives to lend his voice to the mission of applying lessons to prevent similar future tragedies. He was primarily responsible for the development of the Race Riot Commission report formed in 2000, and published in 2004, to thoroughly investigate the tragedy and locate survivors.

Enter another unsung hero, Kevin Matthews, grew up in Greenwood, a few blocks from the storied site. He calls it "hallowed ground" for those connected to the history. Greenwood was never restored to its prosperous beginnings due to the absence of riot clauses in insurance policies. Also, Tulsa city officials refused the aid and support promised from around the country to rebuild after the destruction.

As a young man, Matthews began his own business, Kevin's Cleaners, in the heart of Greenwood. Later, he joined the local fire department and learned what it meant to be a leader of teams. Eventually, he became Oklahoma Senator Kevin Matthews, with a vision of hope to restore Greenwood and Black Wall Street to the collective consciences of people in Tulsa, America, and around the world.

The planning for the 2021 Tulsa Race Massacre Centennial began in 2016, with Matthews as a key figure. As an Oklahoma Senator, he introduced House Bill 17, which authorized $1.5 million from the state budget to tell the story of the race massacre. What originated as an effort to raise five million dollars culminated in raising $30 million worldwide. A state-of-the-art museum was funded, then constructed, called 'Greenwood Rising' at the famed corridor of Greenwood and Archer streets where the destruction commenced in 1921. In addition, people can walk along a Pathway to Hope, which culminates at nearby Reconciliation Park.

Matthews doesn't want people to be ignorant of the fact this happened or for the event to be forgotten. He called the 100-year celebration of the massacre an opportunity to bring economic development, healing, and education to the state of Oklahoma and all areas affected. The hopeful twist is that Greenwood has become a model of reconciliation for the country and the world. What was "Tulsa's dirty secret" for decades became a teaching moment for current and future generations.

Advocates of Black Wall Street now abound, expressing a fervent hope that racial divisions can be repaired and restored by whites and blacks alike, working together. Funding and interest from around the globe poured in as the centennial commission moved forward with plans to commemorate in a large way the 100th anniversary of the Massacre in 2021.

It is an example that building relationships and having dialogue around solutions can make a difference, Matthews said. What about Black Wall Street, has it died? No, the spirit has not died. People are amazed that Charlie Wilson of the Gap Band, John Starks who dunked on Michael Jordan, Wayman Tisdale, and Kenny Monday the Olympic gold medalist are from Tulsa. I could go on and on about how many outstanding black people that have made a difference in the world are from right here . . . and so while there are some terrible things that have happened here, the people that are black that come from here, that have that Black Wall Street spirit, continue to get back up. We continue to succeed, and we continue to fight. That's the Black Wall Street spirit, when those homes and businesses were burned down and the insurance claims didn't pay out, they took the money out of their own pockets. They rebuilt again. And when it was destroyed again, they rebuilt again. That Black Wall Street spirit is the reason I'm here today.

I want [people] to take away that no matter how intelligent you are, no matter how many degrees you have, how many books you've read, you haven't really learned until you can learn about other people. Sit down and learn about other people. That is the ultimate in intelligence and education to me. Books can take you different places, and that's a great education, but building relationships with people that can be advocates for you, people that can be sounding boards for you, and to broaden your horizons I think is the essence of wisdom.

Every generation is not hindered by what the previous generation experienced. They're a lot more fearless. They're a lot more capable of keeping relationships globally, and I hope that this work enhances the opportunity of African Americans and others that believe in what we're doing, to be able to lead us in ways that we haven't seen in the past.

Learning this history made me more active in advocacy. The tragedy, as well as the triumph of Greenwood, aka Black Wall Street, became my story and expanded my world. I've been a presenter at the annual John Hope Franklin Center for Reconciliation symposium in Tulsa. I also created a short form documentary on the subject. Identifying with those who suffered—victims and descendants—is a necessary component of hope. At the same time, all good people are victims of this kind of tragedy. Conversely, all who choose to can become part of the solution of providing hope for generations to come.

Exhortations to Excellence on Hope

> **Never give up, for that is just the place
> and time that the tide will turn.**
> **–Harriet Beecher Stowe**

They say you can live only a few days without water and a month or two without food. I add that you can't live a meaningful life without *hope*. Without this essential virtue, you're just walking through life, going through the motions. Hope is like breathing; absolutely necessary. It raises the standard of giving and of living. There must be a payoff for what you believe and to that which you aspire. Risk and reward, hope for gain—human beings were created for the positivity these provide. This transforms just getting by to a thrilling adventure ride. Hope gives us the upper hand; the inside track to a purpose-driven life.

Hope carries the idea of extending or reaching forward with a desire or expectation of obtaining some good or worthy objective. Having hope gives us confidence that what is desired is not only possible but likely. Thus, pleasure and joy accompany hope—they're tied together—unlike mere wishing. Don't forfeit your expectation of good things to come. Hopefulness is connected to the confidence, pleasure, and joy of leading an extraordinary life.

Being hopeless is being stripped of what you need most—and too often substituted by despondency, depression, and despair. Conversely, hope will go a long way toward dispelling those intruders. Stay ahead of the curve by fanning the flame of hope each day. That's in your power. On a scale, how are you doing today? Take the time to replenish the stocks. Whether it's in an occupation, education, social setting, or related to health matters, hope is a priceless asset to protect and maintain at all costs.

CERTAINTY OF HOPE

Psychologist Dr. Charles Snyder defines hope as the capability to derive pathways to desired goals and motivate oneself via agency thinking to use those pathways. Hope links to a sense of optimism and directly influences self-esteem. Research shows those persons with high levels of hope have better outcomes in academics, athletics, physical health, and improved psychological well-being. Less hope closes pathways to more desirable outcomes, lowering personal esteem. According to Dr. Snyder, future research should encourage understanding the necessity of hope and helping people pursue goals that are suited to their individual abilities, skills, and aptitudes.

> **Even in the mud and scum of things,**
> **something always, always sings.**
> **–Ralph Waldo Emerson**

Hope transmits life, light, and love like the sun. It brightens the day by sheer attitude alone. There's a sense of lightness, rather than heaviness. It's like opening the window shade to the soul. The eyes reflect the promise of hope or betray that it is sorely lacking. Being a hopeful person equips you to impart the same outlook to others and be a light for those in need. The sun benefits other heavenly bodies and the essence of life on Earth. You and I need the sunshine that hope provides. You're a better person for this essential virtue and are diminished in its absence.

When I ponder hope, I think of something sure and steadfast, rather than haphazardly wishing upon a star something that might come true. It's not the lottery where I have little to do with the outcome. This hope is a strong, firm infusion of positive expectation. I am persuaded that something can come from nothing. I'm fighting for it. I'm willing to stake my life on it and work toward the realization.

Hope is a master motivator. Its object might be on the other side of the rainbow, but I know it's there. In any case, the process starts where I am today, square one. Hope's initial payment is deposited here and now. It's like punching a ticket or booking the flight in advance. I have every right to anticipate the ride if I've paid the fare. The prospects for hope are like that—reliable. There is anticipation of the materialization in advance. Plans are altered and built around it. Then again, hope can spring up out of nowhere, in any kind of circumstance. There's nothing like the exhilaration of the unexpected this kind of lifestyle permits.

INSTANTANEOUS CONFIDENCE

Hope is a reality of which you can be firmly persuaded and has the power to motivate and move you to places you've never been. Embrace what you perceive from a distance. Talk freely about it before it happens. You feel the effects up front. It shapes both short and long-term plans. This prompts a fitting, whole person response.

Hope is an essential virtue. You are a partaker and steward of what you've been given. Hope has a way of bubbling from the inside—like a spring—flowing out to make connections in the world. *Be a bridge crosser, a breach repairer, a healer.* Hope doesn't die unless you permit the fire to be extinguished. Even then, it can rise from the dead. The eye is singularly focused convinced of something beyond the veil of consciousness. Hope, when tied to belief, sparks vision. But where there is no vision, people perish—along with their fondest dreams.

> **If it were not for hopes, the heart would break.**
> **–Thomas Fuller**

To be apathetic is to be withdrawn, disinterested, aloof, uncaring, and detached. Hope throws open windows of possibility. I heard someone say recently, "Today is different than yesterday. I must be the one to *make* it a new day."

Hope sends up the sails and keeps you on the straight and narrow.

A hopeful person is characterized by desire, drive, passion, curiosity, eagerness, and the yearning to overcome. Show me a hopeful person and I'll show you one who puts their best foot forward every day. When the deck is stacked against you, you can still thrive. Conditions don't always have to be rosy and the stars don't have to be aligned, because no life is untainted by adversity. The best of intentions encounters opposition. Don't be surprised or taken off guard. *Engaging the good fight of hope is one you can win.*

READY, SET, DON'T GO

One of the most beautiful cities in Israel is Joppa on the Mediterranean Sea. I eagerly anticipated the visit, having never been there before. The sheer situational beauty exceeded all expectations. That day, the sky was as blue as the sea. I had read the Bible story about Jonah and the great fish, and wondered what that day was like for him before the clouds gathered and changed his life forever. Some of the quaint, antiquated buildings stood as they had for centuries, built on a slope descending to the water's edge. Standing on the bank, I saw Tel Aviv in the distance. The shoreline curved around toward the large modern cityscape of Israel's second largest city. The whitecaps made for a stunning vista from the cliff where I stood. The waves incessantly crashed against the rocks below.

Joppa is still a port city today. Fishing boats were everywhere; hundreds of them. It was fascinating to walk and explore the various sizes and shapes of all of those different boats. Some of them were modern. Others were old and dilapidated. Some were well-built. Some were constructed of resourced odds and ends. The creativity was totally impressive. This flavor of fishing took me back in my memory to Jonah's unlikely adventure, where he would learn profound lessons. The hope he was willing to extend to others would return to him manifold.

I looked out across the Mediterranean and imagined Jonah paying his fare, boarding the ship, and setting sail on the open sea. He was despondent and wanted to get away—as far away as possible. Soon, the raging storm threatened the hope of the crew surviving. Jonah believed that his running away from what he knew he was supposed to do with his life was the source of their adverse circumstance and requested that they throw him overboard. Reluctantly, they did.

Miraculously, Jonah was swallowed by a great fish, which in a paradox saved his life. It's one thing to read the story, but it must have been another to have been *the* player in the drama. This was an epic story of despair—but came with a plot twist to the credit of the protagonist. All seemed to be lost in the belly of that fish. Seaweed was wrapped around his head. I'm imagining the darkness of being enclosed and the sounds of the sea and the creature itself. Jonah was at death's door. *Time to reflect.* He described his soul as fainting within him. His life was ebbing away, and he would have died but for what he did next.

On the third day, Jonah had an epiphany—a pathway and strategy became clear. First, he vowed to do what he previously promised—go to Nineveh and help other people. "I will pay that which I've vowed," he said.

The second was to give thanks—even during the trauma of a near-death experience. "They that observe lying vanities forsake their own mercy," he concluded.

Hope supplied him with great confidence—which returned in the form of personal well-being. Yet even if he had died, he died a changed man. His attitude turned in an instant, which is an indicator that he had total charge of this personal asset. You, too, can adopt the right attitude every time, regardless of the intimidating circumstances. That's the power of hope to immediately affect even the smallest of moments.

The great fish vomited Jonah onto dry land, as the story goes. He hit the ground running and headed to Nineveh to pay forward his vow to help others. Jonah must have been moving at a fast pace, because he arrived two days early on what was normally a three-day excursion.

Hope provides an energy that you can feel head to toe. Despair causes energy to deplete in buckets. Jonah became the superhero of Nineveh when he delivered a hopeful message. They were grateful for his visitation, which ultimately turned their lives and city around.

Like that great fish gave up Jonah, many great problems will give you up. They loosen their grip after you've found the pathway to solve your problem and create a brighter future. One of many outcomes of hope is the resolve to serve others' needs above your own. This disposition makes you the proud owner of the hope you distribute. When you drive hope all around town like a vehicle during the day, you get to park it in your garage at night. Check under the hood from time to time to be sure it's optimized.

Hope is a sweet spot you create for others and yourself.

Here's a tip from Jonah's unlikely adventure: when you run away from the call to develop others, you deprive yourself of the opportunity to scale your purpose. But when you run toward the people you intend to help, it will fill you with the energy of hope and put a spring in your step. Running toward heartfelt goals and objectives with the good of others in mind foreshadows an extraordinary life.

PASSENGER OF HOPE

You were born for hope. It's an aberration to live without it. Troubles don't define you. You see beyond difficulties, even the impossibilities. If things have gone awry, it's possible to remain optimistic until things turn again for the better. There's something good around the corner that you didn't expect or take into consideration at the outset. You worked through and seized the moment at the right time. Someone might observe your strenuous trials, yet you have relevant, *inside* information. Understanding the diamond of hope in your possession means you don't throw in the towel—and you steadfastly believe in what you don't see with the eye.

You have a preference, attraction, fascination, hunger, and thirst for hope. It draws you all the way in. It nourishes the soul, keeping you on the lookout for those you can assist. The strongest people in life are characterized by this essential virtue. Weak people have little to none. Automobiles don't run without fuel, no matter how fancy they are. Humans don't get far without hope, no matter how much state-of-the-art talent or ability they possess.

Refuel at pitstops along the way. Keep hope alive. Use the small moments as *springboards* into inspiration that will take you farther than you could achieve on your own. Viewing the horizon, not the terrain, helps you avoid the pitfalls and trappings—or climb out of them when you've stumbled in.

Hope is the pillar that holds up the world.
Hope is the dream of a waking man.
–Pliny the Elder

THE TREE OF INFLUENCE

You don't serve yourself in the larger scheme of things. When you expand your vision, you realize there are people in the future who will benefit from your legacy today. You serve people around you, with a view even to those you haven't met—yet. There are places you haven't ever been or seen but you're on the way—blessed for the journey. There are many who need what you have to offer. You never know whom you might affect by investing in one who will touch the world like you touched them. You can't see the full fruition of promises down the line, but they can be previewed through the uncanny ability of the mind's eye.

Hope and its fulfillment are equivalent in nature—two forms of the same thing. They exist on opposite sides of the ledger. Though you encounter setbacks, they don't defeat you. They provide a golden opportunity for your hope to shine.

Recollect your prior vows and commitments to become thankful. Pick up where you left off before you got into trouble. Regardless of the circumstances, there are choices to make to turn your ship around. You're positioning yourself by changing your inward disposition to hope, which is superior to changing every adverse situation arrayed against you. Even the decision to change has a remarkable ability to alter the immediate matters at hand. When you decided there's a better way, you moved the needle by degrees.

Many of life's failures are people who did not realize how
close they were to success when they gave up.
-Thomas Edison

THE SCIENCE OF HOPE

Chan Hellman was a quiet and withdrawn youth. When he was in eighth grade, a teacher sat down next to him, having no idea what was going on in his life. Pausing a minute, the teacher leaned in toward him and told him he was going to be okay. Those words were timely, infusing hope into Chan's life, making all the difference. Today, Chan credits that teacher for saving his life without even realizing it.

He was a homeless youth all through high school. There were many days he spent wondering what he was going to eat and where he was going to sleep. Yet, homelessness was an intentional choice. It trumped living at home and being part of the family drug trade business.

Hope became necessary to survive and a tool to help him overcome adversity.

Fast forwarding many decades, Chan is considered one of America's top experts on the power of hope. A psychologist, he heads up the University of Oklahoma's Hope Research Center in Tulsa. He's also been a faculty member at the college for twenty plus years. His Ph.D. is in quantitative psychology. He calls hope a 'social gift' because it is sharable and nurtured in the context of meaningful relationships. He says it's a matter of choice that you have ability to focus on what's wrong with a person or what's right with them. Chan learned that hope isn't an accident—it's a purposeful, intentional way of living.

I became acquainted with Hellman's work at a leadership event associated with the University of Oklahoma. I was fascinated to learn there was a man who devoted his entire professional life to the subject of hope. He's making a difference in countless lives across America and around the world. He has found ways to apply principles to raise the quality of living for people who are ready to embrace the challenge.

HOPE CHANGES THINGS

Unsung heroes come along to help in ways you never imagined. Sometimes, helpers don't realize how they are transforming lives without their knowing. Chan returned years later as an adult to thank that teacher for saving his life. Sitting down next to the retired man selling basketball game tickets, Chan leaned in and whispered quietly that he was the reason he was even alive today, then proceeded to tell how and why that was true. That teacher was unaware of what he had done, yet his moment of selfless compassion changed the trajectory of a severely disadvantaged youth.

Chan pays his blessing forward and is an advocate for others who find themselves in hopeless situations of all kinds. He says he can help any child or adult in one hour by the strategies he's developed as a hope scientist. He focuses on those he has an opportunity to touch and the power of imagining the way things *could* be.

> Hope is such a bait it covers any hook.
> –Oliver Goldsmith

The Hope Research Center works with community organizations, serving in areas of domestic violence, child maltreatment, homelessness, food insecurity, and other difficult contexts. Chan suggests those are the ideal situations for the positive influence that hope provides. His passion and mission have taken him around the globe to help people with common needs across diverse cultures.

He teaches that leaders should be hope-informed, and it will in turn improve their teams, as well as culture in the workplace. He says that hope is not an outcome as much as it is a pathway. Well-being is the outcome or goal. Since hope is a pathway, it can be chosen as a lifestyle and immediate improvements can be made by anyone, at any time. Therefore, hope becomes a strategic means to an intentional, chosen end.

Trauma and adversity rob people of hope, whereas Chan's work focuses on the strengths of individuals to overcome their adversities. Trauma in relationships decreases the levels of trust. Therefore, hope as a pathway translates into a positive outcome of building trust. When people learn they can be intentional about hope, it has an immediate effect and becomes a predictor of performance in academic, social, and workplace environments.

Chan emphasizes that hope can and should be taught. He says hope is about three essentials: goals, pathways, and willpower. He described goals as the cornerstone. Next is the pathway or roadmap to actively pursue each goal. Thus, pathway thinking becomes the strategy to pursue and obtain any goal. Through strategy, barriers to hope are identified. Finally, he explains willpower as the mental energy and resources that are committed to a strategy. Pathways and willpower are requisite to achieving the goals critical to one's well-being.

He calls wishing passive, but hope is active.

If you lose hope, somehow you lose the vitality that keeps moving, you lose that courage to be, that quality that helps you go on, in spite of it all. And so today I still have a dream.
–Martin Luther King, Jr.

SMALL DEGREES CAUSE SWEEPING CHANGE

Chan differentiates between degrees of hope by saying higher hope individuals have better coping strategies amid certain stressors. He adds that going from low to slight hope can be a life changer for many. Starting small is a methodical process for goal clarification. First, identify the goal, then the benchmarks toward the objective. He affirms that hope is a belief that can improve anyone's future—and that you have the ability within yourself to make it that way. Hope is an essential virtue to lead an extraordinary life. Use the power of hope for others in need. Hope serves as an anchor and confidence for anyone—making the rewards richer.

For more information about Chan and his work, go to ou.edu/tulsa/hope.com.

Moments of accountability can launch future opportunities. How many lives have you affected by believing and following hope? I'll bet more than you've realized. How many more people will be affected by raising your expectations again?

Who are you determined to help and how?

Hope is a sleeping giant that empowers you through thick and thin.

People are waiting for the piece you contribute to touch their lives.

Hope is a game-changer—for them and for you.

Hope is the thing with feathers that perches in the soul and sings the tune without the words and never stops at all.
-Emily Dickinson

GEMSTONES

- Risk and reward, hope for gain—human beings are created for the positivity these provide.

- Hope transmits life, light, and love like the sun. It brightens the day by sheer attitude alone.

- Being a hopeful person equips you to impart the same outlook to others and be a light for those in need.

- Hope enables you to be a bridge crosser, a breach repairer, a healer.

- The good fight of hope is one you can win.

- We're better persons for the essential virtue of hope and are diminished in its absence.

- You never know whom you might affect by investing in someone who will touch the world like you touched them.

- Regardless of the circumstances, there are choices to make to turn your ship around.

- Even the decision to change has a remarkable ability to alter the immediate matters at hand. You moved the needle when you decided there's a better way.

- Hope is a sleeping giant that empowers you through thick and thin.

REFLECTIONS
HOPE: WIND FOR YOUR SAILS

Identify methods for adjusting position to accomplish the mission.

PROMPT: How can you stay motivated to strive for your goals and help others with theirs?

ACTION: Make a list of activities to do when feeling discouraged.

PROMPT: Reflect on moments when hope has made a difference in your life.

ACTION: Explain the emotions that you may have felt during that process.

Notes:

_____

_____

_____

_____

_____

_____

_____

_____

_____

_____

_____

VIRTUE #7

DILIGENCE: THE WINNER'S EDGE

Why the one drip at a time tool still works wonders

Unsung Hero Story

Diligence is hard work, steadily applied, over time. Hard work alone can become rigid and mechanical, but when passion embodies work, whatever it may be, it takes on a new energy and is difficult to stop. What's the purpose? The goal? Define that and hard work becomes easier because of its connection to a higher purpose.

One of my unsung heroes is Theodore Dwight Weld. He was an unselfish man with an ability to empathize with the sufferings of others. Many believe Weld was the most prominent figure of the abolitionist movement during the mid-nineteenth century. His insistence to keep a low profile made him relatively unknown in the annals of American history, yet he was a consummate unsung hero because he didn't do what he did for the applause. This freed him to apply extra diligence to his all-consuming mission.

Weld was born in 1803 in Connecticut. He attended Hamilton College in upstate New York during the 1820s. Even though his eyesight deteriorated, he began travelling as a lecturer and did so in the southern states, where he witnessed firsthand the harsh realities and cruel atrocities of slavery.

By 1831, Weld was commissioned by philanthropists Arthur and Lewis Tappan to travel and lecture on moral reform, which included slavery. Here's what one of his personal travel logs revealed of his personal diligence for a single year: *4,500 miles total; 2,630 by boat and stagecoach; 1,800 by horseback; 145 on foot; and 236 public addresses.*

Weld returned to upstate New York and came under the influence of Charles G. Finney, becoming his protégé. Both agreed that an institution was needed in the American West where additional anti-slavery lecturers could be trained and raised up. There were hundreds already combing the country thanks to committed individuals who understood they couldn't do it alone. Weld scouted the land, and Cincinnati was chosen as the site for what became Lane Seminary. Weld recruited the faculty, but soon enrolled himself in 1833 as a student. Yet it was commonly held and perceived that Weld was the leader by example of the institution. Students and faculty alike looked to him as his zeal for the abolitionist cause knew no bounds.

Weld organized student debates at Lane in February of 1834 on the two prevailing arguments at the time: colonization versus abolition. For eighteen days, testimony was planned for three hours per evening by various speakers. Harriet Beecher was in attendance, as was John Rankin from nearby Ripley. James Bradley was a young black man, a former slave whose compelling live testimony was featured. After nine days, a vote was taken, and immediate emancipation was unanimously agreed upon by the student body.

The hierarchy of Lane did not agree with the outcome and immediately dismissed Weld from the school. In turn, fifty other students dissolved their association with the college and became known as the Lane Rebels. Weld returned to New York and continued his diligent abolition efforts while the Lane Rebels continued their education in October at Oberlin Collegiate Institute in Oberlin, Ohio, under

Finney, who had taken a departmental charge. Special dorms were built for the Lane Rebels, and many of them eventually rose to levels of leadership in the cause and some fought in the Civil War.

Meanwhile, Weld stepped up diligent publishing efforts as head of the American Anti-Slavery Society in Ohio at half the salary he was offered from another organization. It is said that in one year alone, Weld distributed one million pieces of literature denouncing slavery. By 1836, Weld lost his voice, but that didn't thwart his efforts. He was director of publications for the society from 1836-40 and the editor of *The Emancipator* newspaper. The student debates were recorded in written form by Weld and published in *The Liberator*, widely influencing the nation's perception regarding slavery.

In 1839, Weld wrote a book, *American Slavery as it is: Testimony of a Thousand Witnesses*, which changed the trajectory of slavery in America even further toward emancipation, calling attention to the crimes being committed in those days. True to the title, these were 1,000 real life accounts which had been reported and compiled by Weld from the testimony of people across the country. The details were shocking to the conscience. No, the slaves were not being treated kindly, as had been previously claimed by the slave owners.

Yet the North wasn't altogether innocent, either. Wealthy entre-preneurs owned slaves in the south and placed them on the auction blocks to be shipped south. Hundreds of Blacks were marched in coffle chains on foot all the way from Virginia and other north-ern states to New Orleans and hubs of the lucrative business of slave-trading.

Weld's book became the most widely distributed book on the subject at the time. In between the Lane debates of 1834 and Weld's publishing his book in 1839, Harriet Beecher married Calvin Stowe, a professor at Lane. Harriet Beecher Stowe wrote *Uncle Tom's Cabin* in 1852, in part based on the writings of Weld's 1839 book. Frederick Douglass read it and stated that no slave owner in the South ever refuted the veracity of the accounts that were recorded within the pages. Distribution of the book reached as far as England. From speaking to writing pamphlets and books, to heading anti-slavery organizations, Weld found a way to move the message forward the diligent way—one persevering drip at a time.

During this span, Weld formed a group of lecturers called "The Seventy." These were seventy equally diligent and passionate abolition lecturers. Weld was influential in his recruitment of others—as can be felt in his invitation to throw in and become involved:

"If your hearts ache and bleed, we want you . . . you will help us. If you join us out of a sense of duty, we pray you keep aloof and give place to those who leap into our ranks because they cannot keep themselves out; who instead of whining about duty, shout 'privilege,' 'delight!'"

Lyman Beecher was Harriet Beecher Stowe's father, the president of Lane Seminary in Cincinnati, calling Weld's words during his lectures as "logic on fire." Diligence can be credited for overturning a repulsive system that was taking a tragic toll on the country. Hard work alone would not have sustained; but tied to passion, the work came alive and became a force for positive change. Were it not for diligent people like Weld, slavery may never have been abolished as soon as it was.

Weld's obscurity was not accidental—it was chosen. Often, he shunned cities and population centers to work in outlying country districts, which made the grassroots efforts more effective. The literature, pamphlets, and books did work in the cities. Weld went to areas where newspapers were rare. Many of his works were published anonymously because he didn't care who received the credit. The message was more important—and the reception on a larger scale. Taking the road of humility gave him the unsung status that he preferred.

Weld relocated to Washington, D.C. from 1841-43 to direct the national campaign for sending antislavery petitions to Congress. While there, he also assisted John Quincy Adams when he went on trial for violating the gag rule, which prohibited slavery from being discussed at all in Congress—same diligence, new venue.

This cause was Weld's legacy. When he tied his work to service, it made all the difference. He worked to make others free, which became untiring labors of love and care for other people. Diligence is the essential virtue that turns the table on impossibilities, making them possible through passionate, steady effort over time, as Weld so perfectly demonstrated in his life's mission.

Exhortations to Excellence on Diligence

The leading rule for a man of every calling is diligence; never put off until tomorrow what you can do today.
–Abraham Lincoln

The virtue of diligence is a cutting edge to get things done and puts you firmly in charge of your life, not leaving anything to chance. You've taken ownership. When you succeeded and someone else failed, this may be a key place to check as to the difference why. All things considered, maybe the other person quit early. Maybe they were habitually late or wasted time. Maybe they didn't put their heart and soul into the work, so when the going got tough, they didn't have the persistence or determination to see it through to completion. Nothing can fill the shoes of this sleeping giant. Awakened and engaged, nothing can stand in its way.

You're writing the script for an extraordinary life.

I read a little book in my twenties called *Signposts on the Road to Success*, by E.W. Kenyon, and learned valuable lessons from the pages.

It directed my path to become *self-reliant*, *diligent*, and *punctual*. If I promise to be at an appointment by 2:30 in the afternoon, I do my best to arrive early. It gives peace and a sense of calm to be ahead of the curve and provides composure upon arrival. Conversely, when I'm late or down to the wire, it shows in my demeanor, countenance, and frayed nerves. When I'm early, I convey confidence in who I am in my purpose. I avoid wasting time coming up with excuses. Those who are habitually behind the clock don't consider how negatively it impacts the schedules of others. Maybe it goes unmentioned, but it seldom goes unnoticed. Diligence is tied to being considerate because it matters how you treat other people. A litmus test for the virtue of diligence has as much to do with how you relate to others as it has to do with how you conduct yourself.

Keep both aspects healthy and strong.

THE PATH OF PERSEVERANCE

You're a builder. When your name is mentioned, what associations do other people make? If a pattern of laziness persists, people won't think of you as being successful, no matter how much money you make. These failures wind up as objects of water cooler talk, or eye rolls after you leave. Transmit positive vibes by being diligent, and contributing to the worthwhile progress of others. You care about others' work, not just your own. The diamond of diligence lends itself to building trust in relationships.

When you say you'll do a job, give it your undivided attention. I like to think of every task with a beginning, middle, and end. All three require dedication and persistence. I begin act one with determination. I try to perpetuate the second act with energy to keep it from sagging and losing momentum. I add the finishing touches in the third act to polish the goal and make it presentable. Each task is one whole, divided into equal parts. A diligent mentality has a way of adapting to all three stages as needed, but it's the singular focus that wins every time.

Persistence is doing something despite the difficulty or delay. Single-mindedness is necessary for achieving small or large objectives and pays large dividends over time. Talent alone doesn't win the day, but those with a tenacity to push past obstacles do.

> **By diligence and patience, the mouse bit in two the cable.**
> –Benjamin Franklin

The famous story to illustrate this truth is the classic hare and the tortoise. The hare had greater natural ability and speed but was cocky and overconfident. He took his foot off the gas pedal of consistent effort and paid the ultimate penalty: *defeat*. What the tortoise lacked in speed he made up for with perseverance. Though slower in pace, he crossed the finish line first to win the race.

Success in any endeavor has one commonality—an unwillingness to quit. Your audience consists of at least one—you. Applause or recognition for what you've done may or may not come later, but you've cultivated the essential habit of doing all things well. When you finish one task with excellence, you're fitted for the next. Difficulty can't stop the superhero of diligence because perseverance functions at its best in extreme adversity. Mighty oaks fall by little strokes, goes the saying. Diligence will persist in a course of action despite the stiff opposition.

Keep on.

Enjoyment in any work causes your level of productivity to rise. You want to look back and see the job done with excellence. Diligence is the unsung hero's tool of high achievement, but more than is the personal fulfillment that ensues from a job well done.

Half-heartedness depletes energy. Wholeheartedness—being all the way in—becomes a turbocharger. You care about the objective and the people associated with it.

You're a human being capable of achieving the impossible. One of the great truths is that you can demonstrate diligent leadership in anything and everything—whether you are at the bottom or the top of your team. Employees do well to perform like leaders and leaders do well to serve like employees. Understanding this concept optimizes performance and productivity. Every person understands their role, crossing the finish line together.

Diligence secures rewards—and it's more than the tangible ones. Inner qualities are the big takeaways. Begin with a cut-above attitude and finish with the same. Protect that inward disposition of diligence at all costs and you'll never lack the high achievements you were destined for. It's amazing to think about all you can accomplish, and even more powerful to think what an extraordinary person you have and will become.

> I never could have done what I have done without the habits of punctuality, order, and diligence, without the determination to concentrate myself on one subject at a time.
> –Charles Dickens

EXPONENTIAL POWER OF CONTINUATION

Several years ago, I entered a weight loss and fitness contest. There were some great rewards and prizes for the first, second, and third place winners. The spoils were spelled out in the contest rules and gave motivation. I cared a lot about fitness and health but had been off my game for a while. So, I registered, submitting my "before" pictures and numerous measurements.

This was a ninety-day challenge, so I carefully designed a meal plan and a fitness plan. I'm a runner, so that's mostly what I did for that end of things. I was steady and committed. Once I made the choice to pursue this goal, it made some of my other choices easy. I didn't eat the wrong things, felt healthier in a matter of days, and ran outdoors several days per week. Meeting with a trainer, he hooked me up to a heart monitor while I ran on the treadmill. He marveled that even though he was into Olympic weight training, my cardio fitness was better than his. He was twenty-five years old. I was fifty-five. My metabolic age at the end of that contest was nineteen. I was shocked at that number. But it made sense, because many times when I finished a great run, I wanted to keep on going.

The power of continuation is vital.

After three months, I received a phone call congratulating me for finishing second in the contest. The caveat was that I needed to maintain my current fitness level for three additional months. I was committed. Over the course of those six months, I recorded a 15k run, a half-marathon, and scheduled a marathon to top it off, because I knew I had to elevate the game. When I pulled up lame after the half-marathon, I had to postpone the marathon. Once recovered, I set my own marathon to finish the original goal. I looked at it like a home run, achieving all three races in that six-month span. I had my "after" pictures taken and recorded my new measurements. To cap it off, I jumped into a pool with my clothes on and had a great picture snapped while climbing out on the final day.

At the end of that six months, I received the second phone call letting me know that I had preserved my second-place finish. All totaled, I won $10,000 in cash, prizes, and merchandise. I was beyond thrilled. I was put up in an Anaheim hotel for the convention and awards ceremony. I did achieve nice recognition, but the intangible rewards were greater. I owe that victory to the essential virtue called diligence.

That was several years ago. Though I haven't run a big race in a while, I adapted to running every single day. The goal has changed, but the diligence has not. I've counted more than 1,200 days in a row of running five miles per day. I haven't done this for recognition, but for the health benefits. At first, I merely wanted to break my record of running twenty-seven days in a row. Once I did that, I set a goal of 100 days, 200, then 500, then 750, and finally, 1,000. I'm still going. I'm not doing it for prizes now. I do it for the deep cleansing breath, the movement, the endorphins for the brain, and the focus of not quitting. Even my sleep is better. If you told me I was going to run 5,000 miles in the span of a few years, I might have thought it was nuts. Those miles were divided into steady days on the path and ultimately were steps strung together in succession—a pretty good picture of diligence.

I don't get applause, but I do it anyway.

DON'T FORGET THE HUMANITY

Great football teams play the fourth quarter with as much gusto as the first three. Baseball teams play the ninth inning like the first and the first inning like they do the ninth. The musician plays the last song in the set to bring the house down and places the finishing touches with an exclamation point. Professionals treat each client and colleague like they are the most important one they've had all day—because they are.

Stay the course.
Maybe you take time-outs,
but you never quit.

Diligence is a steady and earnest effort toward a given task. But I want to know how you're treating people in the process. It's the path of least resistance to be self-centered and expect the applause. In the long run, it's easier and more rewarding to share your diligence with others, even if you don't get any applause. Love is the best delivery mechanism.

Who are you helping today? You should help others with as equal a devotion as you do to your own tasks. Ironically, sharing with others will multiply your personal ability.

People who hear about your unselfish disposition may call on you to do the same for them. You've developed a reputation. You don't get excited just about your own goals; you thrill about the aspirations of others and care about things that are important to them.

You win when they win.

Diligence is the opposite of negligence. It means you're all the way in the door and won't come out until you're done. You've passed the point of no return. No one is blessed in what they do without this essential virtue. Anyone great in their field exerts a double portion to achieve excellence. Yet even healthy relationships require diligence to grow, mature, and become as fruitful as they can be.

Prefer diligence before idleness unless you esteem rust above brightness.
–Plato

ONE SWING AT A TIME WRITES THE RECORD BOOKS

Pete Rose is the all-time hit leader in Major League Baseball—4,256 to be exact. He was an important cog in the famed Big Red Machine of the Cincinnati Reds during the 1970s. No matter what Rose did on the field, he did it with extraordinary effort. He gave small things great energy; not just when he got a base hit, but when he drew a base on balls, he sprinted to first base while other players trotted. Rose went above and beyond what was required. He sprinted off the field to the dugout and onto the field from the dugout in between innings.

On Rose's first career at bat, the pitcher walked him, and he sprinted to first base as if he were trying to beat a throw on a ground ball to the infield. On another occasion, during a monstrous home run to the outfield by Hall-of-Famer Mickey Mantle, Rose tried to scale the fence to catch it, even though the ball sailed a hundred feet above the wall. Whitey Ford, the renowned pitcher for the New York Yankees at the time, observed the phenomenon and nicknamed Rose *Charlie Hustle* after viewing the spectacle. The name stuck. Without diligence and consistency, Charlie Hustle would have been as average as Clark Kent. With it, he came bursting out of the phone booth with an 'S' on his chest. Putting diligence on a pedestal elevated Rose to being one of the best to ever play the game, and no one had more fun in the process than he did.

Rose was asked about his high-energy approach to playing baseball, and he explained that he didn't want to lose his job to another player in the wings jockeying for his position. He refused to toss the privilege of playing to chance, so he did everything with twice as much energy. He never looked back. Hustle increased his productivity on every level. He tried to make himself indispensable—and he succeeded.

Rose hated the bench and almost never sat there.

He treated every detail of baseball like his life depended on it and learned the value of giving small moments undivided passion along the way. He truly loved playing the game. There are a lot of things that could have been awarded credit for his tremendous success, but this essential virtue of diligence was key.

Rose played the game with enthusiasm, and it was contagious. He was an integral part of three World Series championship teams and was a seventeen-time all-star. A switch hitter, he adapted according to the need of the moment. Never a power hitter, he only hit 116 home runs during his career, but he chipped away at the plate and into the record books forever. He was a Gold Glove winner twice for his high on base fielding percentage. Upon retirement, his percentage was more than 99 percent, a major league record at the time. He stayed on top of his game and played to the maximum in the smallest of moments. The consistency carried over to the largest moments on the biggest stages.

TURNING DILIGENCE INTO FUN

From a fan's point of view, Rose was one of the most exciting players to watch. He was obsessed with excellence. To the casual observer, Rose was not likely to be the guy to break the all-time hits record that had been held by Ty Cobb since the early 1900s. He wasn't an imposing figure or an intimidating athlete. But he had an extraordinary attitude, which got the ball of his high-performance rolling.

Records are accumulations of steady and consistent effort over time. At the end of the day, it wasn't Rose's raw talent that made the difference, it was the nine-letter essential virtue called diligence. He went against the grain and that defined his own greatness. No one can say that number '14' did anything by accident. Diligence gave him a razor-sharp edge.

Diligence begins internally and shows up on game day no matter what. Rose kept up the pressure to improve and translated that onto the field of play. What Pete lacked in ability, he made up for with diligence, which paid rewards throughout his lengthy twenty-four-year career.

> No work is insignificant. All labor that uplifts humanity
> has dignity and importance and should be undertaken
> with painstaking excellence.
> –Martin Luther King Jr.

The quality of work is just as important as the quantity. Always give an extra dose. Go further than what is required or necessary. Be a *finisher*. Afterward, improve. Diligence crosses the Ts and dots the Is. Leave no stone unturned. Be thorough. Review to be sure nothing was omitted. See your reflection in the results.

Are you proud of what you've accomplished? Does it make you happy to put your signature on your work or performance? Are you eager to share what you've done with an audience? These are good signs. To be hesitant is a signal that you should keep working until there is positive affirmation from the subconscious mind that it's been done well. You're ready to submit the work to another set of eyes and are open to feedback because you took it as far as you could on your own. Listen and take heed. Go back to the drawing board when necessary.

When you are engaged it shows. Diligence pulls the best tools out of you. Sometimes you're surprised that you were able to pour more from the tank than you thought. You can't tap the deepest resources without a predisposition to finish strong. Diligence leads to additional discoveries and places your best treasures on display. Discovery happens while you're moving. Make sure that you empty your tank on the road of life, not stalled out on the berm.

> Cultivate the habit of thorough work. Reason makes the plans. The strong one carries them through. It is easy to do it when you have the right mental attitude toward life. The secret of winning is action. Your best will give you life's best.
> –E.W. Kenyon

REAPING THE REWARD

Be selective about undertakings. Choose a few good arrows rather than a quiver full that might not find their mark. Kenyon emphasized that it helps to choose your work rather than to have work in which you have no interest thrust upon you. What you love will awaken your natural abilities and talent to achieve. Then add the *sizzle* of a great outlook.

The root of the word devotion is *to vow*. You are committed to something greater than yourself. There is an honor to doing work with persuasion. Your attitude of diligence is the greatest asset in your relational bank account. You may be disadvantaged in other ways, but not in this one. Your diligence is your own, like your hands. Doing things with diligence sets a precedent for future positive experiences.

You are a member of the club that elevates the quality of work. Others are proud to work alongside you. You are proactive and intentional. You're a consummate teammate, which makes you an unsung hero for people in many ways. Sometimes it goes unrecognized and underappreciated.

But you do it anyway.

When you exalt diligence, it will promote you. Actions and thoughts merge and synchronize. The reward is cryptically built into the work, and passion cultivates it along the way. Whatever a man or woman sows, he or she shall also reap. Stay alert and focused. You're translating your inner world to life's staging area. The sleeping giant of diligence is activated by your dedicated mission of serving others.

Conversely, a lack of diligence will bear its bitter fruit. Believe in negatives and you receive a crop of negatives. Believe in positives and you'll reap that harvest. In the meantime, the quality of work rises by levels. It brings the rest of its team of virtues alongside and overcomes obstacles that attempt to separate you from your goal. But you counted the cost already and were prepared to go over the top.

> Stick to a task, 'til it sticks to you.
> Beginners are many, finishers are few.
> –Anonymous

PROFILES IN DILIGENCE

Phillips Brooks lived in the 1800s and became a clergyman of Trinity Church in Boston, Massachusetts. Brooks was a speaker and writer but wasn't always identified that way. He was first fired as a school-teacher in Boston at a young age and took it hard, thinking he had failed miserably. He questioned whether he would ever amount to anything. He wrote, "I do not know what will become of me and I do not care much. I wish I were fifteen years old again. I believed I might become a stunning man: but somehow or other I do not seem in the way to come to much now."

This severe setback presented a unique opportunity for Brooks to find a new path forward.

Brooks picked up and started all over again, beginning a lifetime of new achievements and aspirations, graduating from Harvard at the young age of twenty. His life touched the likes of Helen Keller and Anne Sullivan, and he is famously known for his penning of the renowned Christmas hymn "O Little Town of Bethlehem." Brooks encouraged people through writing and speaking that they should view their chosen life's work as a rich source of nourishment for the soul. This is what defined him; not the setbacks or adverse circum-stances. When all else failed, he dug into his inner treasures that make a world of difference. Diligence was an essential virtue for *his* extraordinary life.

For many years, I've had a great admiration for Charles Finney, the second President of Oberlin College in northeast Ohio near Cleveland during the nineteenth century. He had a way of teaching that evolved from his study of law. The way he spoke and wrote was as if he were speaking to a jury. His comments about diligence are striking. I've never heard anyone teach this subject the way he did a few centuries ago. Therefore, I'll give the flavor here.

He taught that idleness was inconsistent with those who seek to please their fellow man. He wrote that diligence is necessary in the pursuit of any calling and that employment, whatever it may be, should not become a snare to the soul. "The love of our race will certainly lead us to exert ourselves to promote their happiness. Idleness can only come from selfishness," he said.

Idleness is also injustice, according to Finney. Other people have a right to expect the diligent use of abilities to promote commonly held interests. He went further to say that every degree of slothfulness is harmful to the world. The duplication and 'scaling' of idleness would cause the ultimate destruction of the universe. Finney stated:

> You are bound to do all the good you can in every way, both to the bodies and souls of men; and this obligation is entirely inconsistent with any degree of slothfulness. Idleness is as inconsistent with health as it is good morals. True devotion must, of necessity, be the supreme devotion of the will, extending to all we have and are—to all times, places, employments, thoughts, and feelings.

The virtue of diligence has provided you with an extraordinary life. Your commitment to excellence is equally beneficial to others as it is for yourself.

You've taken the lid off the deep treasures.

You've found joy in work and service.

Diligence.

There is nothing which persevering effort and unceasing and diligent care cannot accomplish.
–Seneca the Younger

GEMSTONES

- Diligence is a cutting edge to get things done. This essential virtue puts you firmly in charge of your life, not leaving things to chance. Take ownership.

- A litmus test for the virtue of diligence has as much to do with how you relate to others as it has to do with how you conduct yourself.

- Taking your eye off the ball of diligence takes a toll on *anything*. It's means you are taking a rest, perhaps like the overconfident hare.

- Cultivate the essential habit of doing all things well. When you finish one task with excellence, you're fitted for the next.

- One of the great truths is that you can demonstrate diligent leadership in anything and everything—whether you are at the bottom or the top of the team.

- Protect that inward disposition of diligence at all costs and you'll never lack the high achievements you were destined for. It's amazing to think about all you can accomplish.

- Even healthy relationships require diligence to grow, mature, and become as fruitful as they can be.

- The essential virtue of diligence makes you a winner in every endeavor—and you'll be proud of the extraordinary person you've become in the process.

- Diligence leads to additional discovery and places your best treasures on display.

- A lack of diligence will bear its bitter fruit. Believe in negatives and you receive a crop of negatives. Believe in positives and reap their harvest.

REFLECTIONS
DILIGENCE: THE WINNER'S EDGE

Explore why the "one drip at a time" tool of diligence still works wonders.

PROMPT: Reflect on moments when diligence has paid off for you.

ACTION: Make a list of steps to take when working on a goal or task.

PROMPT: Think about a goal you have accomplished despite obstacles. What kept you motivated and what did you learn from the experience?

ACTION: Write down one goal you want to achieve and what steps you can take to persevere towards it.

Notes:

_____

_____

_____

_____

_____

_____

_____

_____

_____

_____

_____

_____

VIRTUE #8

CREATIVITY:
SETTING GENIUS FREE
This is the way to smash the box of limitations

Unsung Hero Story

In the summer of 2017, I traveled to Israel to attend a program at Hebrew University called "The Jerusalem Project," working with journalists exploring the Israeli-Palestinian conflict. We traveled throughout the country, visiting with Israeli and Palestinian leaders, gaining insight, attending conference meetings, and asking questions. Anyone I talked to or heard speak on either side of this issue agreed that it's complicated. Creative solutions are certainly desired and needed.

I came across a creative project in the heart of Jerusalem, one of the world's most fascinating and controversial cities. I witnessed a microcosm of hope with all ethnicities represented, while in the Old City there were flash bombs detonated during the week. On nearby Ben Yehuda Street, there had been horrific bombings years before. Kikar Hamusica, translated "Music Square," is a shining example of using creativity in a collaborative way. There were solo performers, bands, violinists, pianists, guitarists, and vocalists. All the cultural barriers disappeared and the fuse of division was removed for those soothing, impactful, and healing moments of time.

I had a bird's eye view from my second story apartment. With the windows open and the breezes blowing through, it was truly magnificent. I talked to one woman who moved from France to Jerusalem to start her bakery and coffee shop at Music Square. Another woman served Italian food buffet style. They both loved being part of such a meaningful vision. A variety of restaurants, bakeries, and coffee shops surrounded the staging area and the tables in the audience were shared by all the businesses in the square. The concept was brilliant. The musicians and vocalists rotated every few hours, so you could hear multiple artists per day in every genre—which leads me to the story of Nir.

Nir Sarussi, a participating artist at Kikar Hamusica, is the one of the most talented violinists in the world. But it doesn't stop with his high-level talent and skill. When he got close to a table, he serenaded the people who were sitting there and they responded by clapping, jumping to their feet, and dancing. That's where passion and creativity kick his gift of performance into overdrive.

The joy was contagious.

I asked Nir about his approach and the relationships he develops in real time while performing. He explained, "Music has the power to bring people together and to 'break walls' and it is my honor and pleasure to be part [of the Kikar project]. When I recognize the origin of the audience, I play their unique folk music. I just love it when they all dance together. People from Greece, from England, from Russia, and more—they all dance together to the sounds of the various folk music being played."

Nir used to perform every week at Music Square. "It is believed that this place, Kikar Hamusica, will be a center of the music world, that people come to Israel from all over the world to enjoy this good atmosphere," he said.

Nir is from Afula, a city near Tiberias on the Sea of Galilee in northern Israel. As a nine-year-old boy, he went to a local conservatory to learn the art of playing keyboard. After a short audition, the teachers said that he possessed absolute hearing and a very high sense of beat and music. They offered to teach him the violin instead of the piano. Nir accepted that challenge and right away felt like it became a *gift* from heaven. That's where his passion was born to play music—and to live it out from the heart. His father encouraged him and told him that if he was faithful to his homework, he could soon have the 'candy' called the violin.

Nir played faithfully. As the weeks turned to months and the months turned to years, he knew that playing violin was his destiny. The connection Nir experienced to the violin made him feel like it was part of his body, to the extent that he could feel the vibrations through his physical heart. He describes the sensation of when he takes the bow—that he feels the duration of the strain vibrating even through his house. Nir calls the violin an emotional instrument which has fueled his personal creativity. He came to the place of realizing that he absolutely couldn't live without the violin.

At the same time, playing music competitively didn't seem to fit. It was confining and restricting, stifling his creativity yearning to get out. Finding expression of that energy set him free to become one of the best violin artists in the world. He didn't arrive at that level by trying to be like anyone else. He found what it was that made him come alive—which has made all the difference.

Nir enrolled at the Jerusalem Academy of Music at age twenty-one to build on his rising talent. Yet the emotional relationship with the violin and his connection to people soon set his world ablaze with a passion beyond words. Here is Nir's reflection on creativity which mirrors who he is as a person:

> Creativity for me is a few things: to take something from nothing in order to invent something in the music itself—or putting the notes together to create new music. You can take familiar

music or popular music and give it your own interpretation. In this way, you connect with listeners and allow them to become part of your activity in the show.

Nir plays across musical genres. He says his music is intended for everybody. Audiences can be local in Israel or at a venue anywhere in the world. He's played for Jews who have traveled from afar to Israel, politicians from America, even collaborating and jamming with renowned political leaders. Greek music, French music, Romanian music, Irish, German, ethnic—country, pop, Balkan, bluegrass, classical, Irish, German, and Asian—but don't forget the gypsy music. This style found a special place in Nir's heart.

Nir brought his unique interpretation to the piece. He says he focused his effort on music that was 'interesting' to him; what really grabbed him. In his concerts, he plays without sheet music and if he misses a note, he improvises to make up the difference.

Performing at Kikar in Jerusalem allows spaces for creativity and spontaneity because the audience is different every day. Nir plays to individuals and is inspired by them, taking their energy and converting it into a one-of-a-kind experience.

Nir's joy is in creating.

His wife, Naama, says, "I think everyone in the audience feels that Nir is playing just for them. They say things like, 'Thank you for giving this piece. It was amazing. It was exactly what I needed, and I felt it was dedicated to me.'"

"I play for all the people so that I know it makes them happy. I play them something that reminds them of their home and culture," Nir adds.

In addition, he's inspired by the music he chooses to play. He likes to be challenged. Even a new arrangement of an old song lights his creative fire. "This is why God gave me the oxygen to continue—to create and to play—and every concert is different."

When he plays for children, he looks directly at them. He creates a feeling that they are a part of the space. Nir has creative tricks up his sleeve for children to keep them amused and engaged. He might make animal noises of cows or birds with the bow of his violin, or maybe the sound of a train coming down the track. He dances with them and it makes them happy. He has a special affinity for the kindergarten age. They get very excited about his performances.

At times, he plays at outdoor festivals in Europe to 30,000 people, or maybe at an outdoor Jewish festival in Israel. Yet there's an equal amount of joy and fulfillment if he performs for one person inside an ancient cave in Jerusalem's Old City.

The story goes that the cave may have been used as a tunnel by King Tzidkiyahu, the king of Judea who escaped from the Babylonians in 586 BCE, from Jerusalem to the Dead Sea located about forty miles away. This was the cave where Nir performed for a Russian Jew. In the dark and silence, 200 meters inside, Nir began to play the violin with no amplifier, just the magnificent acoustic sounds reverberating in the natural rock beneath the ground. He adapted and created in the moment, choosing to play ancient temple music. Nir recalls the uniqueness of that experience. He says these slow and touching types of songs are ones that get passed from fathers down to their sons. These are the songs that moved the Russian Jew to tears. It has been said that if you were silent in the old days, you could hear the resonance of the music travelling through the rock from the vicinity of the nearby temple.

Nir plays also for connection and feels it is his duty to make people happy. His songs heal people while crossing bridges and divides at the same time, setting an example for others to follow. It brings people together, giving them joy. Sometimes, that has meant playing "Sweet Home Alabama" with a former American governor who played along with his guitar.

On another occasion, Nir traveled to the island of Crete in the Mediterranean Sea off the coast of Greece with his wife. He saw an old violin hanging on the wall and asked the owner of the tavern if he could play it. As he listened to the locals play, Nir joined them playing a local Crete rhythm. The people were amazed at how quickly he adapted to their musical style. Other musicians gathered around as he improvised, and they played Cretan music together. They sat together at a table and spoke for hours after that, enjoying each other's company. The result of this unrehearsed connection was understanding and sharing across cultures.

Nir played a concert for Naama's grandmother, who was over eighty years old at the time. After the concert, she felt "as if Nir added ten more years to my life." And after ten more years, Naama's grandmother did pass away.

"People tell me that when I play for them, I give them courage. I give them life. This is something that I want my children to believe in and continue to do in the way that they go. Do what they want to do but share the smile and happiness with their friends in the world wherever they may be."

Nir draws inspiration from his homeland. He says Jerusalem is a spiritual and emotional city.

> You can feel it when you come here. You feel the places in the stone, in the streets, and the smells. It's a very unique atmosphere—an inspirational place, like none other in the world—no other place like Jerusalem.
>
> I have a lot of stories about what music is doing for people around the world. I can tell you that at one of my last shows, I was playing for old people. After a great show, a very old guy came to me and said, "I have Parkinson's, and nobody knows that I couldn't move for the last eight years. Tonight, after eight years of suffering with Parkinson's, I danced to your music.

Nir has unsung heroes, too. When he was twenty-one at the Jerusalem Academy of Music, there was a teacher who played the accordion; Balkan music in particular. This teacher observed Nir playing and took him aside. "Listen, I feel that you're a good person. I want you to play with me in my ensemble. It's gypsy music and I want you to come and tour with me in Canada."

"I told him, 'You don't even know me. I don't even have a passport. I have never flown to another country.' Then I started to play with him. When I played with him, it reminded me why I wanted to play music to start with. I discovered gypsy music was the best music for me. It's calm. It's not coming from the notes of the sheet music. It's coming from the heart. I performed with him in Canada and then in another musical in Europe. All totaled, it was a twenty-country festival, and in every country, we played and danced."

Thus, Nir's association with bluegrass was formed. "It changed my soul and my musical direction, because when I started to play at the music academy, I thought maybe I would be a violinist in the Israeli Philharmonic Orchestra. And since I met that accordionist, who was my teacher, I realized I didn't want to play in the orchestra. I needed to be in touch with my audience. He taught me and gave me the opportunity to play with him on television and radio and we became a very popular band in Israel. So, in the last twenty-five years, I have collaborated with the best artists and singers in Israel and from around the world."

Take a page from the book of Nir: when in doubt, improvise and create something new. You find your one-of-a-kind niche when you turn your talent, skill, and ability into serving other people by tapping your own creative powers.

At the very least, make someone smile.

Exhortations to Excellence on Creativity

The aim of art is to represent not the outward appearance of things, but their inward significance.
–Aristotle

You are endowed with remarkable stores of creativity. It's a triumph to make worthwhile use of them. Sitting on that fortune, you have something rare and special to offer, and if it's not given, the world misses out on your wealth. Yet there's always something more to conquer, more genius to cultivate, more fulfillment to experience, more service to render. Creativity has a built-in reward system when engaged. The fruits and benefits manifest along the way.

Creativity varies from person to person, but you have something extraordinary that makes you tick. Whatever grabs and ignites within you is likely a golden ticket to be cashed at the window. You're the artist letting it out. Recognition of gifts comes by a heartfelt inclination, an affection, a hunch, the still small voice that urges you forward and provides additional direction.

Purpose is the hub of the wheel, and creativity your means of making it move. These are unique knacks for solving human problems. People have answers. Someone sees a need and fills it. Understanding individuality goes a long way toward carving a creative niche out to benefit others. What a boring world it would be if you were just like your neighbor.

You're not a clone. You're a creative.

What you live and breathe all the time are strong areas of passion. What is your magnificent obsession? That is your tailored gift. The essential virtue of creativity blazes its trail, and your life seems to find a way. Your objective is to remove the obstacles. Sometimes that means blocking out the negative voices—or listening for the purpose of making you better than you were before. Dreaming leads to creativity and creativity leads to productive dreaming.

POWER OF INDIVIDUALITY

Michelangelo described creativity as a vision in the rock that needed to be let out. Release the *genius* out of your vision, whatever it may be. Genius is the tactical edge that moves your life toward unique aspirations and goals. Can you look at others for the purpose of what you gather from their story rather than being like them? I've never seen a Hall of Fame football player who made their way to Canton by being most like Green Bay Packers quarterback Bart Starr or Chicago Bears running back Walter Payton. I've never seen any baseball player enshrined at Cooperstown by imitating the New York Yankees home run king Babe Ruth. Being great is never a matter of imitation, which is the sure way to failure. There's a negation of personal talent that occurs while copying someone else.

> It is better to fail in originality than to succeed in imitation.
> –Herman Melville

Yet, the excellent character traits of athletes can be emulated. What elevated their games to such a high level? Studying and following those qualities is a worthwhile endeavor, but you don't have to be an athlete to practice shared principles of success. Hard work, practice, diligence, vision, and dedication applies to any aspiration. Players' love for the game can be duplicated. The cut-above attitude can be applied and made your own. Sometimes it involves being able to listen to others' instruction and input. Be a student and make it your own. Let virtues embody you without positioning yourself to be a mirror image of others. Whatever makes you a better individual is the sure path to unfettered freedom and an extraordinary life.

You can encourage someone's dream by giving them a clear recognition of their gifts. It does the heart good to treat someone else's aspirations as being equal to your own. It's a great habit and a setup for adding more belief to your own mission. You've connected to others you know, and the attitude you deal out is the one that comes back. You must believe you are worthy of your own dreams coming to pass if others are worthy. You know how much it has helped you when someone believed and took an interest in you. Laying your head down at night after contributing to someone else's life makes the sleep sweeter.

Be the world champion individual with a rich life source of meaningful relationships all around. Recognize strengths that make you unique and be grateful for those. Capitalize on mistakes. It's not always how you succeed, but sometimes how graciously you fail that determines a healthy inward life. This can be risky, because someone might not approve of what they see. But hold steady. Someone will appreciate what you have to offer, and it will be a life changer for you when it happens.

VISIONING ABILITY

Creativity mirrors who you are on the inside. See your face in the work. You are the originator. You imagined and fashioned what you saw in your mind's eye. It resonated with you to the extent that you believed it would find an audience. The size of the audience didn't matter as much as the creative process it took to get there. You loved the journey. The love and devotion mattered. The blood, sweat, tears, and sacrifice which engraved your name on it mattered.

The fulfillment comes when you obey your inmost inclinations, whether it is the beautician, the homemaker, the book, the song, the painting, the speech, the craft, the product, or the athletic achievement. A creator is the artist, author, musician, and producer. A creation is the design, the production, or the work of art; the beginning and end of something beneficial for others. Creators draw inspiration from everyone. They are resourceful with no limit on what they use for fuel.

What is genius but the power of expressing a new individuality?
–Elizabeth Barrett Browning

There is a biblical account of creation that serves as an intriguing model for those who aspire to take this essential virtue of creativity to the next level. The raw material of the universe was brought into existence first: light, water, land, sun, moon, and the stars. But something was trapped in the rock, so to speak, like the sculptor sees when he gazes upon stone. Something lived in the eye of the beholder, the Creator. Design and organization were unfolding in real-time, from days one through six. On the seventh day, God rested from his work. "Behold, it was very good."

On day six, God created people that would have the capacity to do some creating of their own. They were endowed with similar abilities on a smaller scale, yet it would affect the entirety of their individual worlds.

Adam was first in the sequence. He was lifeless until God breathed into his nostrils the breath of life. At the point of that inspiration, man became a living soul. Next, Eve was formed from the rib of the man, equally miraculous. Each was instructed to be fruitful, multiply, and replenish the Earth. It wasn't enough for the couple to subsist. They were to excel, to go above and beyond expectations. They were blessed with essential virtues within that set them apart from the animal kingdom. They could limit themselves only by good or bad choices. Whereas they were instructed to tend the garden, they were also to cultivate the beauty of an inward life. Part of that beauty is the one-of-a-kind creativity that bursts the barriers of your own life.

EMBRACING UNIQUENESS

Adam named every animal in the kingdom, symbolizing a level of authority and sovereignty. He and his wife cared for every plant and tree in the garden. They were to be fruitful, and part of that invitation was the far-reaching call to live creatively for the common good of all. They carved a unique niche, just like you are carving yours.

Congratulations on being fruitful and multiplying in your individual world.

I heard someone say many years ago, "God don't make no junk."

Creativity is a vehicle to travel to the destination of your wildest desires, dreams, and imaginations. For maximum effectiveness, it must be turned toward others rather than being spent on self.

You have DNA that no one else on Earth can duplicate. Your fingerprint is uniquely your own. There isn't another like it, nor will there ever be. Your smile is different than anyone else's. Your laugh is different. Your hair texture and color are your own. No one else walks like you, runs like you, or stands like you. Your voice is like no other. I can hear you, yet not see you, and still know you by name. Mastering life means freeing the essential virtue called creativity—tied with a short rope to your one-of-a-kind personality.

Adhere to the love you have to offer, and you'll never be short of the creativity needed to accomplish your loftiest objectives. Put another way, the sleeping giant of creativity will never fail if you determine not to fail its parent of love. Self-love is indispensable to nurture creative forces. You know you're deserving of the highest and best life has to offer. Your creativity is the vehicle that can help you get there. There's no way but up from where you are standing.

The bottle of the creature cracks and dries up,
but the well of the Creator never fails.
–Charles Spurgeon

CREATIVE PERSPECTIVES

I attended a creative conference in 2015 in Oklahoma City called the Creative World Forum, an annual event that changes venues every year. There were entrepreneurs and business leaders from all over the world in attendance. I gleaned nuggets of wisdom from many of the speakers. The gathering was a collaboration of innovators, policymakers, business leaders, technology experts, and trailblazers for the exchange of ideas and solutions related to global problems. The following are thoughts and reflections shared by those leaders in the think tank at Oklahoma City, which included companies like the Imagination Institute, Lego, and Disney.

Here's a montage of thoughts on the subject:

The best indicator for lifelong creativity includes deeply loving the work you do. Following that is persistence, clear purpose, deep thinking, openness to change, and risk-taking. Creative people are comfortable with being a minority, even if it's a minority of one. They take charge, own their identity, and their dream of the future, which brings imagination to life.

Part of the creative process in problem solving includes dealing with the inevitability of failure. Testing out ideas is beneficial. Keeping the good and discarding the bad is part of focusing your path forward. Dealing with failure in a positive way is vital. Be resilient in the face of defeat. You don't know what good thing is just around the corner when you absolutely refuse to quit. Failure is never a destination, only a necessary part of learning.

Be fearless. Creativity is the most desired quality in people that are hired by companies like these. Creativity isn't solely about talent. The way you think about a thing sets you apart by unlocking the latent power of the imagination. When you look in the mirror, see yourself as an inherently creative individual capable of transforming the world. Be an innovator for life. *Creativity is king.* It's not what you have but what you do with what you have that makes the most difference. Creativity changes leadership and teams for the better—no matter what field of endeavor you are in.

Follow your passion and creativity will come easier. If you do the work and provide the sweat equity, inspiration will follow in time. Never wait on the inspiration. Put your hand to the plow and work hard. All the creativity you need will follow.

> Talent hits a target no one else can hit.
> Genius hits a target no one else can see.
> –Arthur Schopenhauer

MULTIPLYING TALENTS

When you work diligently, talents appear, some being unrealized until a demand is placed on them. Thus, creativity is multiplied through being faithful with what you have. The success carries over and lends to the next opportunity. Being creative means following the initial commitment, whatever that may be. You're born with gifts and work hard for others. Therefore, creativity is a blooming tree that you are privileged to nurture and cultivate.

One of the thrills of my life has been acting and performing. I've been in several stage productions; mainly comedies. My creativity was found in the process of doing them—all because there was a need presented. *Sow an act; reap a harvest.* Another thrill was writing shows for kids. Then, I did it for an organization's ten-year anniversary. Next was a birthday celebration, and finally a wedding event. Each had its unique creative demands. Necessity truly was the mother of that invention. You don't have to be born with a silver spoon to stretch further than you ever have before. Be proactive and intentional. Creativity serves as a function and ally of the devoted and focused inward life.

Be a creative role player. Success in life is based on how you inter-act with the persons, places, and things around you. Wisdom is to understand others' lives—then comes your meaningful contribution to help make those lives better.

Creatives are the up and comers.

Being connective with creativity for the well-being of other people may be the shortest distance to personal fulfillment and extraordinary achievement. Switching the vantage point to the purest unselfishness possible sets the genius loose that will in turn change the world—whether that world is large or small.

The creative mind thinks in terms of images, pictures, and illus-trations. The imagination becomes larger than life, more than words alone. Powerful images become driving forces to propel you through the door of your calling. You can articulate the vision of what you want to contribute to humanity. The still, small voice within is an affirmation that you're on the right track. I like to call it an inward applause. When you write it down and speak it out, sharing with others at the appropriate time, you give it wings to fly.

> **I dream of painting and then I paint my dream.**
> **–Vincent Van Gogh**

CONCEPTS OF CREATIVITY

When you initiate a creative project, make sure to have a predeter-mined resolve; a theme of an idea. With that firmly embedded in your mind, you'll find visual aid and support for what you want to convey to an audience. When you're open and receptive, ideas will jump out, and if one grabs you, it's probably worth acting on. Start the creative preparation early so that the idea can germinate over time. If the idea has legs, it will make it to the finish line. But if it falls by the wayside, then maybe it wasn't strong enough to start with. Let that one go. Or give it another try if it gains strength again.

Allow the layers to stack and accumulate to reinforce a message. Keep the ones that stick and allow the idea to be clothed, so to speak. Be yourself—making the idea more powerful. *You're the greater gift than the idea.* You give birth and make it live. No one can act it out like you, because it dwells deeply in your being. You're the most connected to it. Be willing to appear foolish if need be. People appreciate when you're bold enough to step out of your boat and walk on the waters of impossibility. To be sure, stepping out of the boat is better than staying safe inside the boat—and much more fun.

You are the person who gets to drop the seeds in the ground and watch them grow. When you talk about your vision, be accurate in the things you say. Be honest and truthful with whatever creative gift you possess. Learn from the people you serve because you're not an island to yourself. If you're open to feedback, you're going to be better than you would be alone. Creativity functions in the context of meaningful relationships. There will always be a give and take; an exchange. Your vision will come to completion.

Weigh your creative idea to gauge its strength. Most people have a knack for weighing the buying decision, a professional outcome, or a problem during a crisis. Discard what you don't want but keep what is beneficial. Generally, I've found it better to err on the side of acting on a creative idea that passed the weight test rather than not acting.

Be an observer and seeker of creative ideas everywhere you go. Be receptive to the ideas that come your way. I like to think I'm learning amid all the processes. With that attitude, your creative inventory will expand and grow and develop over time.

An attitude of surrender helps to discern what is best suited for your target audience. When you get that affirmation during a reflection period, it's most often a sure-fire sign that it is a reliable prompt. Ask yourself, does the idea communicate? Can you see it to completion? Take that idea and bounce it off someone you trust and be open to the feedback. If it genuinely sounds good to someone else, then go for it. Fruits that accompany a good, creative idea often include a sense of wisdom, humor, individuality, boldness, and audacity. When the idea passes the checkpoints, it's gaining momentum and becomes more tangible by the moment, looming larger in the crosshairs.

Every piece of your life, past and present, counts. You sow yourself wholeheartedly for the idea to shape and form. Find the need of your audience, those you want to help. Fill it with a beneficial message for that moment. There is life inside the package of that idea. People have needs—and your life is an answer to many of those. Match needs and problems with solutions and you can't go wrong.

ENGAGE AND CONTRIBUTE

You have a course for your creative life, and you're following the one that fits.

You and your gift make a difference. The world will not be the same because you came along. Break free from what you have known yourself to be before. Strike out from the shore and try something new. Become more useful than you have ever been.

Creation is expression, mirroring what is on the inside of you. It's life and power that cannot be denied. It's a spiritual ability encountering a physical, touchable world. Creation is arranging something in such a way that it makes sense and communicates a specific message to the senses of others. Creation can be considered as illustrating and demonstrating what you have to offer. Creation is the overflow of the heart to duplicate in some measure what you know and have experienced in your life. That becomes valuable to the world at large.

> Creativity: An idea is a curious thing.
> It will not work unless you do.
> –Hannah Whitall Smith

Creation is a corresponding action, like artists transfer a picture from their imagination to the canvas. We know what was in the artist after we see the manifestation. How closely does that image resemble the original? The artist is pleased when that desire has been satisfied.

Maybe you're not a painter. You might be a teacher, a mom, or a dad. You might be a coach with a team and a vision, or a business owner with a team and a vision, a leader with a team and a vision, or a project manager with a team and a vision. Maybe you are an integral part of a team and want to perform your individual role and function better. The closer the outcome matches your original vision, the more successful you will be. No matter what context, you're creating and manifesting essential virtues in life and relationships every single day.

THE LASER FOCUS OF SERVING

You are the icing on the cake. In one sense, you experience unspeakable joy for being creative. Conversely, you become a joy for others by using your creative gifts. Like other essential virtues, creativity finds its highest life in the expression of love. When you're determined to live with an unselfish motive, you'll never lack the creative means it takes to be a hero for someone. This is your ability; your privilege and honor.

Great restaurants not only have excellent food ingredients and preparation processes in place, but they also excel in service. All would be in vain if the execution of service bottomed out at the table of the customer. The same is true in any creative endeavor. You need excellent, well-chosen ingredients and components in your projects—but do not stop there. Effective preparation time will enable you to have the best attitude and motivation to serve others at the table of their individual needs. The desire to serve enables you to see goals clearly—then to achieve them. First the blade, then the ear, then the full corn in the ear—the unfailing law of growth.

Seven creative elements I've tried to incorporate into many of my own creative presentations are: color, music, words, objects, design, images, and gifts. Each is a vital part of human expression. Color captivates and grips the attention. Music is a marvelous and amazing proof that creativity was placed squarely into the heart of human beings; one of the most precious gifts bestowed upon mankind. Words should be filled with meaning and truth. They should be reliable and trustworthy, expressive, creative, accurate, and honest. Creatives are fond of arrangement and order. Design brings together the various components into one organized element of communication. Image is the root word of imagination; therefore, pictures have ability to ignite and inspire something within that is powerful. Each gift has personality, potential, unique talents, and abilities. These are the elements that bring the intangible concept of meaningful service into every creative opportunity.

Creativity is a muscle exercised to help and serve others. Being a creative artist is a matter of self-expression. Go above and beyond what is required and discover something within. The creation is a mirror image reflection of the creator. Brace yourself for a new journey into the center of what you were destined to do on a grand scale. Dream big, throw off the restrictions, and manifest that compelling image that lives inside of you. Use whatever it is for the best possible outcome. Contribute your treasure toward someone who needs it the most. Creativity is a superpower—and makes your life extraordinary.

This gift brings inspiration like none other.

The gift is you.

Any work of art is great when it makes you feel that its creator has dipped into your very heart for its sensation.
–Fannie Hurst

GEMSTONES

❖ Understanding individuality goes a long way toward carving a creative niche to benefit others. What a boring world it would be if you were just like your neighbor.

❖ You can encourage someone's dream by a clear recognition of their gifting. It does the heart good to treat someone else's aspirations as being equal to your own.

❖ Dreaming leads to creativity and creativity leads to productive dreaming.

❖ Mastering life means freeing the essential virtue called creativity—tied with a short rope to your one-of-a-kind personality.

❖ The sleeping giant of creativity will never fail if you determine not to fail its parent of love.

❖ Creativity is multiplied through being faithful with what you have. The success carries over and lends to the next opportunity.

❖ For all the wonderful means to convey a creative message, be yourself—making it that much more powerful. *You're the greater gift than the idea itself.*

❖ People have needs—and your life is an answer to many of those. Match needs and problems with solutions and you can't go wrong.

❖ Creation is the overflow of the heart to duplicate in some measure what you know and have experienced on a personal level.

❖ In one sense, you experience unspeakable joy for being creative. Conversely, you become a joy for others by using your creative gifts. Like other essential virtues, creativity finds its highest life in the expression of love.

REFLECTIONS
CREATIVITY: SETTING GENIUS FREE

Investigate the ways to smash the box of limitations.

PROMPT: Reflect on moments when creativity has made a positive impact in your life.

ACTION: Make a list of activities you can do to express and encourage a culture of creativity.

PROMPT: Realize that there are answers and creative solutions to solve any given situation in your life.

ACTION: Think of a time when a thought dropped inside of you that resolved a seemingly insurmountable situation.

Notes:

_____

_____

_____

_____

_____

_____

_____

_____

_____

_____

_____

_____

_____

VIRTUE #9

GRATITUDE: THE EQUALIZER
Extreme benefit of a healthy attitude for a balanced life

Unsung Hero Story

Many people would be surprised to know there are thirty-nine federally recognized Indian Nations inside the state of Oklahoma, each
having their own government. I lived in northeast Oklahoma for
decades without knowing the individual stories of how each tribe
came to settle there. When I learned about the forcible removals to
the state, my education expanded greatly. I never looked at another
Native American the same again. Oklahoma was the territory where
tribes from around the country were sentenced—that land beyond
the Mississippi, where they "wouldn't cause any more trouble." Then
the treaties were broken. When oil was discovered, it wasn't long
before the Oklahoma Land Run ensued.

It was easy to see how the *Myaamia* [Miami] people *could* have
been bitter about the cruelty they suffered and endured during those
decades. In a twist of expectation, I learned from Chief Douglas Lankford that he was still *grateful*. I could feel it in his smile, demeanor,
warm acceptance of me as a person, and his upbeat sense of optimism about the future.

I learned a lot more about the Miami story and why they are thriving today after my conversation with him.

The origin of the Miami indigenous people was downstream from the Great Lakes in Indiana. Miami Nation says every place they've ever lived is their true homeland—including parts of Indiana, Ohio, Wisconsin, Illinois, Kansas, and Oklahoma. They were forcibly removed twice; once from Indiana to Kansas, and a second time from Kansas to Oklahoma. The tribe experienced tremendous suffering during its removal westward.

Here is the story:

"Myaamionki" means all the places the Miami people have ever lived. Saakiiweeyonki was the original Miami village established in the Great Lakes region, near where the St. Joseph River empties into Lake Michigan. The Miami numbered about 24,000 people prior to the turn of the eighteenth century. By 1795, their lands encompassed Indiana, western Ohio, eastern Illinois, lower Michigan, and lower Wisconsin. Beginning with the Treaty of Greenville on Aug. 3, 1795, massive cessions of territory were forced on the tribe.

More land cessions happened between 1805 and 1834. Finally, the Treaty of 1838 created the Great Miami Reserve, a 500,000-acre reservation in Indiana. The Removal Act of 1830 by President Andrew Jackson had a bearing on the eventual removal of the Miami.

The Treaty of the Wabash allowed five years for the tribe to relocate. Chief John Baptiste Richardville died in 1841, shortly after signing the treaty. By this time, half the tribe was exempted from removal by private land acquisitions and changes in citizenship.

On Oct. 6, 1846, just over 300 people were rounded up from villages and herded onto canal boats at gunpoint by the U.S. Army in Peru, Indiana. They were shipped from there on a month-long journey on the Wabash-Erie Canal through Fort Wayne, Indiana, to Defiance, Ohio, at the convergence point with the Miami-Erie Canal, then traveled south to Cincinnati where they were transferred to the steamship Colorado.

Cargo was listed in that day's publication of the Cincinnati Gazette. *"134 barrels of whiskey, ten sacks of 115 pounds of wool, eight barrels of varnish, two Indian ponies, Miami Indians — 225 over and seventy-eight under eight years old, forty-nine perch stones for pigs,"* the newspaper reported.

From Cincinnati, they headed west to St. Louis, traveling the Missouri River to Kanza Landing, the beginning of what would one day be named Kansas City. Sugar Creek was their eventual destination, fifty miles to the south. There, they began to adapt to the new land and build homes. The 500,000 acres promised in the Treaty of 1840 turned out to be 350,000 instead. But even that was short-lived.

A local trader witnessed the arrival of the Miami at Kansa Landing. Many tribal members burst into tears because of the trauma of separation from their traditional land in Indiana. When the trader witnessed the trauma of tribal members begging like children to be returned to their home, even he cried.

The "permanent solution" called for by the Indiana Legislature lasted a little more than twenty years until the Treaty of 1867, which called for a second forced removal, this time to Oklahoma. Government leaders had not realized what they had in Kansas at the time when they promised it to tribes. Therefore, the treaty in perpetuity was soon broken. Kansas was excellent farmland. There were also mineral deposits and natural gas, which made it extremely valuable.

At that point, tribal members were given three options. They could denounce their Miami citizenship and stay in Kansas. They could join the Peoria tribe, which had already moved to Oklahoma, or they could acquire land in Oklahoma and continue to be the Miami tribe. The leadership chose the latter option, maintaining the identity of the tribe. They bought land from the Peoria for their reservation and moved the tribe to Oklahoma.

By the time the Miami arrived in Oklahoma in 1867, they numbered fewer than one hundred. The Miami and Ottawa chiefs agreed the town would be named Miami and the county would be named Ottawa—both names which remain today.

Chief Douglas Lankford says they will never forget their past and will always have a foot there. Indiana remains their ancestral homeland, and that will never change. "We leave the past, but the past never leaves us," Lankford said.

Speaking of their removal, Chief Lankford said, "That was a very traumatic time for our ancestors. There's an account where they were getting ready to get on the boats and our ancestors reached down and grabbed handfuls of dirt to take with them because we were tied to the land. That's what we knew. We were living in Indiana and throughout Ohio, and all that region we roamed. When we moved to Kansas, it was wintertime . . . I believe 1846 was the beginning of the removal, and then in 1867 we were forcibly removed again. It began the move to Oklahoma . . . we never really forget even though this is home now, both of those locations are considered homelands."

Chief Lankford is thankful despite the tragedy experienced during the nineteenth century. He considers it an honor to take the role of a servant leader while tribal enrollment steadily increases month by month. "It is a servant position. It always has been. The chiefs of the past reflect that in their behavior and how they acted. I always try to be a good servant. I cook at cookouts. I'll push a broom if needed. I'm not afraid to move benches. Being chief isn't president. It isn't exalted."

While the revitalization efforts of the nation have thrived through promoting their language and culture, Chief Lankford says it's a great time to be Myaamia. Ten to twenty people are added to the rolls every month. Now, the nation focuses in giving priority to education, learning the language, and bringing back their traditions.

Another item on Chief Lankford's gratitude list is the association Miami Nation has with Miami University in Oxford, Ohio. He says it's entirely unique, a one-of-a-kind relationship in the United States among tribes. "Miami University has been so good to our nation. It's a very special relationship. Without the university, we would not be where we are in our revitalization efforts. So, we can't thank them enough.

"Ribbon work is coming back, and our bowl games are coming back. Our storytelling is in full force. We're beginning to stomp dance again . . . it's kind of that snowball rolling down the hill. The snowball's getting bigger now. It used to be small and it's slowly gaining. But it's exponential growth now."

Chief Lankford has his unsung heroes, too. "The reason I feel like I'm such a good leader is my family that supports me . . . I depend heavily on the people around me as any good leader should. And that's why it's so very hard to take credit. I can't take credit for the great things that are happening. It's a group effort. I'm just the fortunate one that gets to be called the chief or Akima."

Chief Lankford points to community events as being of great interest and relationships being a top priority. "They're really important because it's hard to do anything by yourself. I believe we are good neighbors in this community. We're good neighbors to our tribes in this area."

I asked Chief Lankford if he was bitter about the past misfortunes of the Miami people—before, during, and after the two removals from Indiana. His response was surprising. "I'm a little different than most. There is a hole from the past. I never wished the past away because I would wish myself away. Things have to happen. There's a reason that we're all here today. It would wish away a lot of things if I wished away all of our past. Our past is something to be learned from. You don't make the same mistakes again. You have to learn. And that's what I try to do. Every culture, every country, everybody has bad things in the past, but it's what brings us to who we are today."

Chief Lankford personifies gratitude. He's an unsung hero for their nation, not doing what he does for the applause. He was enthusiastic, kind, sincere, and generous. To hear him talk about the privilege he has of being a leader is worth emulating. With pride and gratitude for their rich roots and traditions, Miami Nation landed on their feet, moving forward with the care and concern for every tribal member.

The venue for their annual celebration changes every year to a different specificity of their ancestral homelands. They forever remember and honor their roots—past, present, and future—no matter where they gather. During my time of interviewing Chief Lankford, no matter what we talked about, gratitude exuded from him in the way he conducted himself and treated others.

Exhortations to Excellence on Gratitude

> Gratitude is the sign of noble souls.
> –Aesop

Gratitude is an essential virtue of the human heart that goes against the grain and poses a threat to the enemy of a negative outlook. It's the ace up your sleeve that can turn things around, no matter how grim or dark they appear. It's a disposition and action under pressure. Gratitude doesn't just happen. It's a choice. Even in defeat, gratitude can spell the difference in how a setback is managed. What can you identify to remain thankful for? Stick with it. Don't let anything end on a bad note. You get the last word so give it a positive plot twist. You get to write your inner script while the circumstances play outwardly. You're making things better by pure disposition. Your attitude is the solver of the problem.

You can always find something within to be thankful for. Make a list. No matter what the difficulty or adversity—nothing can control your life without your tacit consent. The level of gratitude you demonstrate will influence the amount of grace you distribute to others. This attitude becomes crucial. Gratitude holds the best cards in the deck—and grace plays them on the table one deliberate action at a time.

You can remain focused on the positive—though you're aware and well-acquainted with the negative. Even in victory, it's important to exercise gratitude and not gloat at anyone else's expense. Be humble rather than proud. This diamond of the heart allows you to be spontaneous and unpredictable according to the needs of the moment. Even when hemmed in, bad things can't make you turn tail and run. Stand firm and undaunted, even amid the wreckage of seeming failures.

GRATITUDE TURNS INTO GRACE FOR OTHERS

Grace is the gratitude extended for the purpose of including others in your blessing. Acts of benevolence trace to a thankful motive. At the core of gratitude, there is a determination to benefit, not harm, others. Therefore, grace finds its inexhaustible source in the vast ocean of love. The absence of gratitude can be a precursor to a hard fall. Sooner or later, unthankful attitudes have a way of catching up. There's a price to pay for not integrating this essential virtue into the fabric of your life. You owe unswerving allegiance to what grace has provided. The debt remains outstanding but is paid forward to others through a thankful lifestyle. You didn't earn grace, nor did others around you. It's a gift equally shared.

> Virtue and genuine graces in themselves
> speak what no words can utter.
> -William Shakespeare

Grace portrays kindness, pity, or pardon to one who didn't expect it; unmerited favor. This can turn the table on a situation otherwise trending badly. To be gracious is to never take anything or anyone for granted. Gratitude has an uncanny ability to keep you from sinking into life's deepest pits. It undergirds, feeds, and drives you to greater heights. This sleeping giant has you trending upward.

Accentuating the positive is an important attribute of this essential virtue. When the glass is half-empty, you are grateful for the half-full. The cultivation of a thankful attitude will keep the inward oil changed. They say the squeaky wheel gets the grease. Here we could say the squeaky wheel gets the 'grace.'

GRATEFUL PEOPLE TREND UPWARD

Don't avoid the negative situations that pop up in your life, but deal with them in a positive way. You're not burying your head in the sand; you're aware of the factors, positive and negative, yet choose a road of unencumbered freedom. To roll the proverbial boulder on others in many cases rolls back onto you over time, so don't do it.

Free people are better than bound ones. There are plenty of snares along your journey already, but gratitude frees you from the daily trappings. It doesn't make life a bed of roses, but it does enable you to do some nice gardening along the way. Green thumbs don't work with perfect gardens, they work with imperfections—which makes them experts at what they do. It can be said they work with those as a matter of course. They find a need and tend to it.

Keep working the imperfections with a proven model.

Gratitude changes things, yet I've observed behavior where people have opportunities to drop their grievances but throw stones anyway. Then they pick up their neighbors' stones and throw those. Oddly, they're not convicted by the hardness of heart and inhumanity. Some up the ante by labeling with false accusations, all the while ignoring personal wrongdoings. They plug their ears to their inward voice, reload, and fire away. Then they gather up the same stones and start all over again.

All people welcome a reprieve. You know you aren't deserving of one because you've been guilty. Yet who doesn't welcome the officer giving a warning instead of a ticket when you were caught going sixty miles per hour in a forty-five miles per hour zone? Sometimes a second chance is in order; a brand-new slate when you weren't expecting it. Sometimes it's forgiveness for a mistake, misjudgment, or wrongdoing. Who doesn't welcome the opportunity to take a deep cleansing breath and not have to suffer the punishment? I haven't seen anyone turn away such a favor when it's offered.

Life isn't about being whacked with a mallet every time you come up on the short end. You need grace, but equally need to provide the same to others. Either way does the heart a ton of good. There's a positive to being on the giving end of gracefulness. It refreshes the soul to extend mercy to one who didn't merit any.

> Cultivate the habit of being grateful for every good thing that comes to you, and to give thanks continuously. And because all things have contributed to your advancement, you should include all things in your gratitude.
> –Ralph Waldo Emerson

Gratitude is a prerequisite for good things to come; a real multiplier. You can't deal out what you don't have within you already. There's a conversion and reordering that takes place when you choose gratitude. The bad thing isn't as bad, and the good thing is nothing to boast about. If you're not thankful, you'll take your sour attitude out on someone else down the line, and it's seldom pretty. Love has its own reasons—and it's not based on what is earned or deserved. Doing a good deed for the day can become a cherished habit; a lifestyle that completes you. That habit is going to accumulate exponentially and tip the scale in your favor.

BREAK YOUR GLASS CEILING

I attended a luncheon to hear a talk given by Porter Moser, head basketball coach at the University of Oklahoma. I learned that day that he knows something about timeless values. He lives his life and coaches his basketball teams by the same principles. When lifestyle and vocation connect, watch out; you're living an extraordinary life.

Above all, Porter esteems his players as important and lives with energy and kindness. He's grateful for the opportunities he's been given—even more for his players. People are like a sacred trust which involves honor—and that attitude is paying dividends for him. He's considered one of the great coaches in the game.

Previously, he coached the Loyola-Chicago Ramblers to an NCAA Sweet Sixteen and the 2018 Final Four. Not all head coaches are known for the essential virtue of gratitude, but the great ones know there's no better way to build a sports team. Achievement has roots in understanding how one player completes those around him. They're about the team—and how they can be a better contributor. Teammates who hate each other will probably not be standing at the end of the tournament. A lack of gratitude will show up in how they treat each other during crunch time. Those who love each other will show as much grace to the least team member as they do to the greatest. No cog in the wheel is unimportant. For Porter, building outstanding young persons is a prerequisite to building winning programs.

Players improve through practice, but attitude in practice is most crucial. Their future gametime performance is tied to the price they pay in sweat, but the sweat is tied to the thankfulness they must demonstrate for each other and their coach. They can see in their mind's eye taking the winning shot at the buzzer. All the previous hard work pays off in that moment. When opportunity knocked, they were ready—both physically and mentally. Perspiration paved the way for inspiration. They say you'll never work a day when you're doing what you love. Mark it down—they're grateful.

Porter learned these vital principles in part from his own father, who was a business owner with many employees. He practiced the art of finding value in everyday people. You can't value people without being grateful for them. That essential virtue trickled down. Porter himself always felt valued by his father. Gratitude levels the playing fields in life. Find worth in others and comprehend your own. Porter reflects on comments he heard from others about his dad—he had a way of making a person feel like the most valued person in the room. Gratitude is an essential virtue, setting the stage for better things to come. A lack of gratitude shows down the line in ways that can sink the ship, so to speak.

> As we express our gratitude, we must never forget that the highest appreciation is not to utter words, but to live by them.
> –John F. Kennedy

Porter wants to know everything about his players because he can't treat everyone the same. People are different. What motivates one may not motivate the next. There are things in a person's past which may affect how they need to be led and being favorable toward them helps the greater cause. Mentorship happens through the consistent leveraging of appreciation and value. Gratitude is a diamond of the heart that gets things done.

CHANGE THE ATMOSPHERE

Porter believes that how you think affects everything. How you feel determines how you act, which in turn defines the person. Positive energy is integral to his mentality as a coach. He says there's always something for you to lift your head and smile about. He points to gratitude as an indispensable asset to have and says it's nearly impossible to be grateful and negative at the same time. In fact, he keeps a gratitude journal so that he can write down three things he's grateful for every single day. Only time will tell the true value and worth he has created by a selfless investment in his players as individuals. Porter is a prolific builder of lives and teams.

> Before you go to bed, write down three 'gratefuls' for the day and three 'did wells' (they can even include something as simple as doing the laundry)—the results can be amazing.
> –Carol Burnett

Gratitude is figuring out what's right. It has an aura, and its absence can be felt. Balance life in every aspect. Spend time figuring out which person or thing needs the energy, favor, kindness, and cheerful disposition. You're a person of gratitude, not a tyrant, whether you are in the position of the follower or leader.

When you weren't appreciated, how did it make you feel?

Don't do that to others.

Turning bitter waters to sweet will happen with a commitment to gratitude. This path is one you have to choose to walk. You have far more ability than you've realized. If a person operates on 10 percent of their mental capacity, how will the essential virtue of gratitude scale exponentially?

Even under pressure, you can make this virtue sing. Showing favor can be a constant in your life, instead of an occasional whim. It's within reach always. Gratitude will make you a person of vision.

Forgiving is a byproduct of the inward life, the fruit on the vine. You are called to integration, and gratitude helps you live in a secret place the ungrateful know nothing about. There, complaining is minimized. Show me a person who doesn't show gratitude and I'll show you a person not experiencing the best life has to offer. Show me a person who isn't experiencing grace and I'll show you one who doesn't give any away. This is what takes you out of the mundane into an adventure where inspiration holds the wheel.

I can recall employers from years gone by who ruled with an iron fist, but when what they doled out in suffering came full circle, they hoped for a better outcome in vain. What has been set in motion through bad habits can't always be reversed on a dime. There are consequences to poor choices. Extending to others what you want to receive is the Golden Rule, doing to others what you would have them do to you. When the shoe is on the other foot, be consistent. What you give you can expect for yourself. Lead with your best. Gratitude might be considered a great equalizer in life's complex relationships. The person who has little can be grateful and stretch that even farther. Yet the person who has much is equally grateful and understands the call to share—in goods, serving, or mentoring.

> So much has been given me I have no time
> to ponder over that which has been denied.
> —Helen Keller

DESIGNED TO BE A THANKFUL PERSON

A person of gratitude keeps the best interests of others in mind. One's actions follow closely to intentions. Grace makes you a more attractive person. Cruelty makes people cringe. Why is the monster in the movie so hideous? Have you noticed they're never grateful? The monster seldom makes a character change. They make excuses. They blame. Taking responsibility is much too difficult.

To show gratitude is to honor and respect others. Villains never do. These features work hand-in-glove. Dishonor is a spiraling black hole from where no one benefits. In such circumstances, forge a personal path to grace—even if it's not afforded to you. That's the good news. If grace isn't available, create some.

No one can stop you.

Be courteous, pleasant, and kind. To leave off gratitude is to leave life's greatest treasures untouched in the vault. You can't control the choices of others, but you can control your own. Grace has built-in rewards, and withholding it has dire consequences. Don't move the goalposts to make life more difficult for people. There's nothing worse than being crushed by the insensitivity of one who doesn't care. Since you have one opportunity to make a good first impression, err on the side of showing favor. That's what you'll be remembered by. Birds were made to fly, and gratitude makes you soar to heights unknown.

Pride blocks people from the grace that could be theirs. Self-exaltation kicks out their blessing by uprooting them where they were planted. No one in their right mind pulls everything out of the garden prematurely. Gratitude is intended for the humble person, not the arrogant or proud. Showing favor and kindness becomes as natural as breathing. He who exalts himself will be humbled. He who humbles himself will be exalted. I've been mean and I've been kind. Kind is better. At the same time, I've been treated with cruelty, and I've been treated favorably. Grace is better. I've been rejected and I've been accepted. Acceptance is better. And if I want to be accepted, I'll need to be good at exercising the same.

> Reflect upon your blessings of which every man has many—not on your past misfortunes, of which all men have some.
> -Charles Dickens

LESSONS FROM MASADA AND THE DEAD SEA

When I visited Israel, one of the fascinating points of interest was the Dead Sea, the most beautiful silver sea imaginable due to its high mineral content. Miles and miles of majestic mountains contrast with the glistening water below, and when the sun bounces across the surface, the visual effect is stunning. That is enhanced and appears more spectacular from the top of Masada, the ancient fortress hand-carved into the mountains.

The history of Masada is as captivating as the view. A siege ramp was built by the Romans to scale the fortress and slaughter 1,500 Jewish people. But rather than allow themselves to be killed by the Romans, every person committed suicide, a terrifying story to model the bankruptcy of grace in life and relationships. The presence of gratitude transforms into grace—how you deal with others. If grace had been practiced in those moments of time, life could have been respected and shared. Since gratitude and grace were absent, lives were unnecessarily extinguished. Therefore, gratitude is a responsibility. Humanity either benefits or suffers in proportion to the practice of this essential virtue.

TRAVELING IN THE RIGHT DIRECTION

Yet there was a second lesson about gratitude I was about to experience in real time.

It was a scorching day, so very hot. From the top of Masada, I shot video in a circle—north, south, east, then west—a mesmerizing view. I had a towel on my head to keep from being fried. Sweat was pouring from my body, but I wanted to keep going. It's not every day you get such an opportunity. I could feel my face beet-red from the heat. I couldn't wait to go from the top of Masada down to the beach. Dipping in the water would be such a relief. When my wife and I concluded our exploration of the fortress, we took the cable car down to the ground level. We were twenty or so miles from a small town called Ein Bokek; the only question was how we were going to get there. We didn't anticipate there being a problem. There are buses running constantly and cabbies are in abundance. They jockey for position, waiting for tourists to come down from the mountain, then offer their services.

One of the cab drivers offered a ride, but when he said he was going the opposite direction to Ein Gedi, I declined. I approached one of the buses instead, but it wasn't going the right direction either. The driver saw me turn away from the bus and offered once again to take us. I told him where I was going and he said that if I rode with him, he would take the couple in his car to where they wanted, and then drop us off afterward. I finally agreed, so we piled into the back seat, knowing it would be a temporary delay.

However, after dropping the couple, the driver tried to talk me into going to Ein Gedi, still in the opposite direction, instead. I told him that I didn't want to go to Ein Gedi. He already knew that when I got in the car. I wanted to go to Ein Bokek. He said, "No, you go to Ein Gedi."

I countered again, saying, "No, I want to go to Ein Bokek." That's when the cabbie told me I was a bad customer. He wasn't grateful for my business, like he could have been. He wanted me to serve him rather than the other way around. I was prepared to pay the fare, but he needed to follow through with his word. He was angry and you could cut the air with a knife. No more conversation. He turned the car around but didn't take us where we wanted to go. He didn't drive us to Ein Gedi or Ein Bokek. We were far from our destination when he let us out of the cab to walk. When I went to pay, he charged us double. I told him that he promised a certain amount, but he insisted on the higher price.

My wife was upset with the plot twist and told me not to pay him double. But when a fellow cab driver joined him, I felt a bad vibe coming from both, and it wasn't loving favor or gratitude. You can feel it when it's there—or not. I told my wife we needed to pay the fare he asked, even though it was double. That satisfied him and we walked by foot to an entirely different beach on the Dead Sea that we hadn't planned for. We were grateful for the opportunity to go to the beach, even though it wasn't according to the original plan.

BEST BARGAIN EVER

I liken the difference in elevations between Masada and the desert to the virtue of gratitude or the lack thereof. Masada reminds me of gratitude because both are high points for perspective. You can see anything and everything from those plateaus. The vantage point in life changes entirely from a perspective of gratitude. Conversely, a lack of gratitude takes an unexpected toll on the senses, like an arid desert.

Minimal water flow, combined with the depletion of minerals, caused the level of the Dead Sea to diminish over centuries. Similarly, people are designed for a flow of grace—a mutual exchange. When gratitude doesn't pour through, it diminishes the person. The level of life decreases and depletes like that beautiful sea.

They say there is danger of the Dead Sea eventually drying up. Similarly, many people feel dried up in different ways and don't know where to turn. You don't want to be that person. Gratitude is a good place to start all over again.

It wasn't that we were going to have to walk for miles, but it was the idea that the cab driver could have been grateful to have us as paying customers. He promised a result, but once we got in the cab, he changed his course—like a bait and switch. That's kind of scary in the moment—to be at someone's mercy that doesn't have your best interests at heart. But we found our way eventually. Once we got to the beach, we were as hot as could be. Boy, did I want to cool off. Mineral mud was for sale to smear over your body before dipping in the sea. So, we covered ourselves in the mud and couldn't wait to rinse in the water, but the hot sun combined with the extremely hot water of the Dead Sea was unbearable. Forget cooling off. That wasn't what I anticipated. I was burning up, floating, relaxed in the salty sea. But I loved the torture. The minerals were excellent conductors for the brutal heat, and it felt like the hottest bath I've had in my life. Imagine being in 105-degree heat and then climbing into a 105-degree hot tub.

All that to say gratitude is a preferred method of living, above all else; it will raise the elevation of any given perspective. My cabbie chose pride above gratitude. I knew he wasn't thankful for the business I gave him. Therefore, he did not render his service accordingly. An ungrateful disposition won't help him and will likely carry over into a future transaction.

I was burned three times on that journey: once at the top of Masada; once covered in mud-slathered gratitude, floating in the Dead Sea; and once by that crooked cabbie who insisted on taking me where he wanted to go. Here's the thing: grace will take people where they want to go, and pride will drop them where they have no intention of going. Pride charges twice as much as what you want to pay and takes you half as far as you want to go. Put another way, the selflessness of gratitude will take you farther than you asked at a fraction of the price. *This essential virtue is a bargain, delivering the goods for an extraordinary life.*

> Gratitude is the single most important ingredient
> to living a successful and fulfilled life.
> –Jack Canfield

GEMSTONES

- Even in defeat, gratitude can spell the difference in how a setback will be managed.

- You make things better by pure disposition. Your attitude is the solver of the problem.

- At the core of gratitude, there is a determination to benefit—not harm—others. Therefore, grace finds its inexhaustible source in the vast ocean of love.

- Gratitude is a prerequisite for good things to come; a real multiplier. You can't deal out what you don't have within you already.

- Gratitude might be considered a great equalizer in life's complex relationships.

- Forge a personal path to grace if it's not afforded to you. If grace isn't available, create some. *No one can stop you.*

- To leave off gratitude is to leave life's greatest treasures untouched in the vault.

- Birds were made to fly, and gratitude makes you soar to heights unknown.

- People also are designed for a flow of grace—a mutual exchange. When gratitude doesn't pour through, it diminishes the person.

- Gratitude will take you farther than you thought possible at a fraction of the price.

REFLECTIONS
GRATITUDE: THE EQUALIZER

Analyze the extreme benefit of a healthy attitude for a balanced life.

PROMPT: Reflect on moments when gratitude has made a difference in your life.

ACTION: Make a list of people you are grateful for—tell them.

PROMPT: Reflect on a time when you showed gratitude in your life. How did it make you feel?

ACTION: Write down one thing you are grateful for today and how it makes you feel.

Notes:

_____

_____

_____

_____

_____

_____

_____

_____

_____

_____

_____

_____

_____

_____

VIRTUE #10

FAITHFULNESS: THE GREAT CONNECTOR

Advantages to being a strong finisher of tasks, missions, dreams, and objectives

Unsung Hero Story

Faithful people are reliable. You can count on them when the going gets tough. They do what they say. They are there when they are needed. When called upon to do something out of the ordinary, they adapt. Faithful people have an uncanny ability to lean on love as a primary motive, and because of their willingness to serve, find a way to follow it through to completion. You can see the intention reflected in the result.

When I hear the word "faithfulness," I'm reminded of Hedda Sharapan's steadiness over the course of decades. She grew up in a small mill town in western Pennsylvania and graduated from Carnegie Tech, now Carnegie Mellon University, with a degree in psychology.

As a young girl, Hedda dreamed about having her own television show, *The Happy Hedda Show*. After college, she went to Fred Rogers, asking for advice about working in children's television. This was before *Mister Rogers' Neighborhood*, but she knew his name because he was the puppeteer, musician, and co-producer behind-the-scenes of a local WQED station children's program years before. His suggestion was that she should consider pursuing a master's degree in childhood development from the University of Pittsburgh. Hedda says she now understands the wisdom of the advice he gave her then.

Over the years, Hedda learned from Fred that the question is not, "What can we produce for young children?" but if we want to produce meaningful television, the question is, "Who are young children? What makes them happy? What makes them sad or mad? What do they think is funny? What are their concerns? What helps them deal with their feelings?"

Fred obtained funding for *Mister Rogers' Neighborhood* in 1966 during Hedda's second year of graduate school, and asked if she would help him with the new program. She was able to accept his offer (with no pay and no staff) because they were taping at night, and she could still attend her graduate classes during the day. She says that she could see that Fred was making manifest what she was learning in her child development courses about what helps children grow—like rituals, transitions, relationships, dealing with feelings, curiosity, and the difference between make-believe and reality.

Hedda was part of the first taping of the *Mister Rogers' Neighborhood* program in October of 1966, and has been involved with the work ever since. She wore many hats and functioned in a variety of roles: assistant director, assistant producer, associate producer, director of early childhood initiatives, and more, demonstrating the concept that faithfulness makes people resilient and adaptable according to the needs of a focused mission.

On one occasion, Fred put a note on one of Hedda's drafts, calling her "a great synthesizer." Similarly, when Hedda offered a draft of her writing about his work for articles or professional journals, she would place a note on it that said, "For your elevation."

As a result, with his whimsical humor, Fred would sometimes sign his revisions for Hedda as "Your elevator operator."

Faithfulness and commitment created a synergistic effect, where every person was valued for their unique contributions. Even with their small band of twelve to fourteen people on staff, there was an abundance of unsung heroes that made *all things possible*.

Hedda's faithfulness resulted in her being a script consultant for the award-winning PBS kids' series, *Daniel Tiger's Neighborhood*, produced by Fred Rogers Productions in Pittsburgh, Pennsylvania. In addition, she writes the Fred Rogers Institute newsletter every month, *What Can We Learn from Fred Rogers*, distributed to nearly 10,000 subscribers. She has spoken widely across the country to early childhood professionals and general audiences, reflecting on Fred's messages and how they are timeless and relevant today. She is a senior fellow at the Fred Rogers Institute at St. Vincent College in Latrobe, Pennsylvania, where she was awarded an honorary doctoral degree for her efforts of applying academic and professional expertise to the creative work as a whole. From 1970 on, she was speaking and writing about Fred's work and creating materials for early childhood professionals. Her passion became a lifelong mission to help early childhood professionals, religious groups, and general audiences reflect on what they can learn from Fred Rogers' timeless wisdom that affected millions of households over the course of years.

In total, Hedda worked with Fred Rogers and his rich legacy for fifty-six years. She hasn't ceased serving after his passing to help others continue to learn from him. Her passion became a lifelong mission to help others find meaningful messages in Fred Rogers' life work. The practice of essential virtues has led to an extraordinary life she wouldn't trade.

When I first met Hedda to learn more about Fred Rogers and her work with him, she began by asking me questions so she could get to know more about *me*. She said that she learned that personal nature and disposition from Fred—to begin by being interested in other peoples' stories. Often, staff members joked that reporters who wanted to learn about Fred came away from their meeting with him learning more about themselves—because he truly wanted to know their stories.

Hedda's story provides a unique glimpse of what it must have been like to be part of that lifelong mission of service to children and their families. The current team at Fred Rogers Productions still produces award-winning children's programs—illustrating that faithfulness, steadiness, and consistency over the long-term produces extraordinary results. There's still a continued striving to be excellent. Faithfulness as a diamond of the heart is difficult to quantify—because it's a gift that keeps finding new ways to give.

Together with many other talented and like-minded individuals in the organization, Hedda has helped blaze a trail and built meaningful relationships along the way with a motive to serve. Like the timeless messages from *Mister Rogers' Neighborhood,* faithfulness contributes to personal fulfillment, remarkable achievement, and endurance of timeless values.

Faithfulness can adapt itself to new opportunities when necessary. For example, some of the puppet characters Fred created, like King Friday and Daniel Tiger, originally were used on the *Children's Corner* with Josie Carey program as early as 1954, then again through the *Mister Rogers' Neighborhood* episodes, and some still live in the current programming of Fred Rogers' Productions after Fred's passing.

When faithfulness is tied to a passionate mission or cause, it becomes a rich legacy—more alive than ever because of people like Hedda. Maybe you lost a job or an opportunity through no fault of your own, like I did many years ago. But you shook the dust off and carried faithfulness into your next endeavor, and perhaps made it better than it was before. The essential virtue of faithfulness makes an extraordinary life possible for anyone.

Exhortations to Excellence on Faithfulness

> By faithfulness we are collected and wound up into
> unity within ourselves, whereas we had been
> scattered abroad in multiplicity.
> -St. Augustine

Faith and faithfulness are heads and tails of the same coin. They are two rivers that merge into one mighty purpose. You can determine a lot about one by reflecting on the other. Faithfulness, according to *Webster*, is an essential virtue to see things through to completion, steadfast in affection or allegiance, firm in adherence to promises or observance of duty, consistent and true to an original objective. Faith is the intangible that overcomes trials and obstacles—turning the impossible into possible.

Does what you do correspond with what you claim? If so, there is an integrity that speaks louder than words. If not, there is a disparity that shows up down the line, leading away from its greater potential. Call it a hiccup that can trip up. Faith and faithfulness unify actions.

A grain of faith as tiny as a mustard seed can move a mountain. Therefore, faith is an essential virtue, and its corresponding faithfulness proves how much you genuinely possess. Faith is a choice, a steadfast belief in the practical matters; a spiritual reality. Faithfulness is a natural ability, carrying the objective into effect.

Faith is the stage. Faithfulness is the actor.

Faith paints a detailed picture of the desire and states what it believes. Faithfulness is the strong one to see it through. Together they turn ordinary tasks into uncommon achievements. At the same time, they improve a sense of personal well-being. A faithful person is a focused person. You are at one with what you do. Faith draws on a power greater than self. You are limited alone, but become unlimited when faithfulness kicks into overdrive.

> Faith is the pierless bridge supporting what
> we see unto the scene that we do not.
> –Emily Dickinson

PERSPECTIVE IN THE DETAILS

Many years ago, I had a brief, one-year stint as a furniture salesman. That experience helped me understand that small tasks were worth expending great energy. I endeavored to demonstrate this disposition to the customer, even if I was selling a nineteen-dollar hat rack—the least expensive item in the store. I decided to do small things as if they were great and great things as if they were small. This commitment balanced the scale for me—being committed to do everything with excellence, both large and small.

As a consumer, it's easy to pick up on a salesperson's attitude. If the attitude is good, it will pay off in the long run. If the attitude is bad, it will boomerang in more ways than one.

There were virtually a few dollars of commission with selling a hat rack. I remember some of my colleagues shrugged off a sale like that. They were waiting for the big one to leap upon them. But for me, I learned that treating a small sale as large cued the customer that I wasn't trying to move on with bigger fish to fry. I reasoned that you never know what can come out of caring for a prospective buyer. I managed the hat rack sale as if it were a ten-thousand-dollar bedroom set. Treated well, that person might return for a larger ticket item and not hesitate to ask for me by name—or at least recommend me to a friend.

Regardless, taking time with people is always the right thing to do.

I flipped the script on a common misconception that big commissions were wrapped up in big sales. The reverse was true. Big commissions were wrapped up in small steps of faithfulness. When you attach value to the essential virtues, rather than the external results, results inevitably improve.

In the opposite vein, I determined to treat a ten-thousand-dollar bedroom sale as if it were a nineteen-dollar hat rack. I took the bigger sale with a grain of salt, like it was no big deal. I did this to keep my head in the game and not skip smaller steps of service a customer would appreciate I take on their behalf. There wasn't any part of the sale that was unimportant. And the customer knew that from the way I treated them. I wasn't in a hurry, ever. I took the time and made the relationship a priority. If I knew I had done everything I could, I moved on. How I interacted with the buyer mattered. Attitudes trump performance, but at the same time cause it soar.

> The man who moves a mountain begins
> by carrying away small stones.
> –Confucius

Faithful people are fulfilled people.

Treating the bedroom sale like a hat rack freed my mind. The nerves were gone.

I shared this concept with my regional manager at the store, who oversaw hundreds of salespersons, and he liked it so much that he asked if he could use it in his trainings across many states. What it helped me do was not to show favoritism with people or customers—a dagger to optimal performance. It's the golden rule—if you want people to treat you as important, treat them the same way.

I finished the year as the top salesperson in the store. Integrating this concept into my daily customer experiences was one of the main reasons why. Anyone can thank the customer who bought from them. The acid test is in being gracious and thanking those who don't.

THE BIG PICTURE AND THE PROCESS

The same concept holds true with athletics and performances of any kind. The big field will never intimidate an athlete that puts his or her heart and soul into the small performances—even on the practice field when no people are watching. The smallest moments pay off in the NBA Finals, the Super Bowl, or the World Series. Small deposits can be recognized as precipitators of great success. These moments stretch you and make you an extraordinary person. Practice the virtues that elevate your life—and the lives of others.

Faith is believing in a large, overarching objective. Faithfulness is action in small, doable increments. Faith is stretched over a long period of time. Faithfulness is carried out as a day-by-day proposition. To be faithful is to complete small tasks well. These are the training grounds for the bigger things to come.

A faithful person doesn't live just for today. Their vision is bigger and more encompassing. Every action sets up a more hopeful tomorrow. Faithful people are visionaries. Everything counts, whether others recognize the value or not. The rewards keep on giving—more than that, you become an extraordinary person. You do what you say you're going to do, and it builds integrity within yourself and a trust with others.

Whether it's faithfulness in business, academics, service-related endeavors, or friendships, people and teams require your best. Put that foot forward and expect the same in return. Complete processes with excellence, energy, kindness, and love. You may not see the fruition in advance, but you can still be polite and gracious. You are steadfast and consistent, no matter what. Faithful people are never shocked when something good happens, because their actions and expectations paved the way. When the positive unfolds, be gracious.

> A little thing is a little thing, but
> faithfulness in little things is a great thing.
> -Hudson Taylor

THE FINE ART OF FOLLOWING THROUGH

When I met Gene Hughes, we sat down for a conversation. One thing that struck me was his kindness. He was considerate, respectful, and after we talked, I came away with the distinct impression that he was a faithful man in each individual area of his life. Sometimes emphasis is placed on one area at the expense of another—and that was not Gene. He is nearing 100 years old, and the smile on his face seems ever-present. I learned that he wants to be remembered that way. I thought he was doing a pretty good job.

As an entrepreneur, selling wasn't his end game—but to be an extraordinary person was. That included how he relates to family, personal health, and relationships. Dealing with a personal health crisis eventually led him to expand that vision to include others. The longevity of being part of a company that has spanned six decades includes important values like faithfulness. He came to be trusted by others and was reliable over the course of many years.

Integrity has been a big word. His steadiness in one area has equally worked wonders in all the others. When allowed, faithfulness connects people to everything important at the same time. This has helped him keep his eye on the ball, not elevating success above what it means to be a fulfilled individual and a genuine helper of others.

His sickness story is what changed the trajectory of his life from being a high school teacher to becoming the founder of a business that rapidly rose to become one of the most reputable companies in America.

When he was sick with an ulcerated stomach as a young man, someone suggested he try capsicum (cayenne pepper) for the symptoms and pain. The effects of taking it by the spoonful helped his stomach and he made a full recovery. Even though it's not guaranteed to help everyone, it helped him. Gene's wife suggested that he capsulize the cayenne pepper to make it available to other people. He followed the advice and formed Nature's Sunshine Products (NSP)—the first company to capsulize herbal supplements. That was 1972 in Utah. Fifty years later, NSP is a leading brand of natural health products that are rooted in science. He went from a high school teacher to being an entrepreneur that has delivered results—and stayed on his capsicum capsules permanently.

MULTIPLICATION OF CONSISTENCY

Gene told me his initial investment was in the millions of dollars for equipment, research, testing, and development to ensure the purity and reliability of products to the end consumer. Once the demand skyrocketed, they almost went out of business, not being able to keep up with it all. But it was worth pushing through and enduring the early tests.

Today, NSP is in all fifty states and thirty countries around the world. They've stayed true to the goal of keeping the loyalty of customers. There are more than 500,000 customers and distributors throughout the world. Product innovation includes daily essentials, weight management products, vitamins and minerals, targeted combination products, and more. Annual sales have gone from $100,000 in the first year to $325 million in 2015 when we sat down together.

Stringent quality, safety, and purity have been watchwords for the company to build trust with those who have returned as repeat customers due to a consistent track record over time. Gene emphasized that if anything is foreign in a product, it's returned immediately. His vendors know that NSP will not buy an ingredient unless it's proven to be the best available. Consequently, they have a squeaky-clean reputation. Quality control guides the company and its decisions. In addition, they are staffed by reputable researchers, scientists, doctors, and renowned health experts.

Like his business, Gene's life has been reliable, steady, dependable, and consistent. He demonstrates that what is good for the personal life will apply across genres, including the professional. *Forbes* magazine listed NSP as one of America's top 100 trustworthy companies in 2013. They've built on that firm foundation to the tune of more than 350 wellness products.

In the twilight years of his life, Gene hasn't lost the touch. He and his wife Kristine endeavored to leave a legacy for others to benefit long after they're gone. Gene lost Kristine a few years ago to sickness. Make no mistake, faithfulness for Gene includes his seven children and dozens of grandchildren. He wants to be a good patriarch to the family. He exercises every week. He wants to be remembered as a good man whose primary objective was to render lasting service to others, and his future is to render more of the same. Helping others has raised his quality of life beyond what he could have achieved on his own.

Gene's smile still lights up a room—another consistent character feature that has lent to his extraordinary life. He's thankful for the health and wealth he's helped deliver to families. At the same time, he is grateful to the people who have helped him. It's a two-way street. He says integrity, service, and quality have been cornerstones of everything he's done. His seasoned company has stayed on the straight and narrow with the commitment to being the safest, most reliable, and effective health products in the world—beginning and ending with an essential virtue called faithfulness.

FOOTPRINTS AND BREADCRUMBS

Faith sees through the fog. Faithful people are not presumptuous or entitled but believe strongly enough in their objective until they possess it. These order the footsteps in the direction of what you desire the most. Faith manifests possibilities. Faithfulness keeps those desires from dying unborn. Demonstrate faith by acting on what you claim. Faith may be invisible to the eye, but faithfulness is how it ultimately comes to pass.

Have a master plan. Then let everything you do reflect predetermined values.

Olympic athletes train for their hopeful goal in the early stages. In their mind's eye, they transport themselves to a future goal and work backward from there. Steps are calculated according to the overall distance to the objective. They have an unseen obsession. It drives them day and night. They believe wholeheartedly in the goal and sacrifice everything to achieve it. They are steady and move consistently toward what they desire. They start well, enjoy the process, and thrill at the culmination of the dream. No part is unimportant. Being faithful in small things sets them up perfectly to be faithful in much.

Few people see the micro advances you've made, but in hindsight, the vision comes clear that seeming inconsequential steps paved the way to your achievement, and it shaped the person you have become. The faithful practice of essential virtues leads to your extraordinary life.

Be purposeful, targeted, and intentional. Faithful persons stand out from the crowd. Sometimes you will be present after everyone else has gone home. Make sure you are driven by an unseen taskmaster—the inner self. A faithful person perseveres. Be loyal, reliable, and exact.

Your conscience affirms when you've done all you could. You must be thorough and leave no stones unturned. Welcome scrutiny and embrace the challenge to be better. You want everyone around you to benefit from the completion of your task.

> Faith makes the discords of the present
> the harmonies of the future.
> –Robert Collyer

There's a Japanese phrase, *kaizen*, defined as continuous improvement. Toyota Motor Corporation adopted this motto in the development of their automobile line. Because of this commitment, Toyota separated themselves from the competition over decades as a company worth emulating around the globe. They called their steady mission QDR—quality, durability, and reliability. Nothing was more important than these guide stones. Everything was evaluated through the lens of whether a product would stand their rigid test—yet be better again the following year. If an idea contributed to improvement, it was implemented. If it didn't add value, it was eliminated.

How much more can *you* improve? Yesterday's faithfulness isn't enough for today's objectives, ambitions, and achievements. When you consider an option, ask in advance—does it contribute to your overall improvement? If so, you add it to your repertoire. And if it doesn't contribute, kick it to the curb.

THE GIFTS IN STRUGGLES

The metamorphosis of a butterfly begins as an ordinary caterpillar. It's in a cocoon, preparing for something great. It has an instinctual vision or dream of what it can become. One day, it will fly. But for the moment, it's stuck on a tree. It's all a matter of timing. The caterpillar has struggles you can't see. It's isolated. It's closed in and confined.

You could say it's trapped, but there's more going on behind the scenes. The walls of the cocoon are pressing in and declaring the caterpillar will be trapped forever. But the limitations are truly gifts, designed to give the wings sufficient time to develop.

What would happen if the caterpillar was cut out prematurely? What if the slow process of growth was bypassed? When a cocoon is cut open early, the creature will fall to the earth and die. It needs the constraint to grow. But when the wings are given the opportunity to develop, they break through the walls of the cocoon, giving the butterfly strength enough to fly. No longer is the butterfly limited to what it was before.

> There is no normal life that is free of pain.
> It's the very wrestling of our problems
> that can be the impetus for our growth.
> –Fred Rogers

This is the limiting realm for people. There's a higher destination you were born for; something greater than you've ever been. You know you can fly. You are patient and authentic. Don't pretend before you've had time to grow. You're not fake, trying to pull something over on others before the due season. Being genuine is a choice. Fly when the time is right, and the strength to achieve is inherent. Be the best version of yourself in the moment. The cocoon is your friend. In the same manner, you don't return to your former self after you overcome formidable trials.

Empty promises are ultimately exposed. Be faithful with what belongs to others, and you will find it easier to be faithful to your own cause. You're not numbered with those who fabricate stories, leverage good will, and exploit others for personal gain. To be fake is to weave falsehood to try and make good on a poor imitation. Many die inwardly, wishing they could take certain actions back, especially when those actions lost them everything—including families, friends, or livelihoods.

Faithfulness is the real deal and benefits others. Will people profit in some way from what you're doing? That's a great sign. You'll be validated and affirmed for this virtue, but exposed if you are being phony. A person of faithfulness is focused and has the wherewithal to overcome anything that life throws at them. Trials and tribulations don't have to be your undoing but can instead be a catalyst for growth and change. You can't alter circumstances, but you can alter your approach and proximity to them. Every day is its own challenge. Faithfulness is a powerhouse that defines you as a person. Faithfulness keeps you steady and becomes an anchor for your life. It's a path paved with answers, and not always the obvious ones. You'll be remembered for the things you finished, not what you started. Like the butterfly, your most beautiful and genuine gifts can emerge from your biggest struggles.

THE FINISHERS

You can be tossed around like the waves or firm and unwavering. You can regroup and find peace rather than thinking your circumstances are going to align perfectly. The essential virtue of faithfulness will prevent you from being sunk by difficulties. Wisdom is available to straighten the thinking process, making you singular in purpose again. Make a good first impression. I've never seen a person of faithfulness that was dishonest, so never lead with deceit; only bring the essential virtues of character. Don't claim one thing and then act the opposite.

The bow of faith is for aiming and the arrow of faithfulness for following through. You are the archer of your life. No one aims and plucks the string for you. You are plucking faith arrows with each steady, consistent action. Faithfulness hits your bullseyes.

> Faith is the strength by which a shattered
> world shall emerge into light.
> –Helen Keller

Faithful people are patient; a byproduct of not selling out when things go awry. Trials are a proving ground; an opportunity to demonstrate commitment as a finisher. Which is going to win, the person or the adversity? The reward for not throwing in your towel early is that you can be a fulfilled person, not wanting for anything. You don't have to change everything around you, but only discover an ever-present fountain to complete you.

Have you thought about the loved ones in your life that have been faithful to you? Sometimes it's good to take inventory. Be sure that no stone is left unturned when it comes to appreciating those who didn't give up on you. It can be easy to forget or take those heroes for granted.

When you say something, faithfulness calls for honesty and accuracy. If you can't follow through, admit it as soon as possible to be accountable. Words matter, because you are creating harmony and agreement between what you say and what you do. Transparency allows you to pick up and do better the next time. Believe there's always a way because there is. Don't start projects and leave half of them undone. The same holds true with dreams. Pick them up, wherever they lie, and realize it's never too late to achieve them. Faithfulness should never be misappropriated as a tool for evil. Be a genuine advocate for others—and do it all for the sake of love.

Faithfulness is an *essential virtue* for an extraordinary life; proof that you are going to be a positive influence wherever you render service. From every mountain of completion, there's another one in sight for you to seize upon. Faithfulness guarantees personal fulfillment, remarkable success, and a brighter future than you imagined.

People can count on *you*.

You are numbered with the faithful.

You are a finisher.

> Make faithfulness and truth thy masters.
> Have no friends unlike thyself.
> Be not ashamed to mend thy faults.
> –Henry David Thoreau

GEMSTONES

- Faith paints a detailed picture of the desire and states what it believes. Faithfulness is the strong one to see it through.

- To be faithful is to complete small tasks well. These are the training grounds for bigger things to come.

- Small deposits can be recognized as precipitators to great success. These moments stretch you and make you an extraordinary person.

- Sow yourself in an unselfish way whether there is a promise for gain or not.

- Faith is stretched over a long period of time. Faithfulness is carried out as a day-by-day proposition.

- Faith manifests possibilities. Faithfulness keeps those desires from dying unborn.

- Faithfulness benefits others. Will people profit in some way from what you're doing?

- You'll be remembered for the things you finished, not what you started.

- Words matter because you are creating harmony and agreement between what you say and what you do.

- The bow of faith is for aiming, the arrow of faithfulness for following through. You are the archer of your own life.

REFLECTIONS
FAITHFULNESS: THE GREAT CONNECTOR

Examine the advantages to being a strong finisher of tasks, dreams, missions, and objectives.

PROMPT: Reflect on moments when faithfulness has brought you success.

ACTION: Make a list of steps to take to stay faithful to your commitments.

PROMPT: Your faithfulness determines what level of faith you have in the process, keeping your word, and your relationships.

ACTION: Where can you demonstrate the virtue of faithfulness in your life?

Notes:

_____

_____

_____

_____

_____

_____

_____

_____

_____

_____

_____

VIRTUE #11

MERCY: CUTTING EDGE HUMANITY

Open invitation to the secret rapid rewards system for maximized living

Unsung Hero Story

Unsung heroes show up in unexpected places. Jessica is a nurse. Hospital workers observe suffering on a wide scale every day and have the unique opportunity to personify the essential virtue of mercy. In fact, hospitals are the only organizations I know that contain the literal word. They reach out in ways where they often aren't applauded. But they do what they do anyway. When they combine essential skills with compassion, it sparks something special.

When my father became ill, I decided not to take risks. I'd rather see him alive than at a funeral, so I travelled from Oklahoma to Ohio to be sure I left nothing undone or unspoken. I spent the night in the hospital while he was bedfast and on oxygen. Neither of us slept a wink that night. I never imagined being in a situation where I needed to place drops of water in my father's mouth to satisfy his thirst. Yet if I gave him too much, he would choke. During the night, I reminded him of the dream I had years before where he was on the other side of life, holding the unique, meaningful white placards face-down in his lap. These were the things he had done through love and devotion that mattered on an eternal scale.

The next morning, the nurse Jessica came in to sit down with Dad while I was still in the room from the night before. It surprised me that she asked if he were to die that day, who would he want to be with him? I didn't know he was that close. He replied that he wanted my mom and his four kids to be present. That proved to be a timely question, as she had a gut sense his time was drawing near.

Jessica was on duty for the day shift and told me she had conversations with him during that time. "He said that he came walking into the hospital and knew he wasn't going to be able to walk out again before he died." Her care and comfort made a big difference.

Later in the day, our family followed through with his wishes to be at his bedside, which would not have been possible without Jessica's insight into the situation. The sands of time were dropping through the hourglass and none of us knew how close he was to the end. He could barely speak through that oxygen mask, but did anyway—for about an hour and a half. This was his opportunity to share his inmost heart and thoughts—and it was a wonderful time. We laughed, reminisced, sang, and prayed together.

Here are a few of my dad's thoughts during those cherished moments:

I'm moving to a different place.

That's all death is really.

I'm moving to a new home where death is overcome, and real life has begun. I'm glad I had you all.

I'll be there and you'll be here. From here to there there's simply no way to define what that is.

The wonder of it all.

There is going to be revealed to me the very secrets of life.

By the time we wrapped up that sharing time, it was early Sunday evening. As we each filed out of the hospital room, he called out, "Promise that you all won't leave me at one time!"

So, a few returned to alleviate his sudden trauma of feeling abandoned. Not long after that, because of being awake all night, he was exhausted. He finally drifted off to sleep for several hours.

My mom and brother had decided to spend the next night with him. My sister and I were going to go home and rest, but then I realized I forgot the car keys. When I came back upstairs to the hospital wing to retrieve them, I found Jessica crying in the nurses' station. When I asked her what was wrong, she told me she didn't believe Dad would last through the night. After conversing for a about fifteen minutes with Jessica, my sister and I decided to not go home after all. We were prepared to sleep in the lounge area, but that never happened.

About 3:00 in the morning, Dad awakened with my brother in the room. He was emphatic, "I'm done! I'm done! I'm done!"

The family was immediately called into the room, as the reading on the oxygen machine steadily declined. He had lost consciousness but was still breathing. He was resolved and ready to go, though. There was a calm and peaceful look on his face as the inevitable was happening before our eyes. My belief is that he knew we were there and ultimately got his wish.

At 3:30 in the morning, my dad took his last breath. Thanks to Jessica, we were able to spend the last hour and a half together as a family, which would not have been possible otherwise. Gathering in those wee hours of the morning wouldn't have been possible, either. Jessica didn't have to care like she did. She could have done her duty and called it a day. But she went above and beyond with an essential virtue called mercy. She became an unsung hero—a helper—as well as Cindy, the night nurse who was on duty when he passed.

Nurses' personal connection to families makes a difference—even when they don't get the applause they deserve. We couldn't have scripted a better outcome to the credit of two nurses who went the extra mile. Here's what Jessica had to say, "I was there to be a part of your dad's final decisions on his final day and was very blessed to meet your family to help all of you coordinate his final wishes."

I asked Jessica how she knew he was going to die. "Part of it comes with experience. I was watching his struggle, and part of it was the conversations he and I were having. He seemed to be saying good-bye. I asked him, 'Do you want the scientific information about what's happening to your body?' He said, 'yes.' So I went through things that we see as the patient is getting closer to their time. He had some of those symptoms. And I was telling him that he might see somebody that I can't see, and that he might hear somebody talking to him that I can't see. And that's okay. That doesn't mean they're not there—but they're not there to talk to me; they're there to talk to him. I could tell that his lungs and his body were starting to shut down, and he was so tired. Breathing is very hard work, and to see him struggle to breathe, made him not want anything to eat or drink. It was oxygen that he wanted. He was so parched. He did have that dilemma, 'I need to eat. I need to drink, but I can't.' And then it was just a feeling. He was finally going to reap the joy that he had given others, and I could tell he was transitioning emotionally. But it is scary, because nobody knows exactly what happens in those final moments, and nobody knows how it happens. So, I answered as honestly as I could to the best of my knowledge. I was blessed that he felt comfortable enough to ask me those questions. I'm honored that you allowed me to be a part of that."

Jessica rendered service while having physical challenges in her own body. She set her own interests aside to focus on someone else's needs above her own. "I've had some struggles with my health . . . it means a lot to be reminded that I actually helped somebody, and that it's not always just going in and passing pills. It's good to know that I was able to help your dad and your family understand what was happening. You've reminded me of the good parts of being a nurse. I do consider that a good part. To help them so that they're not scared or alone is a huge part of why I wanted to become a nurse; to take care of someone the way I would want my family or myself to be taken care of. I appreciate you reminding me that there are times I get to do that. We get the opportunity to help families say goodbye and to help people as best we can to make their wishes known and to help them accommodate as best we can.

"I was blessed that I received the assignment to take care of your family."

Jessica and Cindy behaved as nurses but heroes in ways only mercy could script.

Exhortations to Excellence on Mercy

> Put together all the tenderest love you know of,
> multiply it by infinity, and you will begin to see
> glimpses of the love and grace of God.
> –Hannah Whitall Smith

To show mercy may be the most boundless virtue of all; love in action. Who can say they have mastered the privilege of life without modeling this diamond of the heart? You're an object of mercy, not wrath. People were born for the beauty and fragrance of the rose, not the thorns lining the stem. Mercy is a golden opportunity to make good on love's grand promises. Have you considered how you can demonstrate more mercy to others? How can you experience more of this rich provision for yourself? This is the two-pronged secret blessing of the ages—a shared blessing.

The good news is that what you share will be partaken of simultaneously. You eat a portion of the pie you serve to others. Conversely, what you're not willing to share with others will short-change your life. I don't know why this is true, but I'm glad it is:

you are shaped by the essential virtues you freely and willingly extend. *Not many things endure forever but mercy does.*

Mercy is cutting-edge humanity. It makes you wealthy where it counts most—in the heart. Your bottom line as a person is increased and enriched. You're better off by practicing this master stroke than leaving it tucked out of sight and mind. It's like leaving your best Christmas gift unopened. Can anything effect more miracles? Think of the story someone will have to share because of the compassion you show.

THE SUPERPOWER OF IDENTIFICATION

Mercy seldom gets the credit for who you are and what you have become, but it makes the man or woman stronger than anything else can. Education is great. Entrepreneurship is rewarding. Serving a great cause is fulfilling. There are outward reasons for success, but this inner virtue of mercy speaks louder than all. Mercy is an indispensable sleeping giant of a role-player. They say when a person is confronted by death, their life passes before their eyes. Everything comes full circle. Time slows to a crawl. Deep introspection happens in these moments. When it comes to life goals, tackle *mercy* as a priority. Don't wait until you're on your deathbed to examine the circle that is your life. For me and for you, the time is now.

Blessed are the merciful for they shall obtain mercy.
–Matthew 5:7

To be merciful is to show pity, sympathy, and feeling for others' suffering. In today's world, suffering abounds. The only question posed is the nature of the difficulty. It could be a family problem, a job loss, a personal crisis, the loss of a loved one. Extraordinary obstacles require extraordinary virtues to get you through. Somehow, these character traits burst through the barriers of limiting beliefs. Mercy is the action you take when you feel those emotions of empathy. You are touched with the feeling of another person's infirmities. You imagine what it must be like to be walking in their shoes. You might not know the suffering of your friend, neighbor, or family member—until you ask the hard questions. When you learn the story, you care. You treat it like it is your own. You have the remarkable ability to identify with the crisis of another and not shun the opportunity to fill shoes you never dreamed possible.

Your superhero status is elevated to new levels when you do this. Do not just put on airs; but instead remain rooted, grounded, and connected. Mercy is more than mere words. It's a yearning, a burning, and learning to do the unusual thing. The pain of others intersects with your life because you bring something to the table that they need. I've heard it said that all people are broken in some way, and I think that resonates at the deepest level. Life's conquests encompass how to heal others, including ourselves. Solve problems for others and endeavor to make contributions to that end. Consider acts of mercy as a preparation for adverse times to come in your own life. There will never be a point where you're not in need of this virtue that makes a world of difference in the human condition.

That's when you think to yourself, *wow, I needed that.*

SHARE AND LIFT THE BURDENS

Mercy is compassion; an action. This is your ability to lift the downtrodden. Determine that you're not going to cross the finish line of life alone. You're bringing others with you. Make a habit to thank someone who contributed to your victories—both big and small. Do the necessary soul searching and introspection. Identify someone who helped you—but don't stop there. Make a fresh commitment that you're going to be there for others going forward. Do a kind deed, one at a time. It's going to ignite you and become a lifestyle. Mercy might be the best habit ever acquired and perpetuated by human beings. Patent that and make it your own. This goes beyond the intellect to the muscle memory of life. People feel you. This is your new transformation and trajectory; to reposition yourself for others is your arc of growth.

The answers to life's struggles are often closer than you think. How often are relationships murdered or extinguished through the lack of mercy? People should be treated like assets, not liabilities. Such are the dangers of unhealthy competition. To show mercy is to show forbearance. There's no need to be ruthless, merciless, and heartless. There were other ways to deal with insecurities instead of compounding them. Mercy can turn things in the right direction and become a bridge to a better future. Make intentional requisitions on the rich mercy available to you. This is the best way to right wrongs in every case.

To be empathetic is to identify with how another person feels. The antithesis is to be callous, indifferent, and unfeeling. There are cases where people begged for their lives and were denied in a violent act of murder. There are innumerable accounts where a person was so crazed in the moment of passion that the heart cries of the victim didn't register. No amount of pleading or reasoning could stop the aggressor from following through. Mercy could have been the hero, and withholding it made the perpetrator's positive influence diminish.

> **Sweet mercy is nobility's true badge.**
> **–William Shakespeare**

FIRST THINGS

When charting life goals, include mercy at the top of it in permanent marker. I wonder how many to-do lists include resolved plans to practice this regularly. How can your life change by keeping this in your daily thoughts? What potential pitfalls do you avoid by consistently following this essential virtue? How much adversity could be avoided by a new lifestyle of being there for others in ways you hadn't thought of before?

I have a hunch that one good thing will lead to another, and before long you will see the string of pearls across time. You get to where you want to be because of an initial small decision that you stay true to.

You feel what others feel when you focus attention on them. *Identification*. You pick up their burdens as your own. What a magical thing, to take ownership. You may seek answers during crises, but a right attitude is worth its weight in gold. Make a difference in someone's day, year, and life. Maybe it's being present in the moment for someone that didn't expect it. That person will feel the effects of mercy much longer than the time it took for you to extend the kindness.

As a teenager, I grew up in Port Huron, Michigan, in the thumb of the mitten on Lake Huron. In the winter, it was cold. The water of the St. Clair River flowing from the southernmost tip of Lake Huron was frigid. It never did warm up, not even in the summertime. It was so cold it would make your feet ache. But in the winter, the river would at times ice over, even though the current was so swift. The deep freeze could last for weeks or months. I remember one year when the season was particularly harsh. When the ice broke up, many weeks passed of hearing the ice moan and groan at all times of the day or night, but eventually, the harsh winter gave way to the warm thaw of spring.

Similarly, mercy has the warmth to make cold hearts live and thrive again. This is a day and age where feelings are raw. Many have been damaged. Some have become numb to the pain. Yet showing mercy can melt the ice block. Reach out to touch a person in need who wasn't expecting it. Mercy can mean remitting what could legitimately be held against another. It does your own heart good, not to mention the effect it has on your recipient. Doing so will help you lead a more focused, integrated life, concentrating on what matters most—essential virtues.

To excite the feelings of mercy is like discovering oil on the property where you reside. It was there all along. You can do whatever you want with what you've found. To that point, people who discover the hidden wealth of mercy become the richest people in the world overnight. *Mercy is better than money.* At the end of your days, when your life passes in front of you, how you've shown mercy and compassion will trump how you've spent a material fortune. Remain committed to a lifting lifestyle, rather than being a burden or weight upon others.

> Believe, when you are most unhappy, that there is something for you to do in the world. So long as you can sweeten another's pain, life is not in vain.
> –Helen Keller

THE WAY OUT FROM WITHIN

Years ago, I had a vision in a dream. I was in a dark pit; so dark that I couldn't see my hand in front of my face. I couldn't see in any direction—front, behind, left, or right. I was enveloped by darkness. I looked straight up, craning my neck. Far above there was a circle of light at the top of the shaft, but there was no way to get out. There wasn't a ladder or stairs. Literally, there was no way to bridge the gap between here and there. I was stuck at the bottom. There was no hope. The darkness on every side of me was like impenetrable walls. Momentarily, I saw two faces, one on each side of the circle of light. They were peering down from a place of judgment. The faces were condemning, expressing disdain and contempt.

I remember feeling that they weren't wrong. I knew I had flaws. I knew there were things I had done that weren't good. Yet they showed no mercy. They weren't going to do anything to help me out of the pit. They mocked, sneered, scoffed, and ridiculed. I later wondered how blameless they considered themselves to be. Yet it didn't matter. They chose judgment when the reciprocal would have been the better choice.

There was a transition. I looked up one more time and saw a third face appear between the other two. My attention was drawn to the center, and I didn't look any longer at the two condemning faces. No matter what I had done, the third face spoke volumes more than the other two combined. I knew who it was even though no words were spoken. There was something striking about the eyes. I'd never seen eyes like that before. They were liquid pools of love. There was no condemnation, only compassion. He identified with me, knowing my estate at the bottom of that pit, and loved me anyway. He saw right through me. If eyes are the windows to the soul, his were wells of compassion where there seemed to be no bottom or end—in a literal sense. Words aren't adequate to convey how true this was in the moment.

Truth be told, the number of people in your life that don't believe in you may outnumber those who do by a two to one margin. I learned a lesson that no matter what opinions or perceptions live in the minds of others, there was someone who knew about me and cared anyway. This is the best example of mercy I can convey because it's etched in my consciousness forever. Those eyes told me everything I needed to know. *And the silence.* Nothing needed to be spoken. I'll never forget that visual, no matter how much time slips by. It's just as vivid today as it was twenty years ago. It felt as if he saw every fiber of my being. By the peaceful look on that man's face, nothing took him by storm. Where I couldn't fathom the depths of him, he fathomed the entire depths of me. Nothing was covered or hidden.

And that was a gift.

I still didn't know how to get out, but it became a moot point. Numerous lessons could be derived from that vision. One could be that I needed to learn how to live in the pits of life with the knowledge that someone loves me the way I am. That there would be others placed in my life who would do the same and share that mercy. They would be unsung heroes in my life.

That you have mercy at your disposal is both a privilege and a responsibility. You can be the condemner or the one who shows mercy. You can be someone else's unsung hero. Which side will you take, the light or the darkness? Maybe there's a lesson that you can't allow negative opinions to dominate your thinking. Maybe you don't totally escape the darkness in this life but are looking for answers and ways to navigate life with its inherent possibilities.

Adopting mercy as a way of life will take you farther than you can go otherwise. Be a person who doesn't condemn. There are plenty of those already. Be the exception, not the rule. Be a person who understands and identifies with the suffering of others. You'll be like the man in the middle that I saw in the dream at the top of the circle of light. You'll share the ability to see through the lens of mercy rather than harsh judgment. Mitigate suffering wherever you can, whenever you can, however you can. Choosing mercy allows the how of accomplishing that to come into full view.

> I have always found that mercy bears
> richer fruits than strict justice.
> –Abraham Lincoln

ILLUSTRATIONS OF MERCY

Charles Grandison Finney was born in 1792 in Litchfield, Connecticut. He went to law school but didn't ever practice as an attorney in court. Instead, he used those specialized skills to speak, teach, and expose corruption in the public arena during the nineteenth century. When he taught in mass indoor and outdoor meetings, he laid out a case in detail as if he were a lawyer. He described his method of speaking to people as if they were jurors, processing and rendering a verdict, appealing to their sense of reason. He was also a prominent figure in the abolition of slavery movement during the mid-1800s. I call Finney an unsung hero for the cause, as he would later petition

Abraham Lincoln for the immediate emancipation of three million slaves in the South. But for the tireless efforts of Finney, history may have been written differently. Finney had numerous essential virtues working to his advantage—courage, honesty, diligence, love—and mercy. They have a way of banding together like a team. These made a difference in his ability to influence people and effect sweeping change across the United States.

Here's a piece of Finney's story:

He was a fiery lecturer and revivalist who travelled throughout New York state, then New England. He later fanned out across the Midwest and other parts of America to vocalize the atrocities of slavery. He went on to pastor a church in downtown New York City, where eight antislavery societies met on a regular basis. They broadly published literature that was distributed across multiple platforms to inform and educate the public. Propagandists had claimed the slaves were treated humanely. Finney trained hundreds of workers whose voices brought the stark reality of the opposite to bear. These crimes were largely covered up. One way to do that is to not count the deaths. The numbers were never published and that, in a twisted way, absolved guilt and accountability for those terrible deeds.

GRASSROOTS LEADERSHIP

Mercy led the way in Finney's mission, but also his sense of justice, which paved the way for mercy's exercise. The Lane Rebels from Cincinnati enrolled themselves at Oberlin University in Oberlin, Ohio, near Cleveland, to be under the tutelage of Finney. By that time, Finney was the head of the theology department and later became Oberlin's second president. Finney had extended the invitation to the students from Cincinnati. Additional dorms were built on campus to accommodate them.

> The law works fear and wrath; grace works hope and mercy.
> -Martin Luther

Mercy was at work among students and the faculty. America's first Black graduate came from Oberlin. Like Cincinnati and Ripley, the town was a hotbed for abolition. Who knew that the freedom of slaves in America would come down to unsung heroes such as Finney, Weld, and Harriet Beecher—or the students and faculty at a college like Oberlin. The students were as fiery and committed as their mentors. They were emancipation heroes, even though Lincoln received the lion's share of the credit. There were pockets of opposition to their cause, even in the North, but the theme of abolition was carrying the day.

The Underground Railroad was an example of people pitching in and combining their energies for a great cause. No one person could do it alone. The secret railroad was one of mercy and kindness. One of the most prominent routes began in Ripley, on the banks of the Ohio River. The railroad passed through central Ohio, where I went to middle school and high school, though I didn't understand the significance at the time. The route culminated in Oberlin, considered an entirely safe town, one of few that existed. The Lane Rebels fit in perfectly.

THE OBERLIN-WELLINGTON RESCUE

John Price was a fifteen-year-old boy from Mayfield, Kentucky. He escaped his master and moved to Oberlin, where he began to enjoy his new-found freedom. After settling for some time, Price's owner representative and a federal marshal approached the young man to trick him into returning to Kentucky. They didn't identify themselves but offered him twenty dollars to work in a field. When Price took them up on the offer, they kidnapped him and took him ten miles south to Wellington where they rented a hotel room. The following day they planned to continue the journey south through Columbus to return Price to where they believed he rightfully belonged—on the plantation in Mayfield.

The students and faculty of Oberlin, as well as the citizens of Wellington, got wind of the scheme and were outraged. Gathering townspeople, they went to Wellington where locals added to the number and joined them in surrounding the hotel where John Price was held; roughly 230 people in total. Several entered the hotel room from the second floor and took the boy back, returning him to Oberlin. One of the professors kept Price overnight. The following day, a group took him north to the Canadian border, releasing him once and for all. No one ever heard from Price again, and there are no historical accounts as to what he did with his life going forward. But he was free, and the essential virtue of mercy was personified.

Mercy is an act.

This event became known as the *Oberlin-Wellington Rescue*. Court trials in Cleveland, Ohio, ensued. The federal marshal and slave owner from Kentucky were charged with kidnapping. On the other side, about thirty-five citizens of Oberlin and Wellington were indicted for violating the Fugitive Slave Act of 1850—which stated it was against the law to provide haven to fleeing slaves. Two of those individuals went to trial. Eventually, charges were dropped on both sides. And Oberlin became known by many as the town that started the Civil War. Freeing one boy contributed to the release of three million by the mercy of those who refused to tolerate their untold suffering any longer.

Unlikely and courageous students helped shape and write American history books. Finney petitioned Lincoln with hundreds of signatures from Oberlin, asking for the immediate release of the suffering slaves. I've seen a copy of this original document. Many of these items are retained in the Oberlin archives. Harriet Beecher Stowe, writer of *Uncle Tom's Cabin*, was eventually invited to the White House by Lincoln after the Emancipation Proclamation was signed. He asked, tongue-in-cheek, if she was the one stirring up all the trouble. But it was truly the essential virtue of mercy stirring in the hearts of those who cared.

> If God is infinitely merciful, we need not wait in the use of means, to move him to the exercise of mercy; as he is continually using means with us to make us willing to accept or bring us into a state of mind in which it can be consistent for him to exercise mercy.
> -Charles Finney

THE CENTRALITY OF MERCY

Mercy is a triumph over justice. It's the central point of life and meets people where they are, even when it's ugly. When people fail, they need covering and protection. They are honest about their need and responsible for self-correction. The Hebrew word for mercy connotes kindness and compassion. This virtue will accomplish good like none other and endures for time and eternity. Mercy without truth has no grounding—and truth without mercy becomes absurdly mechanical. Who enjoys living in a harsh world of judgment every day?

No one I know.

You know the difference between right and wrong, and not because someone is standing over your head to clobber you. Be inspired from within and endeavor to match your actions to your heart. You're susceptible to making mistakes and rendering poor decisions. At the same time, you're capable of turning the tide by an ability to make renewed dedication through hindsight and foresight. Leverage your personal volition to redirect. You don't do things by your own power. You have many helpers along the way, both internally and externally. There are essential virtues within and unsung heroes without. All of these synergize your way to victory.

Mercy covers the vital and vulnerable areas of a person. Mercy is the crux of living—how you receive and extend this virtue to others. Protection stretches across this new lifestyle and takes you farther than you dreamed possible. When you look back, you will wonder why you didn't act sooner. The benefits of mercy are immeasurable.

Without mercy, you run on your own steam, susceptible to the harshest blows. Eventually, you run out of gas and reach an end. But the life of mercy is the safest route to happiness and the richest life to lead. Mercy travels wherever you go like Mastercard. This is a seismic shift. The seat of mercy has been transferred to the heart of humans who personify essential virtues. Wear mercy like a cloak. Distribute mercy like it's your business. Intercede for others. Become an advocate.

Be an entrepreneur of this essential virtue.

This is the most direct route to the center of the universe. When searching for the meaning of life, look no further. Mercy is the essence; a legacy for you to leave to others. When you decide to be an unsung hero, it elevates the circumstance. This is the proven model of behavior that will shape and elevate lives like none other.

You have found the key to unlock the prison doors for others when you have found *mercy*. You walk free with a focused purpose of freeing captives from a variety of adverse circumstances. You can do this in simple ways, whether at work or play. Be sure that the people around you are loved and cared for—*the noblest mission in history for anyone who dares to embark upon it.*

> Mercy without justice is the mother of dissolution;
> justice without mercy is cruelty.
> –Thomas Aquinas

GEMSTONES

◈ To show mercy may be the most boundless virtue of all. It is love in action.

◈ Can anything effect more miracles? Think of the story someone will have to share because of the mercy you showed.

◈ Mercy might be the best habit ever acquired and maintained by human beings. Patent that trait and make it your own.

◈ Mercy is more than mere words. It's a yearning, a burning, and learning to do the unusual thing. The pain of others intersects with your life because you bring something to the table they need.

◈ Mercy is compassion, an action. This is your ability to lift the downtrodden. Determine that you're not going to cross the finish line of life alone. You're bringing others with you on the way.

◈ A person will feel the effects of mercy much longer than the time it took for you to extend the kindness.

◈ You can be the condemner or the one who shows mercy. You can be someone else's unsung hero. Which side will you take; the light or the darkness?

◈ When you decide to be an unsung hero, it elevates the circumstance. Here is the proven model of behavior that will shape and elevate lives like none other.

◈ The Hebrew word for mercy connotes kindness and compassion. This virtue will accomplish good like none other and endures for time and eternity.

◈ Mercy is the crux of living—how you receive and extend this virtue to others.

REFLECTIONS
MERCY: CUTTING EDGE HUMANITY

Identify the secret rapid rewards system for maximized living when you give the gift of mercy.

PROMPT: Reflect on moments when mercy has helped to heal or restore you.

ACTION: Make a list of ways to show mercy to yourself and others.

PROMPT: Think about a situation where you put yourself in someone else's shoes. How did it impact your perspective and actions?

ACTION: Write down one way you can show empathy to someone in your life today.

Notes:

_____

_____

_____

_____

_____

_____

_____

_____

_____

_____

VIRTUE #12

GROWTH: THE GARDEN OF LIFE
Highlighting small decisions that lead to super character transformation

Unsung Hero Story

Mark Frank is a gifted theater coordinator and playwright. He checks all the boxes for unsung heroes and is one of the most selfless people I know. In this day of self-seeking, Mark wants growth as an outcome to everything he does. His priorities are right. His aspirations are aimed at the students and people he serves. He works hard on that dynamic, everything else being secondary. He does wonderful things with no expected praise. He's a consummate professional. But more than that, he's a consummate human being. He'd rather see his colleagues receive their due than to receive his own.

Mark is like the greenhouse. Growth is his goal. Since I've been in it as a performer and seen him in action, I can validate that's true—not just mere words. He's genuine, authentic, and sincere in his quest to elevate people to be everything they aspire to be in those settings. The show is an opportunity to demonstrate that growth. Both the mentor and the protégé benefit.

I remember scouring through the props in the storage area of the theater department. Mark was obsessed in finding something we could use as a pacemaker for eighty-six-year-old Alfie, the role I played. He dug and dug and fished out a bulky clock to put in my front shirt pocket. He started piecing it together with duct tape because it needed doctoring. That's what made this dilapidated pacemaker so hilarious to see on stage. Before long, I looked down and saw his blood on the concrete floor. I looked closer and saw duct tape wrapped around his finger, but he had kept right on working. He had cut his finger open in the process of constructing that prop. He didn't even say ouch—no complaining. The most important thing in the moment was that brainstorm and getting 'er done for rehearsal that night.

That pacemaker was placed in my shirt pocket for the show. When other characters wanted to control Alfie or give him a jump start, they pulled out that clock and turned it up a notch or two, or all the way. That became one of the funniest props ever. It was so ridiculous looking—and perfect.

Mark helped me to be a better Alfie than I ever dreamed. He put *his* creativity into *my* part. It gave me a lot of joy to be in that play. Yet he didn't ask for the credit. His joy was watching the show and my growth as an actor.

He is an unsung helper.

In theater, the show must go on. During the opening performance, Francis, the main character, threw Alfie nearly through a set wall by accident. I was sprawled on the floor, face down. Francis didn't know his own strength. I lay there stunned, motionless. Mark said afterward he was ready to jump in and do my lines. He thought I was literally dead. Mark's a great guy. But he would have done anything to move that show forward. I was shocked he even knew all my lines. He would have taken over—as if it were part of the show.

He is a remarkable mentor.

I got the credit for following his direction, yet he was largely responsible for my development, giving me the liberty to grow. In the lobby after the show, audience members greeted me in the performers' handshake line, but he was backstage thanking everybody behind the scenes. I've heard it said that you can accomplish amazing things in life, so long as you don't care who gets the credit.

Theater is a lot like life.

Mark emphasizes that a cast is going to make mistakes; it's how they deal with them and bounce back that makes the difference. "You're like a motivational teacher. You're always teaching. It's all about them," he says.

There are many unsung heroes in a theater production. Mark says he is resolved to shake every technician's hand, every stagehand, every person responsible for the technical aspects. "I want to make sure they know how much I appreciate them. I think the way you are in life and how you conduct yourself is how you'll be as a director."

Mark describes himself as a mover and a shaker. He's enthusiastic, and the growth of his actors, singers, and dancers is more important than the finished product.

This emphasis is so needed in any profession or walk of life. What is the culture of the business, the classroom, the church, and your home? Discipline and etiquette are required on and off the professional, academic, and social stages. What is the transformation of the person from where they started in the beginning, compared to where he or she finished at the end? If that can be measured and quantified, the leader has done their job. Those who aspire to grow in any field will willingly take direction and learn.

"Put your ego aside. Put everything aside," Mark admonishes. "How you want to be treated is how you should treat others. That's professional. Life is about relationships, and you've got to make sure they're strong."

Mark believes there are positive takeaways from being involved with theater, including ensemble building, life-long friendships, and learning how to better work with people. "Life is way too short. Time is so important. Take the time you have in life and use it for the positive, because you never know when your last day is going to be. Why waste it on the negative? Be nice to people because you don't know what they're suffering from. They could be dying, and you don't even know it. And you were just mean to that person?"

He adds that it is a good idea to compliment someone every day to help a person, or a relationship, grow. "The biggest thing is to respect them, and who they are," he concluded.

Since 1992, Mark has conducted children's summer theatre every year. He calls children's theatre the best part of his job. He told me about a six-year-old named Dirk who played a role in Disney's *Aladdin Jr.* Dirk struggled in finding things he liked to do until he discovered theater. "He says he is going to do this every summer of his life now and anytime he can. He found his purpose. I think there are little kids out there that have never done something like this before. They do it, fall in love with it, and then that's their calling. That's what I like. I like seeing somebody who was not in the arts, even college students and adults that say, 'I'm struggling, I'm depressed, or I don't know what to do.' Then they find theatre and it totally changes their life."

The best thing for Mark in summer theatre is seeing children find their place.

Mark describes the theme of Aladdin as being applicable to people who want to grow in life. "Liking who you are and not trying to be someone you're not. Jasmine is tired of being a princess and wants to be an "everyday" person that is not noticed or recognized. Aladdin, on the other hand, wants to be a prince because he is a street rat. You find out through the play that when Aladdin becomes somebody he's not, it gets him in trouble, and when Jasmine tries to cover up who she is, it gets her into trouble."

Mark says the great lesson in the Disney musical is: "Love who you are and don't try to be someone you're not, because who you are is good enough."

He says generally people can get what they need in life if they work hard. Genie represents the magic in every person, but each individual has to pull it out themselves. "You can wish it to happen and if you work hard, you can get your dreams. But if you lie, deceive, disguise, and cheat, you'll probably end up failing."

He describes people who wish to become millionaires and later become miserable. Perhaps their money is stolen, they lose their marriage or family, or infighting occurs over the money. Regardless of the desire or aspiration, "Be careful what you wish for. Is that what you truly want? In Aladdin's case, he gets his wish and becomes Prince Ali. But he's miserable and realizes he's better off just being himself. Jasmine agrees. She didn't fall in love with Prince Ali. She fell in love with Aladdin.

"A child is there for the ensemble. Very few kids in thirty years of doing children's theatre have I seen out there for themselves. They are there for the whole." Mark says the opportunity to work with kids is mutually beneficial.

"Look, they have changed my life, too. When you have a seven-year-old who you just met six weeks ago come up and hug you so hard you can't breathe, with tears in their eyes, and say, 'I will miss you until next summer,' that's the reason I do it."

Mark says the lessons to be learned working with kids are, "Be patient, have fun, don't take life too seriously. It's okay to laugh." He adds, "They go to the bathroom a lot. You have a three-hour rehearsal and you're going to have seven kids that go the bathroom twenty-one times."

He usually finds out they are not going to the bathroom. They are more likely to be in the staging area dancing or looking in the mirror making faces. Creating confidence in a child to go in front of an audience of 150 people and walk away with the accomplishment allows them to go into any study and conquer it also. He wants kids to understand that they can do anything. "I'm not the message, they are. They can do whatever they put their heart to."

Exhortations to Excellence on Growth

> I'm a big believer in growth. Life is not about achievement. It's about learning and growth, and developing qualities like compassion, patience, perseverance, love, and joy, and so forth. And so, if that is the case, then I think our goals should include something which stretches us.
> –Jack Canfield

My wife is an avid gardener. She spends a lot of time and care in growing things. She plants vegetables for eating and flowers for beauty. She doesn't differentiate when it comes to doing what will allow for maximum growth. Every part of the garden gets her all. Her heart and soul go into every phase of the process. For her, it's all joy, start to finish. There's a time to plant, a time to water, a time to weed, a time for the warm sunshine—and always the right time for tender loving care.

Gardeners don't rush to do everything in a hurry. They're patient and kind with those plants, all the time. They don't rebuke the plants and tell them how no-good they really are and that they'll never amount to anything in life. It would be absurd to make such comparisons. "Why don't you look like that beautiful rose over there?"

Rather, there's a unique vision for every living thing. We could say my wife is an *unsung hero* to those plants. They couldn't be what they are without her. She doesn't ask for the credit. She takes pleasure in the result.

When you go inside a greenhouse, everything is conducive to life. It's a tender, quiet atmosphere. Have you ever noticed how peaceful it is there? The workers don't run roughshod over what they're trying to grow. Every action is intentional and contributes to that beautiful end. Anyone harsh or abusive in that delicate environment will be looking for a new job soon. At the end of the day, they want to do everything possible to nurture a positive outcome.

Be equally committed to the growth of people.

People you associate with every day are like those plants. Your company is your greenhouse. Your business is a greenhouse. Your organization is a greenhouse. Your life is a greenhouse, even your family.

Handle with care.

NURTURING THE PRIVILEGE OF INFLUENCE

Your growth in life as a person, leader, or teammate is in direct correlation to the growth you facilitate for others.

There are some who believe harshness in leadership, for example, is a good thing; a necessary evil. "But look at all I do for you," might be a demeaning statement made to call into question the worth and value of the person they're scolding. Maybe they throw chairs or strike players, thinking it's okay and for the good of the team, when it's only for the good of letting off steam. After all, look at the lofty objectives, they rationalize. But it's a mirage. Selfishness is at the core of all inappropriate behaviors. If it's not mutually beneficial, it's probably not right.

This is a poor substitute for good leadership. They try to win at all costs but lose in the long run. Growth of individuals and the team are stunted by this type of leadership. Consider the boss who acts like a tyrant and thinks they wouldn't have gotten to where they are if they dealt with the 'forbidden fruit of kindness.' *That's weak,* can be the mentality. This is their justification; an admission they know it is wrong. Their conscience is broadcasting the truth of the matter but it's being ignored and overwritten. The very offer of an excuse or justification tips off that they know the right way is available. They can't seem to control their thoughts or actions and opt instead to avoid essential virtues that would lead them to a better way of dealing with those under them.

They could instead leverage love, courage, friendship, hope, honesty, mercy, or gratitude. But those steps to an extraordinary life are totally ignored while they are taking their insecurity out on others. It subsequently makes them the smallest person in the room, instead of the biggest. They could be someone's unsung hero—a true helper—instead, they set the growth of others back a step and their own by two or more.

> The purpose of that apple tree is to grow a little new wood each year. That is what I plan to do.
> -Henry Wadsworth Longfellow

CYCLICAL POSITIVITY

When an employee goes by the wayside, the boss might excuse it by saying they deserved it, or never did fit in anyway. *If they can't stand the heat, get out of the kitchen,* so to speak. But the truth is that the aggressive behavior never did fit. The boss may have created a relational inferno in the company, team, or organization that cut against the grain of everything that leads to a healthy environment. People, who were the most valuable assets in an organization, might have become the victims of bullying, wrath, or anger. Others might have been damaged and succumbed out of fear of losing their positions. Yet the boss is worse off than the fired worker, because they'll repeat history down the line. More suffering is in store when inferior methods of leadership go unchecked.

The cycle repeats when they look for a new employee who will have thicker skin and be willing to sustain the knots on the head and blows to the chin with more resilience and gratitude. *You should take one for the team*, seems to be the thought. Or *he took that one like a champ*. All the while, something died in the relationship and in the company. Uncorrected, it may never be the same again—a slow death over time.

If you're a coach, that team is your garden; your sacred trust. If you are a parent, your home is your garden. If you are a gardener, the plants are your teachers. If you're a teacher, the classroom is your garden. What goes on behind closed doors is something you should own and be proud of. You're building extraordinary people with the building blocks of essential virtues. The people trusted to your care deserve the best you have to offer. You become an unsung hero in the process, even if you never get credit. They will learn by example that treating others with respect is a requisite for fulfilled persons, teams, and leaders.

THE GROWTH CONTINUUM

Have you been there? Ever been fired for doing nothing wrong? Have you been rejected? Have you lost opportunities? I have. Yet there's room for growth each day. I move forward, better than I was before, despite the misfortunes. I want to recognize my unsung heroes and their importance in my progress. Acknowledging those people does the heart good. Gratitude will turn the unsung hero into a sung one. You grow by recognizing the indispensability of people that have been graciously placed in your life. They're called alongside to help you.

By the same token, you're called alongside others to help. Your piece is important to their growth as a person and success as a teammate.

> **It is never too late to be who you might have been.**
> **—Mary Ann Evans, aka George Eliot**

Mister Rogers believed people are located on a continuum of the same line. You have an important place on that line, different than anyone else in history. You can't make someone be on your level, nor can you aspire to a level where you don't belong. Too much growth too quickly isn't healthy, which is why copying others becomes counterproductive. Instead, allow for the wonderful differences on that line of continuum through understanding, respect, recognition, and esteem. Every person's growth is dependent on the growth they facilitate for others. The sense of connection provides immeasurable reciprocal benefits.

THE ENDURING NATURE OF SOWING

How can you utilize these essential virtues of love, courage, honesty, faithfulness, optimism, diligence, hope, creativity, friendship, gratitude, and mercy? Practice them deliberately, putting your best foot forward, one virtue at a time. When you concentrate on one, the others tag along for the ride. There's an attraction since these virtues are family; kin to one another in a literal sense.

At the end of life, you can look back and say you made timeless virtues more important than money, fame, vocation, or achievements. The practice of them makes you better at whatever you do. More than that, it's who and what you become. When you translate inputs into outputs with whole-hearted giving, it facilitates a higher purpose in everything. These virtues never fail because they make you a better person than you were yesterday. They are effective prescriptions for relational health. Be proud of the place you occupy on that continuum. Make sure that you're not standing still but moving in the right direction. No one else can do what you do, quite like you do.

> Twenty years from now you will be more disappointed by the things that you didn't do than by the ones you did do. So, throw off the bowlines. Sail away from the safe harbor. Catch the trade winds in your sails. Explore. Dream. Discover.
> –Mark Twain

To grow is to make steady gains, progressing from one level to the next. You mature, ascend, develop, expand, and increase—to the end goal of being a fulfilled person with an extraordinary life. In turn, everything you do is blessed. But you don't arrive overnight.

To dig up your seed every day to examine it is premature. Keep the good seed in the ground through trust. Be faithful, consistent, and true. Part of that trust is caring for others. The remainder of the blessing is reserved for you.

THE GARDENER'S TOOLBELT

Love your neighbor as yourself. You deserve love as much as anyone else. It's easy to beat yourself up sometimes. Go easy and give yourself some slack. You've more than bloodied yourself at one time or another. Maybe you gave yourself more than one haymaker when you were disappointed with yourself. Sprinkle the secret sauce of mercy and see how you grow.

Relax. Breathe. Forgive. Learn. Develop. Serve.

Learn someone else's story. When you do, your world grows by leaps and bounds. Learn for the purpose of understanding, to the point you're able to identify with and describe it like it was your own story to tell. Their journey becomes your own. If you show great interest, it changes you in the process. People have amazing things to say and share. Some of the most profound lessons come from listening in the moment. The connection compounds your life. Experiences are accessible. You learn in a way that doesn't require you to walk through the same things they did, except by empathy. You feel like you were there. When you share empathy, you lend immediate aid to the sufferer. They grow through your willingness to relate on a heart level.

SHARING AND CARING

Stories transform you through identifying with someone else's pain or triumph. Sharing is truly caring. When you hurt, I hurt. When you're happy, I rejoice with you—not mechanically but humanely. You have a beating heart for a reason. Eyes to see for a reason. Ears to hear for a reason. Hands to touch for a reason. Use all your life on a whole new level for the essential benefits of others.

In the experience of defeat, you learn the value of humility. That way it's easier to identify the area of your life that needs improvement. Perseverance is your strength, and resilience becomes a purposeful, sustainable, and indispensable strategy. You are committed to growth in your world—and that translates into helping people in your world grow by leaps and bounds. You're a caretaker and a caregiver. You found out it's fun to help people progress on their journeys—and in an ironic twist, you are the beneficiary.

**Let's look back at some of the
people you've met in this book:**

Renee was at her lowest moment in life. In her worst moment of crisis, she prayed for her friends not to die, even though the injuries she sustained were horrific. She was honest enough to say she wasn't as strong as people gave her credit for. She wanted to give up, but faith made a difference by turning her attention to the less fortunate. Renee is one of the most courageous people I know. The will to live was gone until she found courage which rose within her broken body and wounded spirit. She could have quit but didn't. But for the essential virtues of hope and faith, she would have stayed in depression—but chose to grow instead. Renee wasn't expecting the gift of courage to come through her ultra-supportive community— but it became a difference-maker.

The gift of courage is *transferable* to anyone in need—anytime, anywhere.

Jim Stovall could have let blindness define him. Instead, he founded a television network and became a prolific author and movie maker. He can't see but reads more books than anyone I know. He practices well the essential virtues in this book. Many people who help him are unsung heroes on his mission. He couldn't do what he does without them. He makes those unsung heroes sing by acknowledging them. Meanwhile, he's using his gift to help people grow beyond their most binding limitations. He grows each day as he reads another book.

> **The conclusion is that growth occurs with the steady practice of essential virtues and extending those on behalf of those in need of them.**

> Unless you try to do something beyond what you have already mastered, you will never grow.
> –Ralph Waldo Emerson

THE RICH REWARDS

The rewards you gain internally for living a virtuous life inspire you to be an unsung hero and not need the applause. Engage character essentials like love—the most underestimated gift in the history of the world. Knowing the amazing results of it will help to reorder everything. People personify essential virtues, and when they do, they become indispensable in their realm. They don't ask for the credit. They're happy in their role and that's the way it should be.

Remember those white placards from the introduction? There are many of those in your lap right now. Take the time to identify them. It might surprise you what counts. There are items written on those cards that you've done through love and devotion that many people don't know about. It doesn't diminish them one iota. You did them out of a pure motive. You might have thought it was nothing at the time, but it's all recorded in a time capsule. Those unsung deeds count even when people don't fully understand.

Do them anyway.

The reward is not always immediate, but it comes eventually, even on the other side. There's nothing you do through love that doesn't count on an eternal scale. Long after you're gone, there will be ripples in the lives you touched by your willingness to help others grow. You become part of the story of many. You make those individuals bigger than they could have been without you. When they think of the good things in their lives, they will remember. They may or may not tell you.

Do stuff anyway.

When all seems lost, hold steady. Something is stirring in you. Be open to the person coming alongside to help you. They might be that special angel in disguise—or you may elect to be that angel and indirectly find your own superpower.

There are no limits to growth and human progress when
men and women are free to follow their dreams.
–Ronald Reagan

Mister Rogers was a hero to countless children. They looked up to
him because he looked up to them. He considered children to be more
important than himself. Fred Rogers was a servant. He used essential
virtues to communicate penetrating messages. He wanted kids to
grow. He used *silence*, understanding that kids are genius enough
to observe and think and read between the lines. In the process of
reaching them, he reached adults, parents, and team members. But
he always reciprocated love. There was more growing to do. Being an
extraordinary person was more important than anything else.

YOUR LIFE'S LEGACY

The legacy of love is big enough for all to participate and mutually
benefit. Emphasize the importance of unsung heroes by saying there
is always someone who loved you into loving and that smiled you
into smiling, like Fred taught.

No one gets all the credit for anything in life worth doing.

But you've done them anyway.

Who are you touching today? That person will touch someone
tomorrow. *And the gift goes on.* Unsung heroes make the world go
around. The way they become heroes is by practicing essential virtues.
These are diamonds of the heart in your possession right now.

Grow through your struggles with character. Go into the phone
booth and come out stronger, more vibrant, more alive than ever
before. Who are the unsung heroes that promoted you to where
you are today? Have you thanked them? Maybe you have already. It

wouldn't hurt to do it again. Maybe it was parents, friends, or associates. Maybe it was a spouse or sibling, or perhaps a teacher, coach, or instructor.

What do you have that you didn't receive? What you know was taught by someone. Your skills were acquired from people who modeled character virtues and set an example by serving. *They cared about you.* Shun the abuse where you've experienced it. Embrace the caring and grow. Grab a hand. Connect to hearts. Use your treasures, heroes of the heart. There will always be those who exalt themselves and humiliate others. But that's not you. Real heroes *flip the script* by humbling themselves to exalt others, which is the straightest line to wholeness, integration, and personal harmony.

Congratulations on your extraordinary life and contributions.

People are waiting for you.

Man cannot really improve himself without improving others.
–Charles Dickens

GEMSTONES

- You can accomplish amazing things in life, so long as you don't care who gets the credit.

- What is the transformation of the person from where they started in the beginning, compared to where he or she finished at the end? If that can be measured and quantified, the leader has done their job.

- Your company is a greenhouse. Your business is a greenhouse. Your organization is a greenhouse. Your team is a greenhouse. Your life is a greenhouse, even your family. *Handle with care.*

- Every person's growth is dependent on the growth they facilitate for others. The sense of connection provides immeasurable reciprocal benefits.

- At the end of your life, make sure that you can look back and say you made timeless virtues more important than money, fame, vocation, or achievements. The practice of them made you better at whatever you do. More than that, it's who and what you've become.

- To grow is to make steady gains, progressing from one level to the next. You mature, ascend, develop, expand, and increase to become a fulfilled person embedded in an extraordinary life.

- You are committed to growth in your world—and that translates into helping people in your world grow—by leaps and bounds.

- Long after you're gone, there will be ripples in the lives you touched by your willingness to help them develop.

- Who are you touching today? That person will touch someone tomorrow. And the *gift goes on.* Unsung heroes make the world go around.

- Shun the abuse where you've experienced it. Embrace the caring and grow. Grab a hand. Connect to hearts. Use your treasures, the heroes of the heart.

REFLECTIONS
GROWTH: GARDEN OF YOUR LIFE

Analyze the small decisions that lead to super character transformation.

PROMPT: Reflect on moments when growth has made a difference in your life.

ACTION: Make a list of activities to do to foster growth.

PROMPT: Reflect on a time when you stood up for your beliefs. How did it impact your actions and what did you learn from the experience?

ACTION: Write down one situation where you can act with integrity and the steps you can take to do so.

Notes:

_____

_____

_____

_____

_____

_____

_____

_____

_____

_____

_____

_____

Epilogue

Ciara works at a local coffee shop, which has thousands of locations throughout the world. But what Ciara brings to work each day is extraordinary. She has a one-of-a-kind personality, disposition of service, and an uncommon love for people.

I can count on her to brighten my day every time I go to the coffee shop. She'll jump out of nowhere to personally prepare my pour over coffee. She knows what I want before I ask and tells the cashier what to enter the system before I can order. She's already preparing my cup before it's rung up on the register.

Then I wait for Ciara to finish the process with tender loving care. She instructs her workers how to do what she does. She brings it over herself and hands it to me with a smile. When I sit down to sip, I look at the cup and read the hand-written note on the side. She always wishes me to have a wonderful day or week. She draws a smiley face, which is a reflection from the heart of this kind and genuine person.

As I sit and enjoy my perfect cup of coffee, I'm reminded of how one person can make such a difference in another person's day. I'm grateful for the extraordinary measures Ciara goes to make me feel like a valued customer—yet even more, a valued person.

People like Ciara are hard to come by. She makes an ordinary day special with her attitude alone. It's never contrived. It's sincere, genuine, and remarkable. There's no question how she feels about serving. She counts it a privilege.

Yet, all that isn't enough. Occasionally, she drops by the table in the course of her other duties to say hello and shares a moment which lets me know that she values our relationship. So many times, this amazing girl has given me a chocolate chip cookie at her own expense. All in all, when I leave the coffee shop, I'm grateful.

Ciara is a dear friend. What's not to love about a person who combines what she does with essential virtues and how she translates that toward others? This is the difference a person can make doing ordinary things in an extraordinary way.

It's not what you do, but how you do what you do, that separates you from the crowd. People like Ciara stand out to me. She makes it her duty to lift others up. When you hug your coffee person, you know it's special. This is the kind of disposition everyone should strive for in the workplace or any place, where human stories supersede the dry mechanics of going through the motions of ordinary tasks.

Why would someone like Ciara extend such kindnesses in a corporately owned coffee shop? But maybe the bigger question is, *why not?* She creates a lasting impression that will not be soon forgotten. Before I leave, Ciara often asks, "When are you coming back?"

And, as you might imagine, I return for Ciara. The last time I was there, she asked, "Are you coming in tomorrow?"

Ciara portrays gratitude for her job, which she has inextricably tied to the privilege of serving and connecting with people. Every workplace can use a person like her.

You are effecting change you desire to see in the environment, whatever or wherever that may be. Transform your position into a meaningful vision, going above and beyond what is expected. It's in your grasp and power to do so. Someone's going to be grateful that you did. Do what you do for the joy and satisfaction in giving, not for the applause. You're going to be incredible. You know stories and have learned of others who not only have strong values but use them every day for good.

The smallest acts of virtue create a mountain of change in the world.

SPECIAL FEATURE

IN-PERSON VISITS

The Jim Stovall Story with Jim Stovall

&

Mister Rogers Story with Hedda Sharapan

THE JIM STOVALL STORY

WITH JIM STOVALL

JIM B. NORTH:

*The first question I want to ask, just in a capsule, is your take on prepa-
ration versus opportunity. Can you expound on what that means to you?*

JIM STOVALL:

Sure. Preparation makes opportunity valid. Unfortunately, a lot of
people aren't willing to do preparation unless there's an opportunity
right in front of them, and the world doesn't work that way. By the
time an opportunity presents itself, it's generally too late to start your
preparation. Success happens when that preparedness and opportunity meet. A lot of people who would tell you they never had a chance
have been presented with many opportunities. They just had not put
themselves in the place to take advantage of them.

JBN:

*Tell me a little bit about your personal background so people have a context
of who you are and where you came from.*

JIM S.

I was born and raised here in Tulsa, Oklahoma. As a young man my
ambition was to be an athlete. I thought I would be a professional
football player in the NFL, and then one year before playing a season
of ball, I was diagnosed with a condition that caused me to lose my
sight. I made an immediate switch and became an Olympic weightlifter and finished my athletic career in that sport. And then I did
lose my sight in my twenties and developed a system so that blind

and visually impaired people could access television. We produce about 1,000 hours a year of accessible programming. Out of that I was given opportunities to speak, and out of that grew books, movies, and my syndicated column. That's kind of a thumbnail sketch of how we got from there to here.

JBN:

Where do your syndicated columns appear?

JIM S:

They appear in about 400 publications throughout North America, Europe, and Asia. Some print—newspapers and magazines—and some are online publications. A lot of them are business/financial, and some of them are just corporate and general interest. Here in Tulsa, I am in *The Tulsa Business Journal*, *The Tulsa Legal Record*, *The Tulsa Beacon*, and *Broken Arrow*. You can find me about anywhere, and anybody anywhere that anyone can't find it, they can just call or email us, and we will put them on the list, and they'll get it via email each week.

JBN:

Now, a little bit about the founding of the Narrative Television Network. What year, what was the process, and how did that work to get this initiated?

JIM S:

We started the network in 1988. That's when we came up with the idea. It was just me and a legally blind woman here in Tulsa named Kathy Harper, who subsequently passed away several years ago. We both had been frustrated with the inability to access television, and we realized there were 13 million blind and visually impaired people here in America and millions more around the world, and television and movies are the number one recreational activity in our society. We began working on our system to add extra soundtracks and started in the home video business and couldn't keep up with demand. In 1990, we had our opportunity to go on television, picked up a national distribution deal, won an Emmy award that year for our first season on national television, and that was the beginning of everything. Then in the late '90s, television switched predominately from analog to mostly digital.

That opened a brand-new world for us because we just created these little soundtracks, and the narrator described what was going on between the voices of the characters in those silent places. Well, there's plenty of bandwidth for that soundtrack to live on that TV show, so now most primetime television that goes into your home or anybody's home across the country is narrated, and there's a button— SAP, second audio program—or languages, whatever it's called on the various televisions. You just push that, and you hear the soundtracks that we created here in Tulsa.

JBN:

What kind of feedback do you get from the blind that are benefiting from this service?

JIM S:

Well, it's very emotional. They're very appreciative. I mean, it would be hard for most sighted people to understand what it's like to live in this society in the twenty-first century if you can't access movies and television. I mean, as we were discussing earlier, it is the number one recreational activity, and if you can't take part in that, you are very separated from society. These little soundtracks make it possible for millions of people to enjoy that, and then a lot of kids who are blind or visually impaired can go to a regular school, if they can access the visual mediums, and we're a big part of that. We do a lot of work for Annenberg and Corporation for Public Broadcasting. We do a lot of educational programming that makes it possible for these kids that are blind or visually impaired to go to mainstream schools and compete with their peers.

JBN:

What are a few brief success principles that you keep in mind when you approach your projects?

JIM S:

That it's not about me. You've got to do what you say you're going to do every time. No one makes money. We earn money, and the only way we earn it is if we create value for other people, and the more value we create, the more money we earn. Anybody that wants to have more success either needs to create more value for the people they currently serve or serve more people. Those things are part of what I do, and I try to stay focused on my mission. I do five things. I do movies, television, books, speeches, and columns.

JBN:

It strikes me that blindness can be a barrier, but it has not been for you. I think anybody has some sort of barrier, and so people need to know and understand how they can break those barriers down. I think the first part of this I want to ask you is: What message would you have for blind people that haven't been able to push that barrier down yet, for lack of any number of things? It would be easy to feel isolated, like you were referring to earlier. What would you say to them or any person that's suffering from such a mental block right now?

JIM S:

Well, focus on your mission, not the method. Blindness is limiting to my methods, but it's not limiting to my mission. When I first went blind, there were several things I realized were not going to be a part of my life. One was that I couldn't drive anymore, except in the movies. I always drive in the movies. In real life, I don't drive anymore, but that doesn't mean I don't go places. I have two million miles with American Airlines. I've been around the world eighty times. I mean, I can go anywhere I want to go, but if I were tied to that method, I'd still be at home.

As soon as I lost my sight, I realized I couldn't read anymore. Well, I discovered audio books and how to make them high speed, and I read a book every day. There hasn't been a day in nearly thirty years that I haven't read a whole book. I read a book this morning, and I can listen to books at 700 to 800 words a minute. Yeah, I can't read, but that doesn't mean I can't be the most well read, literate person I know. Becoming a reader made me want to be a writer.

The third thing that frustrated me is I couldn't watch television and movies, and obviously that created a whole business and career for me. When I took the limiting factors of transportation, reading, and TV and movies, and turned them around, they've served me very well.

JBN:

Yes, they have. It strikes me that sometimes we who have sight can be blind in a lot of areas, not really having a field of view for life as we ought. It also strikes me that a person like yourself who might have a physical impairment has a wider field of view. You do see. The irony of seeing but not seeing versus not being able to see but seeing—do you know what I'm after there?

JIM S:

Sure. There's a big difference between sight and vision. Sight tells you where you are and what's around you; a very handy thing to have. I had it for the first part of my life, and sight is very convenient. Vision tells you where you could be and what's possible, and it's infinitely more valuable if you use it. Sighted people have a tendency, I find, to be judgmental and make snap judgments.

JBN:

Is it possible in a couple sentences to tell me what you feel constitutes a healthy vision? What do you think that means?

JIM S:

I believe the meaning of life is to find our gift, find what it is we've been given. The purpose of life is to give it away. The happiest people you will ever find are those who have found their gift, and then gave it away to serve other people. You will find some very satisfied people. People who haven't found their gift are frustrated, or people who have found it and don't give it away are unfulfilled.

JBN:

What are your thoughts about Helen Keller? She had great accomplishments. She was an author. You're an author. She had great success in life, and yet, she was not only blind, but she was deaf, so that was two barriers she had to knock down.

JIM S:

I have assistance from my colleagues here when I work or work in the studio or travel or things, but I can be relatively independent otherwise. Helen Keller, because she had two profound disabilities, needed more constant assistance. Anne Sullivan helped her. It was chronicled in the movie, the book, and the Broadway play *The Miracle Worker*, and Helen Keller's success is owed as much to Anne Sullivan as my success here is to my colleagues; the people that are the very best at what they do. There's no one in this building where I could do their job. I get all these awards and accolades. I mean, I write bestselling books. Yet I don't know how to type.

JBN:

Do you dictate it?

JIM S:

I dictate everything to a very talented lady down the hall named Dorothy, who is, without a doubt, the best editor and grammarian in the publishing industry. I mean, hundreds of newspapers and magazines after almost thirty years of my columns—I don't even think they look at them anymore. They don't even look at my columns. They just know Dorothy edited it, and it's ready to go.

My publishers that publish my books, same thing. They get a print-ready manuscript. Not because of me, because of Dorothy. I don't know how to spell anything. I don't understand punctuation at all. To me, it's just one long sentence, whatever you're talking about, books or audio. I realize I couldn't write books without her. I do speeches in arena events, and I could not get from here to the event on the coast or wherever we're going.

Then I have colleagues that are very good at helping me understand the stage and where are we going to go and what are we going to do, and we mark that out. We're getting ready to make the seventh movie based on one of my books, and the people at 20th Century Fox and Warner Bros., the great people we work with, I have to trust them and feel good about the actors, directors, the people. Because when you make books that you can't read that are made into movies you can't watch, you have to trust these people with your message.

Helen Keller and I both had our successes owing to collaborating with a lot of great people, but that's easy for me to understand. I'm certain it was easy for Helen Keller to understand. The problem is there are a lot of people out there that have all their senses, but they don't have any common sense, and they think they can do everything on their own, and when you collaborate with the right people, one and one equals ten, because it ceases to add and begins to multiply.

JBN:

Okay, the dynamic of inspiration. You inspire many, but also, where does your inspiration come from? Because somehow there is this correlation. Something ignites within you to tackle these things, so it must inspire you before you're able to inspire someone else. Can you just briefly comment on that? Where does your inspiration come from?

JIM S:

I'm inspired by books I read, the people I meet. My university training is in psychology. I believe one of the most powerful thoughts or ideas that's come out in the last few years is we become like the five people we spend the most time with. For some people, that's a very disturbing thought, and more recently I've seen some pretty compelling evidence that our income becomes the average of the five people we hang around with the most. You tend to perform at a certain level. If you hang around people that talk a certain way, you'll find yourself talking like they talk. If they act a certain way, you will. You take on those characteristics. I get inspired by the people around me. I get inspired by the books I read. I try to realize that we're a computer. What goes in is what comes out. I try to put in some powerful, positive messages.

I also tell audiences, "It's not about me. Please don't miss the power of this message due to the weakness of the messenger. I've not accomplished all the things we're going to talk about. I'm a fellow traveler on this path to where we all want to be. I come here with no answers. I come here with a framework with some questions because I believe everyone that ever hears me or reads what I wrote came with the questions. We don't fail because we don't know what to do. We fail because we don't do what we know."

Everybody that ever reads one of my books or hears me talk or watches one of my movies, they know more than enough to be successful. Everybody that's failing at a job, a career, a business, a relationship, they know what to do. They just don't do it. If anyone will be honest with themselves, when you have a failure, when you have a lapse, when something doesn't turn out the way you want it to, you find yourself saying, "You know, I knew better than that.'"

JBN:

In a few sentences, does faith play a part in what you do?

JIM S:

Sure. I mean, everybody's faith does, and mine does, and you've got to understand there's something bigger than us out there. People relate to that in different ways. There's a big difference between faith and religion, or the huge difference between religion and relationship. Religion is comfortable. You go to this service every week or maybe twice a week and you hear the pretty music, and you listen to these people talk, and that's religion. Relationship usually comes about when you have a crisis in your life, and you have to start dealing with God or your creator in a hands-on, ongoing, moment-by-moment way. For me, blindness catapulted me from religion to relationship.

JBN:

Excellent. Thank you for that. The overarching goal for you in life. Is there an overarching goal that comes to mind?

JIM S:

Yeah. In corporate America ten years ago, this thing emerged, and everybody thought it was really cool and sexy. Got to have a message statement or mission statement—what's our mission statement? And too many corporations would put it on the wall and ignore it. Well, I believe we all need a personal mission statement. What are we doing here? Mine was given to me by my grandmother. She was quite elderly and in hospice care and didn't have long to live, and I remember going to visit her.

She was sleeping, and one of her nurses said, "You know, she's really proud of what you do."

And I said, "I'm not even sure she knows what I do." She replied, "Well, she has this picture of you with your Emmy award right there next to her bed, and everybody that comes in here—the doctors, nurses, and people that come to visit—she always says, 'That's my grandson. He does two things: He helps blind people watch TV, and he travels around the world letting people know they can have good things in their life.'" I thought, "Okay, that's my mission statement," and if I live to be 114 years old, that's probably what I'll be doing.

JBN:

Outstanding. How did you become a great writer?

JIM S:

I'm embarrassed to tell you and anybody else that will pick up on this, that I was well into my twenties before I ever read a whole book cover to cover. In my early years I was an athlete, and grew up here in Tulsa, and as politely as I know how to put it: Nobody really encouraged me to focus on my studies, shall we say. As long as you can play ball at a certain level, it wasn't a big priority.

Then I started losing my sight, so books were never a part of that, but then in my late twenties after I was already blind, I discovered the National Library for the Blind and how to get these audio books, and I worked with some people to make them higher speed so I could just consume these. Conservatively, in the last thirty years, I've probably read 10,000 books.

Well, becoming a reader made me want to be a writer, and I would encourage anybody: If you want to be a writer, be a reader. Not all readers become writers, but all great writers are voracious readers, and that's the key, I think.

JBN:

What do you want your legacy to be? Is there a sentence or two that would capsulate that?

JIM S:

I did the best I could with what I had to help as many as possible, and my legacy would not be what I did, as much as what other people do. I have letters from schoolkids, or businesspeople or people around the world, and I like it when they say, "I read your book and you're great," and all that's wonderful, but the one's I really appreciate, somewhere in the second or third paragraph say, "After I read your book, here's what happened to me."

We all want the flattery, and I get to talk to my readers. I have ten million books in print and my phone number is in all of them, or my email address, and I respond to everybody, so I get that feedback. It's nice for them to say that was a great book or a great movie, so that is what matters to me. I think those people would be the legacy, just like I hope I'm a legacy for Napoleon Hill, Norman Vincent Peale, Zig Ziglar, Paul Harvey, and other people that have helped me in my career, either in person or through their books.

JBN:

What are your concluding remarks?

JIM S:

Too often we're waiting for all the lights to be green before we'll leave the house, and life doesn't work that way. The world belongs to the man or woman with a big dream that'll take the next step and then figure out what to do after that, and if you will live your life like that and find your gift, and then find the most compelling ways to give your gift away, you will have a very happy and successful life.

I always like people to remember that the biggest dream they ever had, the biggest goal, is alive and well, and it would not have been put inside of them if they didn't have the capacity to achieve it. So, the question is never, "Can we?" the question is, "Will we?"

The world belongs to the man or woman who will step out and visualize that goal and take one more step toward it, and then see where they go from there. If you'll just take that next step, sooner or later, you will own your destiny and live a life very few people can even imagine.

**For more information and available resources
from Jim go to: jimstovall.com**

MISTER ROGERS STORY

WITH HEDDA SHARAPAN

JIM B. NORTH:

Hi Hedda. Can we begin by your telling me how you started working with Fred Rogers?

HEDDA SHARAPAN:

It was 1965—before *Mister Rogers' Neighborhood*—that I met Fred Rogers. I had just graduated with a degree in Psychology from Carnegie Tech (now Carnegie Mellon University). That June, while I was waiting to hear from graduate schools, I decided to see what kind of summer job I might find. One of the places I visited was our Pittsburgh public station, WQED, and asked if I could do some work for children's television. The man who interviewed me said that they were not producing anything there for children. And I couldn't teach on "educational television" without a teaching degree. But he said if I was interested in children's television, I might want to talk to Fred Rogers.

We knew Fred's name here in Pittsburgh because he was the co-producer, puppeteer, and musician for *Children's Corner*, our WQED program that ran from 1954 to 1962. He was behind the scenes, but we knew he was a major player on that program. So, I wanted to see what he had to say. At the time, he was learning about children, observing them under the guidance of a child psychologist named Dr. Margaret McFarland. Fred was continuing his studies of children who were enrolled in a nursery school of a church. He met with me in the library of the church, and when I told him I wanted to work in children's television, he said, "If this is what you want, why don't you think about a master's degree?"

But Jim, he didn't say a master's degree in TV production, or mass media, or communication. He said, "Why don't you think about a master's degree in child development?"

What I heard in his advice was that the important question was not "What can we produce for children?" The important question was, "Who are they and what are they bringing to us? What makes them happy? What makes them sad? What are they worried about? What are their concerns? How are they dealing with their feelings?"

So, it made sense to me. Fred had suggested that I do that master's degree work through the University of Pittsburgh, where he was connected to Dr. McFarland, his mentor. She was the head of the Graduate School of Child Development at the University of Pittsburgh.as part of their training. It made sense for me to stay in Pittsburgh and go to graduate school at Pitt. And I would see Fred now and then at school.

In 1966, I was in my second year of grad school when Fred got funding for *Mister Rogers' Neighborhood*. And he asked if I would help as the assistant director. There was no staff, and there was no pay. It was the time of black and white television. We were taping in the evenings, so it worked out well with my studies. I was in grad school in the daytime learning complex child development theory, and I would come into the control room at night where I would watch Fred work on the same topics and issues. He made them manifest. That's the word. He was making manifest all these things I was learning—ritual, transition, separation, relationships, curiosity, the difference between make believe and reality, how to help children feel good about who they are and help them deal with their anger, their sadness, their fears. I was in this unique position to really understand what he was offering.

Now, I think it really is important to give you Fred's background and how he got there to the Child Development Graduate School and to WQED. Fred grew up in a small town about an hour outside of Pittsburgh called Latrobe, Pennsylvania.

Music was his first love, and he went to Rollins College in Florida, where he studied music composition. When Fred graduated college, he was intending to go into the ministry. He grew up in a family that was very strongly faith-based and had close ties with their Presbyterian minister.

JBN:

Why was he at school?

HEDDA:

In his senior year at Rollins in 1950, he came home for spring break and watched some early television programs on the TV set at home. When he saw children's programming, he has been quoted as saying that what he saw were pies in faces and nonsense, and he said, "Children deserve better." And he surprised his family by saying, "I'm not going into ministry. I'm going to learn about television."

After he completed college, he went to New York as an apprentice and then as a floor manager for early music programs.

One of the people he met and worked with occasionally was Gabby Hayes, who was a TV cowboy on Saturday morning for kids. Fred once asked him, "Mr. Hayes, what do you think about when you look at the camera and you know that there are millions of children out there watching?"

Gabby Hayes said, "Freddie, you just think of one little Buckaroo out there."

And I think that's what helped Fred understand that this thing called "mass media" is very personal.

After about two years at NBC, I heard him once say was that he felt commercial television was going towards greed, and away from *gift*. And he wanted to be part of gift. So, he left NBC, and came back to Pittsburgh to help start WQED. This was to be the first community-supported educational station in the country. He was brought in as the first program director, with the responsibility of getting programs in the lineup. Nobody stepped forward to do a children's program, so he paired up with Josie Carey, who was an actress helping to get the station going and doing secretarial work there, to do a program called *Children's Corner*. Go to misterrogers.org and you'll find some of the history and a great video clip. *Children's Corner* was live from 4-5 p.m. each weekday, so Fred was able to go back to his original plan and took his lunch hours doing courses at the Pittsburgh Theological Seminary.

He was working on a master's in divinity (and it took him eight years of lunch hours!). One of his classes had to do with pastoral counseling. The students were to do a case study on an adult. Because of Fred's interest in children and children's television, he asked the professor if he could do his case study on a child. And the professor told him that he needed to connect with Dr. McFarland at the University of Pittsburgh Child Development Graduate School. With her background in child psychology, she would occasionally be asked to speak at courses for the seminary students. So that's how he connected with her. Fred then sat in on many of the graduate school classes, and then he spent a lot of time sitting and observing children under the guidance of Dr. McFarland or the other teachers who would help him think through what he was seeing and what might be below the surface.

Fred used to say when he first started working with children that he wanted to be somebody interesting for them to be around; somebody fun for them to be around. But he said the more comfortable he became with himself and with the children, the more he realized that if he really wanted to communicate, the most important thing was to listen. What made them happy? What made them sad? What were they concerned about? How did they see things?

JBN:

You must have really worked hard on that. Because words really do matter. And the construction of the sentences, I would think, was vital.

HEDDA:

It seemed to me that it was incredibly important for Fred to find ways to communicate ideas, thoughts, and feelings to children in a way that was truly meaningful. He wrote almost all the scripts (almost 900 in all). He did have some help now and then, but he had his hand in every one of those scripts. Besides that, he wrote all the music (melodies as well as the lyrics) and he did almost all the puppet manipulation and voices. He was the host of the program and essentially the executive producer. We were a small staff—twelve or maybe fourteen of us in his small nonprofit company. We were support staff.

I was an assistant producer for the next two years, then found another way to support his work. If people wanted Fred to speak at conferences, they were told that he wasn't available because of production needs, but I was. I started doing professional development and speaking and writing about the program. The way I saw it, Fred was translating child development into a television experience. And what I would do was help people translate it back to child development. I didn't do lectures. What I did was give people a little bit of background about myself and about Fred. And then I showed videos and led them in a discussion about what messages they heard in the videos that could help with their work with children.

There were two things about working with Fred for me. One was that I always felt challenged because I wanted whatever I wrote about his work for professional journals or newsletters to be the most carefully and thoughtfully worded.

Now, the other side is that Fred was an extraordinary appreciator. He really appreciated each one of us on his small staff of twelve or fourteen for what we brought to his work. I'll give you an example. We were sitting around while Fred was thinking of new themes for the next season and saying, "Let's go over some ideas for our themes for next year."

Everybody else started offering him ideas, and I was sitting there thinking, *I don't have a thought. Nothing's coming. I can't. What am I doing here? I'm not really helpful.* So, I went back to my desk when the meeting was over, and on my chair, Fred had put some writing about the *Neighborhood* that I had worked on for a professional journal. And at the top of that he wrote, "Thanks, Hedda; you're a great synthesizer."

I thought it was okay if the others came up with the creative ideas. I had a different role here, and it was one that was appreciated.

JBN:

It's good to know that it's enough to be a helper. It's amazing, like a gift. We all should be helpers in various ways, and to find that way that we can best contribute. And to not feel like you have to go way outside of those ways, that it's enough in itself. It has its rewards, but it's not that you're seeking them. They happen.

Any of us are helpers in some way. Your point is that we all can't do everything. But we all can do something, and to be happy with that, and to be comfortable in our own skin, like you said that he was. He was comfortable with himself. Therefore, he was comfortable talking to children because he wasn't afraid.

Did you have any idea at the time where this would go?

HEDDA:

The amazing thing to me is that this legacy has lived on. Maybe because what we're living in now, people are saying we need this kind of caring about each other; a sense of neighborliness, listening, authenticity, helping, and kindness. We need that more than ever in our world.

JBN:

These things came through that screen in a palpable way, and with consistency. Almost sixty years that you've been doing this, and it's all stood the test of time.

I imagine for you, with all the different hats you've worn, all the different functions that you've had, and your contributions to all of this, that you're adaptable. But it's been with this core of a purpose that I suppose set you up for the ability to adapt because of your understanding of your mission, and your purpose and motivation.

HEDDA:

I had really good mentors along the way.

JBN:

What are you most grateful for with your role and contribution? It's bigger than life. I know it's been an effort of many people. But what about you? What are you most grateful for?

HEDDA:

I'm grateful for the opportunity to have such meaningful work that is helpful for others—and for the chance to have so many years to learn from Fred what it is to do meaningful work. It's heartwarming that so many people care about the kinds of things that Fred has helped us care about. It's really touching for me and humbling, you know. I fell into this work, starting with no pay, no staff, just an interest that grew out of watching early television and as a child pretending about having my own children's TV show in front of the mirror, *The*

Happy Hedda Show. And I'm grateful over the years that I had so many ways to learn about myself, about children, about life.

JBN:

What was your relationship like with him? He's this one-on-one guy on the TV screen. I can't imagine he was otherwise with you. So, what was your one-on-one relationship like?

HEDDA:

I would say it was a relationship of a mentor and colleague. I wanted to learn at the foot of the master. Fred was very warm and caring with all of us, and not just as staff working there. He cared about our families and our needs. When my mother was dying of cancer, I needed to spend a lot of time away from work to help her. She was here in Pittsburgh, and I was the only daughter that was here. I remember going to Fred one day and saying, "I'm really sorry that I haven't been around very much to help. But it's my mother situation." And Fred said, "Hedda, you're doing the most important work there is, caring for your mother now."

And I know he did that with each of us.

JBN:

You used a word a little while ago: manifest. You all have manifested a lot of things with that creative process, not just creativity. It's one thing to build a building, and it's another thing to have a good foundation for that building. You had creativity, but you had depth and authenticity as well, and this thinking through and working through with such careful- ness, which means you did, for lack of a better word, your due diligence. I mean, you really brought both.

What do you think children love about Fred Rogers the most?

HEDDA:

I think it was that he was approaching the show as a "television visit." A visit. It was as if he cared as much that you were there with him as he was there with you. He would say something like, "Did you ever feel like that? Have you ever had times like that?"

And he would be silent, giving his young viewers time to think and reflect. He treated television as a personal medium, not "mass media." He wanted his "television neighbors" to know that he cared that they were there watching and listening; thinking and reflecting. But at the same time, he wanted to make it clear that it was an honest relationship—as a *television* friend or a *television* neighbor. A few times over the years, Fred would say something like, "We're television friends, but I can't see you or hear you through the television. And I wish I could give you this treat that we've just made. But I can be only a television friend."

There's the honesty.

JBN:

I think another wonderful thing about the programs is that he wasn't afraid of silence. I have found that to be a powerful use of silence, because you're allowing those kids to think and feel.

HEDDA:

Silence was really important to Fred. Fred wanted to give adults time to reflect, too, and in his graduation speeches or other speeches, he started to offer that minute of silence. He would say something like, "I want you to give you a minute of silence, a total minute of silence, to think about the people who helped you become who you are." That's what made him so radical. There was a lot of silence on *Mister Rogers' Neighborhood*—and in those speeches.

JBN:

That silence had a way of drawing you in. He had this way of direct appeal. So, it's like he truly was talking to one child.

What do you think the effect of that was; the benefit of that direct appeal? Was it just the way the reception of the child was enhanced, and they felt like they were the only one he was talking to? What was it?

HEDDA:

It starts with a sense of relationship—as a television friend. But remember that Fred spent years training for that, spending the time in the preschools with young children, learning to listen to them, learning to communicate with them.

JBN:

I think that what strikes me most is his trust and faith in children, because I experienced that when I was doing work with kids. I believed they were smart. And I believed I did not have to cram something down their throats. I believed that if they observed certain things, and they heard certain things, they would process that for themselves, and I didn't have to do their work for them. They're much smarter than they're given credit for a lot of times. I find that kids will do their own work of thinking and absorbing what's around them. For me, it was a matter of putting the right things on the table. I felt like a server. It's like a dinner table, if I would just put certain things on the table, I wouldn't have to feed them. They'd feed themselves.

HEDDA:

To think that adults cared about their thoughts and feelings, that's really important.

JBN:

These are messages that we just really don't hear very often. You struck such a chord. I wonder if you might comment on the honesty aspect, because that came through in so many ways, too. It wouldn't quite work the same if it wasn't totally honest. I think you really achieved that. I'm wondering how honesty marked the creation, and the production of the show, and why that was so important?

HEDDA:

I remember hearing Fred saying that he just wanted to be one more honest adult in the life of a child. That was very much a part of what he thought was important.

For one thing, the part of the program in the Neighborhood of Make-Believe was rather tightly scripted, because it was a carefully crafted story for actors and the puppets. But the parts when he was with guests were just authentic conversations. Think about the classic visit with Jeff Erlanger, the boy in the wheelchair—that was unscripted and unrehearsed.

I also think about the time when Fred accidentally buttoned his sweater wrong. He could have stopped the tape and done it right, but he just rebuttoned it, saying, "I thought I was doing that just right."

So, how you allow the honesty without over-stimulating or giving too much that a child couldn't handle, is a real tricky one. How do you talk about these things? In part, you have to care that you're not giving too much. You give a bit and see where the child goes with it. Over the years, he dealt extremely thoughtfully, honestly, and caringly with some very difficult issues—divorce, adoption, disabilities, the death of the fish on the program, and the assassination of Robert Kennedy in the parent special.

JBN:

How do we characterize honesty? Is it the transparency? The word some-times doesn't capture everything, but it came across in your production of the shows, I imagine in all your relationships that way, as a team. Anything further you would say about that?

He was pretty good at the honesty of thoughts and feelings and took pains in being sure that was done in the right way. Maybe honesty is like being responsible with how you think and feel and not hiding it. And you're not trying to overdo it, but there's a certain responsibility.

HEDDA:

Acknowledging feelings, the honesty about that, is one of the most helpful things for any of us. Think about how it feels when someone says, "I understand that you would feel that way. You have a right to your feelings."

Fred always said that feelings are natural and normal. They're part of being human. The important thing is to find healthy, constructive things to do with your feelings.

JBN:

That segues to the next thing I wanted to touch on: respect. Because you say you didn't have arguments on the set or issues as a team. This respect was not something just toward the children, it was toward each other. How did respect, on or even off the set, distinguish and mark what you did and still do?

HEDDA:

This is my only work experience. I went right from graduate school to *Mister Rogers' Neighborhood*. It's empathy. It's appreciation. It's getting to know somebody. One of Fred's favorite books was *The*

Little Prince by Saint Exupery. One of the lines that I remember from it is that one way to build a relationship is to *waste time with someone.* We spent a lot of time together. We often ate lunch together, talking about our families, friends, worries, joys. Getting to know each other helped us respect each other and understand when there were differences and find ways to work things through.

JBN:

Maybe respect can't be looked at apart from care. That's part of it.

I've been in some theater. I haven't been in a lot but have been in enough to love it. I've been in comedies. Nothing thrills me like that. It's hard to describe. They say with good theater, great actors and actresses, are great because they are 'other' oriented. In other words, they know every-thing that's going on around them on that stage, and every other person is more important because only then do you know how you particularly fit.

You're reminding me of that quote of his, "I'll never forget the sense of wholeness I felt when I finally realized after a lot of help from a lot of people, when in fact, I really was not, I was not just a songwriter, or language buff, or a student of human development, or telecommunicator, but someone who could use every talent that had ever been given to me in the service of children and their families."

HEDDA:

That's the thing I wanted to be sure to mention. Dr. Margaret McFarland, a remarkable child psychologist at the University of Pittsburgh, loved being the counterpart to his work. And the way I saw it is that she would give him the roadmaps of child development. If he was going to do a week about food, she would just tell him stories about how children approach food, how sometimes they give it to the mother, or sometimes eat with their fingers, or what it means to be watching your mother's face when she's feeding you. So, she would give him the roadmaps of child development from real family kinds of experiences. And then it seemed that she would back off and say, "Now you take the journey the way that is right for you."

JBN:

Like loading up his plate.
A lot of times in life, we get credit for things. Yet sometimes that credit needs to be dispersed all around. And I think he was pretty good at recognizing that.

HEDDA:

Well, because love was at the heart of *Mister Rogers' Neighborhood. Unconditional love.* As Fred said, it's through relationships that we grow best and learn best. Love is at the center of relationships.

JBN:

You would say this was the overarching, most important thing of all.

HEDDA:

The concept of "Neighbor" [a consistent theme in the programming] has that in it, so do all those words: helping, neighborhood, kindness.

But there's another side to loving that's important to remember– that setting limits is a part of loving. Children feel safer when we are firm but kind in setting limits. Children don't come with self-control. They need our caring help to learn ways to deal with their anger and frustrations, etc.

JBN:

You talked about neighborhood. Regarding the culture that you built there, for all the shows, and everything that you did, there was a palpable

*culture, neighborhood visits, friendship, and then the props that symbolize
these things. How important was this concept? Can you just describe the
culture?*

HEDDA:

Fred intentionally called his program *Mister Rogers' Neighborhood.*
And he created it as a neighborhood of people who cared about each
other. He also loved introducing children to real people. He once
said that he wanted to give children a smorgasbord of people who
found meaning in their lives in different ways. Some of them were
artists, some were musicians, some worked in the factories, some of
them were jugglers, a bus driver, and a plumber. And that sense of
neighborhood is that it takes a lot of different people with different
skills and interests. You know, that's really neighborhood.

The *Neighborhood of Make-Believe* was another kind of neighborhood with lots of different characters with a variety of
personalities—some arrogant, some mischievous, and some timid—
and in their stories we came to see how they had to work things out.
Fred used to refer to those as parables. And with the *Neighborhood of
Make-Believe,* you could have situations with conflicts or upsetting
times, and have the characters figure out how to find a solution. In
a sense, the *Neighborhood of Make-Believe* was a group of puppet
characters and caring adults living together in a "neighborhood"
community, a caring community.

JBN:

*I want to get your comments on acceptance, because Fred had a quote that
stated, "People that make you feel less than you are, that's the great evil."*

Acceptance was so important with this, "I like you as you are."

I'm wondering the importance of that if you have a few comments.

HEDDA:

First of all, feeling good about who you are can help you want to be the best you can be . . . and do things that are helpful and caring, not hurtful.

JBN:

He had this quote, "You don't have to do anything sensational for people to love you."

So just to segue into care, because he's saying how important it is to care for each other. And he called it making goodness attractive. This aspect of care, as he said, is what changes the world. What that prompted in me is that if care is important, then there's a fragility to life. And there's a fragility to children, there's a fragility to me and to you. And if we don't handle each other with care, it's like this box that says, Handle with Care on it. If there's fragile contents, you don't just throw it around. I think that's true with people that there's things inside of them that you can't just shake around and dump the contents. So, as to this aspect of care, do you have anything you would say?

HEDDA:

Part of what I took from Fred about what it means to care for someone means to listen, to honor their story, to respect their story. Fred used to say, "I think of myself as an emotional archaeologist, because I'm fascinated by who people are and what their story is."

I will tell you when he was traveling, and was at a conference or a meeting, people would come up to him and he was so focused on them, it was as if they were the only person in the room. That's how he always was, like you were the only one there. And he gave his full attention. What do they say, "We have two ears and one mouth."

Most of the time, we "listen" to think about what we're going to say next. That's not what Fred did. Fred just listened.

JBN:

That resonates because I have found that to be true. I also love to hear people's stories. And I have found it to be life changing. Because every time I hear someone's story, it makes my world bigger. And if I did not understand that story, I would shrink. So just to understand someone's story taps parts of life that we can never experience otherwise. I have found it shocking sometimes to hear people's stories. It's like, "Oh, my goodness, that literally blows me away."

There's an effect. You see the substance of memory foam, there's always an equal but opposite reaction. There's a permanent impression made in me when I hear someone's story. For lack of a better word, as far as the word "hero," we all have them. I know that he would not want to be heroized. But still, as he said, there's always someone that loved you into loving, smiled you into smiling. And for them, you are a hero. You can call them an unsung hero or a hero or whatever. But it's true that we all have someone like that. And then equally, there's someone we need to be that for. And we never have to have the credit.

I'm sure you all sorely miss him. What's similar and what's different since his passing? You're carrying on his work, and you're endeavoring to continue to build on the foundation that he laid.

HEDDA:

What's interesting is that there are people still using his work. Almost all the episodes are available—some on PBS Kids, some on mister-rogers.org, some on Amazon Prime and in libraries. There are a group of teachers nationally who use *Mister Rogers' Neighborhood* regularly and talk about it with the children. There are still parents and grand-parents who want their children and grandchildren to watch Mister Rogers. I've shown episodes to my grandchildren. It's timeless.

JBN:

I think that's one of the remarkable things; the sense of connection is off the chain. Because of the authenticity, genuineness, and sincerity that made everything work. I think of it like a tree, because, it has a sense of connection at the root. It's also connected with all those branches at the same time, and that's all those people. Then the leaves and the fruit are the results of that organic connection.

I think of it like a greenhouse. You go in there, and it's this environment for growth. Everything that's done inside that greenhouse is done to facilitate growth. And if it doesn't contribute to that end, it's not allowed. Not in a bad sense, but everything is geared for that. What you all have done reminds me of that, because you can't stand over a flower or a tree or a shrub and say, "Now I told you to grow!"

It's like you must give. You must do things that are required for growth. And so, growth is something encouraged. It's not forced. You all did a masterful job of that.

I think the concepts are so important because they apply across the globe. And if we all understood sharing and caring, we wouldn't have many of the conflicts we have on these larger scales today. Because the problem, you can it trace back to an inability to share. I'm not going to share this with you. There's not room for both of us here, when really there is room, if we just all find our place. Then you allow the growth for the other person as much as you do for yourself. These are the basics. And that's why these global crises are going on; it's just this lack of ability to apply these basic things.

I use some words just because I don't have a better one. But you're a speaker. You're a writer. You're an ambassador for this in a way. The word ambassador came to me because, not in a strict sense, but in function you are one.

These are timeless concepts and it's helped keep you stay young. Well, talking to you, like I said earlier, opens my world—the friendship and relationship. There's one more question I'd like to ask. With all you studied on child development, I'm asking a capsule of a huge concept, this inner child. We all have that, right? I know that adults have benefited from what you do. But then also, there's this inner child in the adult that still needs to be nurtured. Sometimes that's been repressed.

HEDDA:

One day, I walked into the office, and in the front room was a friend of Fred's, who was sitting there. I sat down to talk with him, and he asked, "Did you hear about this new song that Fred was writing?"

And I said, "No, what is it?"

He told me the first line of it, "The child is in me still, and sometimes not so still."

So, I went to Fred and said, "I love the thought in these words. How does the rest of the song go?"

And he told me he just got stuck and never finished it. But when you think about it, all we need is that phrase.

I love that concept. The child is in me still. Margaret MacFarland always said that one of the reasons Fred was able to be so authentic in his communication with children is that he could remember what it was like to be a child. He could somehow untangle stuff that happens along the way and get himself back to some of those feelings. And to allow yourself the right to those feelings, and that gives you vulnerability and empathy.

For more information and material go to:
misterrogers.org fredrogersinstitute.org fredrogers.org

Sign up for Hedda Sharapan's newsletter at
fredrogersinstitute.org/heddas-newsletter

The Unsung Heroes of Mister Rogers

by Fred Rogers

The World According to Mister Rogers *(With permission)*

I've had lots of heroes—lots of people I've wanted to be like. To this day, I can still feel the excitement in 1944 as I opened the first install-ment of my Charles Atlas exercise course. I had saved my money ($19) and had sent away for those lessons that I thought would help me look like Atlas himself holding up the world.

In 1944, I was a chubby and weak sixteen-year-old, and Charles Atlas was trim and strong. I did the exercises every morning—some of them even had me hanging on a bar at a doorjamb. Many months and many lessons later, I still didn't look like Charles Atlas. Now, hap-pily, I don't need to. Maybe it's natural, especially when we're little and feel weak, to choose "outside" kinds of heroes and superheroes who can keep us safe in a scary world.

My next hero was a "big man on campus" in our high school: Jim Stumbaugh. He could do anything. A letterman in basketball, football, and track, he made all A's. Both of his parents were teachers, but his dad died during our freshman year. Who knows? Maybe that made Jim sensitive to the needs of a shy kid like me. At any rate, we beat the odds and became lifelong friends. Many years after high school, when Jim's teenage son was killed in an automobile accident, I was there for him. The way he lived through that terrible time and the way he lived through his own years of cancer confirmed my pick of a hero. Jim started out looking like Charles Atlas and ended up looking like Mahatma Gandhi. What's amazing to me is that he always acted like that peace-filled Gandhi.

Yes, Gandhi's one of my heroes . . . Gandhi, Albert Schweitzer, Jane Addams (that tireless advocate of internationalism and world peace), and Bo Lozoff (who helps inmates use their time well in prison). Other heroes are Yo-Yo Ma and everyone else in the public eye who cares about beauty and refuses to bow to fast and loud sensationalism and greed.

Recently I've added an "unknown hero" too. I've had lots of heroes—lots of people I've added to my list: the person who drives the car I saw the other day, the parked car with the flashing lights and the sign that reads, "Vintage Volunteer . . . Home Delivered Meals." So those are some of my heroes now: the Charles Atlases of my elder years! They're the kind of people who help all of us come to realize that "biggest" doesn't necessarily mean "best," that the most important things of life are inside things like feelings and wonder and love, and that the ultimate happiness is being able sometimes, somehow to help our neighbor become a hero, too.

One of my seminary professors, Dr. Orr, often talked with great poignancy about Henry, a student who had come to the seminary with a degree in classic literature and a fine working knowledge of Greek and Latin as well as several modern languages. He remembered this young man as being brilliant and yet always receiving with such grace the offers of others. "He never put on airs," Dr. Orr said. "You always felt he really respected everybody else."

It seems that this young man was a perfectionist. For him, every word had to be just so. It was excruciating for him to give a sermon unless he felt it was letter-perfect; consequently, it took him two months to write one sermon. Even though he tried hard, it became clear to him that he was not going to be suited for the parish ministry. Eventually, he dropped out of seminary and took a job at a local department store.

Dr. Orr didn't hear from him for a long while, so one day, he stopped in the store to see how Henry was faring. It happened to be Henry's day off, but his coworkers talked with Dr. Orr about him. The more they talked, the more Dr. Orr realized that the people at the store knew nothing about this fellow employee's extensive education. What they did know was what had happened in their department after his arrival. "This department was filled with all kinds of jealousy and pettiness. It was a miserable place to work before Henry came," a person told Dr. Orr. "But after he had been here a while, somehow all that miserable stuff seemed to disappear. We all got working together, and well, it's different with him here. He is like a minister in more ways than anyone ever knows. You say you know Henry? Well, you are blessed, too, then."

Dr. Orr finally contacted Henry, and the two of them read Greek literature together for ten years before Henry died. When Dr. Orr talked about him, he would invariably say, "To think there were people at the seminary—and elsewhere—who called it a waste for Henry to have done what he did, working at that department store." Then Dr. Orr would add, "Henry probably had one of the greatest ministries I know. I feel privileged to have been his friend."

ABOUT THE AUTHOR

Jim is an inspirational and motivational award-winning writer and speaker with a master's degree in professional writing from the University of Oklahoma's Gaylord College of Journalism and Mass Communication. He also studied international reporting at Hebrew University in Jerusalem to glean a greater understanding of the Israeli-Palestinian conflict.

Jim's care and connection to others allows him to serve across platforms. He uses his experiences and insights to elevate individuals' lives, improve corporate culture, and motivate a wide variety of groups and organizations to look at their world through a new lens. He also served twenty-five years in the corporate world as a leader of teams. Jim has created his own talk show in a variety of contexts and has served as a pastor and childrens' pastor for many years.

A featured workshop speaker multiple times at the annual John Hope Franklin Center for Reconciliation in Tulsa, Oklahoma, Jim cares about people and has something fresh to offer any audience. He believes that everyone is capable of being an unsung hero, one who positively impacts the lives of others, with a little inspiration and direction using the character virtues we each possess.

A married father of three children and grandfather of four, Jim is living a life filled with possibilities, and his mission is to help others do the same. In his free time, this health and fitness junkie and avid runner enjoys singing, acting, humor, and performing.

**For booking and speaking engagements,
email jim@jimbnorth.com**

ACKNOWLEDGMENTS

I begin with my friend Tony Morbitt. I was twenty years old when he was fifty. He spent significant time with me after he lost his wife to cancer. He spoke about her often. Tony pointed his finger in my face one day and said, "Someday, you're going to write books."

I looked at him with a blank expression, wondering what in the world he was talking about. But *somehow, I believed him.*

My instructors at the University of Oklahoma's Gaylord College of Journalism and Mass Communication are more than mentors. They have provided feedback, instruction, friendship, and enormous opportunities. Mel Odom, Kevin Hahn, Scott Hodgson, Dr. Ralph Beliveau, Dr. Melanie Wilderman, John Schmeltzer, Mike Boettcher, Dr. Meta Carstarphen, and Kim Burke for starters. Professor Mary Anna Evans oversaw the creation and early development of this book, along with Professor Deborah Chester, both seasoned authors.

My Judaic/Israel Studies department instructors have invested in me richly. I learned Hebrew from Dr. Ori Kritz and Yael Lavender Smith, the book of Genesis from Dr. Alan Levinson, and took a graduate course on Jerusalem with Dr. Rhona Seidelman. These rich experiences set me up to go to Israel for my greatest educational and cultural experience.

Jerry Goodwin was my original editor for the journalistic work I began in Tulsa. He once admonished me that I never really knew what might happen by following a given path. I've kept my eyes open for derivative opportunities ever since. Many of those have come to fruition with many more to come. Thanks to Tulsa Community College along with Brian Benson, Dr. Jeanne Urie, Lisa Stefanic, Josh Parish,

Mike McCruiz, Susan O'Neil, and Dr. Jane Varmecky for friendship and mentorship.

Next on my unsung hero list heads with Steve Harrison, a visionary who lent his belief to my project. Also invaluable were Jack Canfield and Patty Aubery. All three reviewed my manuscript and offered reflections and feedback to make it better. Debra Englander was my developmental editor, Cristina Smith my encouraging book and writing coach, Valerie Costa my indispensable, endearing, skillful editor, and Christy Day my creative inspirational cover, back cover, and interior designer who helped prepare this book for print. Sincere gratitude goes to Steve Scholl for proofreading the manuscript, whose rich experience in the book publishing industry made his contribution invaluable. Finally, Geoffrey Berwind, a master storyteller in his own right, reviewed material with me periodically. Each of their selfless-ness, connectivity, and expertise stand out. Special thanks to Maggie McLaughlin for the logistics in positioning the book for its online presence, distribution in bookstores, and global outreach.

I've cherished countless friends throughout my life from whom I've derived courage. To all, plus family and colleagues, you've helped mold, shape, and improve me as a person and a professional, contributing to my life.

My unsung hero wife, Rhoda, has many white placards to her credit. She contributed immeasurably to the writing and production of *Unsung Heroes Wear No Capes: 12 Essential Virtues for an Extraordinary Life*, epitomizing one of the primary themes: "Not everything worthwhile you do will receive applause."

But she did them anyway.

My children are rewards—Phoebe, Evie, and Jason. My grandkids, siblings, extended family, and parents have embodied a special kind of love that endures all things.

Thanks to each valued guest in this book who made it richer with your unique, inspirational journeys: Jim Stovall, Hedda Sharapan, Renee, Chief Douglas Lankford, Senator Kevin Matthews, Jack Shadwick, Jessica, Mark Frank, and Nir Sarussi.

To book Jim for a speaking engagement,
email jim@jimbnorth.com

Additional copies of this book may be purchased at:

Amazon.com
Independent bookstores
jimbnorth.com

I'd love to hear your feedback on how this book has helped you or
someone you know. Please write to me, jim@jimbnorth.com

Made in the USA
Monee, IL
11 August 2023

40821522R00164